GREAT
MILITARY
DISASTERS

JULIAN SPILSBURY

GREAT
MILITARY
DISASTERS

Quercus

CONTENTS

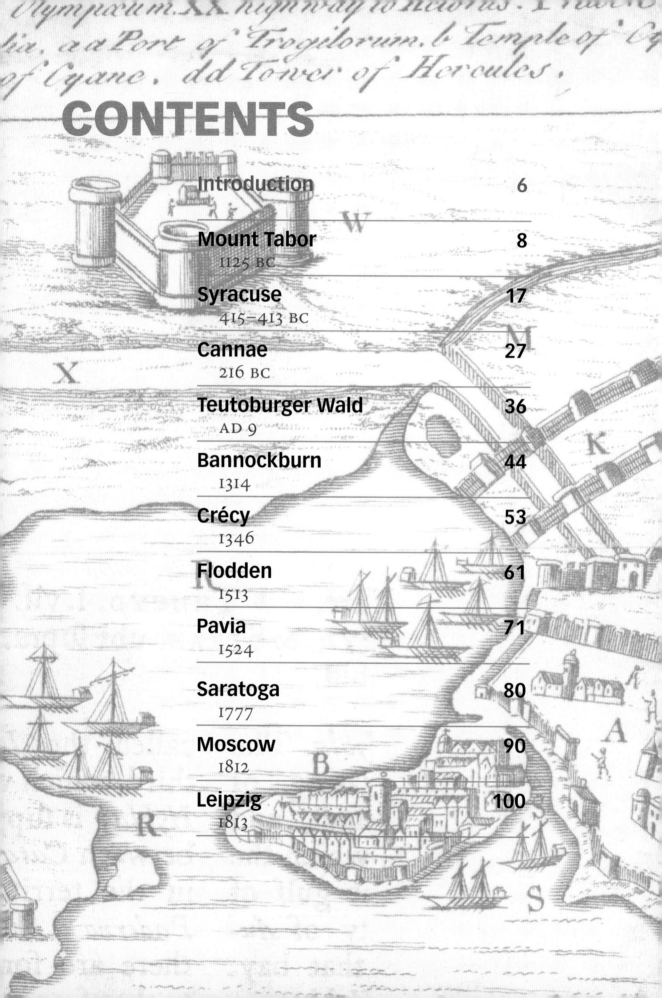

INTRODUCTION

The Germans have a word for it – 'Schadenfreude', defined as 'enjoyment obtained from the misfortunes of somebody else'. Reading of the ruin of grand projects, the destruction of armies and the demolition of military reputations is an abiding – if guilty – pleasure. At one level, this book might be taken as a 'how not to' guide to the art of war. There is something to be said for this. Asked in old age what he had learned from serving with the Duke of York's campaign in the Low Countries (which gave rise to the famous nursery rhyme), the Duke of Wellington replied, 'I learned how not to do it, and that is always something.'

Through the ages, various military theorists have struggled to formulate rules of war. The sum of their conclusions are neatly condensed into the 'Principles of War', currently taught in the British army: selection and maintenance of aim; concentration of force; economy of effort; maintenance of morale; offensive action; flexibility; co-operation; security; surprise; and sustainability. Of course, war being an art rather than a science, applying these principles will not guarantee victory, but following them should help to avert disaster – all things being equal, which they rarely are. In all ages it is possible to identify commanders who have done all the right things for all the right reasons, only to fall foul of that most inexorable of the laws of war – Murphy's.

'Success has many fathers,' it is said. 'Failure is an orphan.' In reality, though, failure – in the form of military disaster – has many fathers, too. The causes of defeat are many and varied. To ascribe any disaster to one cause only would be to oversimplify, but in terms of *major* causes we may identify the following within these pages: over-reliance on technology (Mount Tabor, Flodden, Verdun, Dien Bien Phu); *under*-reliance or misunderstanding of technology (Crécy, Fredericksburg); overconfidence (Sicily, the Teutoburger Wald, Little Bighorn, Isandhlwana, Stalingrad). In some cases (Sedan, Tannenberg), one of the combatants' armies was simply unfit for purpose or (Saratoga, Moscow) unprepared for the problems posed by geography. To the above list might be added: failure to anticipate; failure to adapt; failure to learn; and, perhaps above all, underestimating the enemy.

One man's defeat is another's victory – in a number of cases the defeated army was simply out-generalled. Another guilty pleasure, of course, is to sit by one's fireside, well fed and rested, and second-guess the man on the ground, forgetting that he was as likely as not tired, cold, hungry, misinformed, under pressure and under fire. A habit of thought has developed, especially since the 1930s, that equates 'military disaster' with 'military blunders', perpetrated by (mostly aristocratic) bunglers who led, or more commonly sent, men to their deaths through sheer incompetence. Professor Norman Dixon, in his book *On the Psychology of Military Incompetence*, suggests that military organizations, by their very nature, attract and favour the rigid, narrow-minded and hidebound types who are most likely to lead men to disaster.

In fact, in many of the battles described in this book, the leaders of the defeated side were experienced men of war, well practised in their trade, doing their utmost in circumstances and under pressures that most of us can only imagine. Many paid with their lives for defeats for which they were only partly to blame. All too often the conditions for defeat were created long before the war began by political or diplomatic bungling, neglect of armies in peacetime, or the imposition of impossible tasks on armies and commanders. The real culprits – nameless and long-forgotten politicians – escaped blame themselves by blaming the generals.

Some commanders – Hannibal, Robert E. Lee and Napoleon spring to mind – achieved, for a time, such a reputation that their enemies were half beaten before the battle even started. Such masters of the art of war, though, were often fated to become their enemies' instructors. 'These animals have learned something!' Napoleon commented, watching his enemies' troops manoeuvre in the summer of 1813. Indeed they had – as he was to discover at Leipzig. Having defeated the Swedes at Poltava in 1709 after many years of defeats, Peter the Great of Russia toasted the captured Swedish officers he entertained at dinner that evening as 'Our Teachers in the Art of War'.

Defeat, then, can be the school of victory. Those who survive it can emerge, like Scipio from the carnage at Cannae, to become the eventual victors. Field Marshal Sir William Slim, who led a defeated army out of Burma in 1942 and led it back to victory in 1944–5, described a defeated commander's feelings in his book *Defeat into Victory*. 'Defeat is bitter,' he wrote. 'Bitter to the common soldier, but trebly bitter to his general. The soldier may comfort himself that, whatever the result, he has done his duty faithfully and steadfastly, but the commander has failed in his duty if he has not won victory – for that *is* his duty. He has no other comparable to it.' Slim goes on to describe how the defeated general will blame himself for failing his men and his country and will question his own leadership, even his very manhood. 'And then he must stop! For if he is ever to command in battle again, he must shake off these regrets, and stamp on them as they claw at his will and his self-confidence. He must beat off these attacks he delivers against himself, and cast out the doubts born of failure. Forget them, and remember only the lessons to be learned from defeat – they are more than from victory.'

Julian Spilsbury

'UNTO THY SEED HAVE I GIVEN THIS LAND,
FROM THE RIVER OF EGYPT UNTO THE GREAT
RIVER, THE RIVER EUPHRATES'
GENESIS 15:18

MOUNT TABOR

1125 BC

By the 12th century BC, the time of the Book of Judges, God's promise to Abraham of a land for the nation of Israel was only half-fulfilled. The Biblical representation of 'all Israel' invading Canaan, under Joshua in around 1230 BC, has been rejected by modern scholars. They suggest a far more gradual process, with the Hebrew tribes who had come out of Egypt during the Exodus entering the Promised Land by a combination of peaceful infiltration, assimilation, inter-marriage and, only when necessary, warfare.

The natives of Canaan had been accustomed to nomadic invaders, but these newcomers were different. Previous incursions from the deserts had been little more than extended raids, but these new arrivals showed every intention of settling. What was more, they were a people inspired – by a devotion to one God, Yahveh (Jehovah) – who they proclaimed to be the only true God. 'The moral is to the physical as three is to one,' said Napoleon, and there can be no doubt that when it came to war this fierce and austere creed gave the Hebrews a distinct moral advantage over their sophisticated but decadent opponents. Initially rebuffed by the ring of fortified cities that guarded the Negev and the Beersheba Valley, the Israelites marched first east into the desert and then north. Then, under Joshua, they entered Canaan across the Jordan, north of the Dead Sea.

Barak takes command

There followed an extended period of warfare, which ended (when the Book of Judges begins) in stalemate. Despite early Israelite victories at Jericho and Ai, the Canaanites proved formidable opponents. Secure behind their walled cities, they dominated the coastal plain and the Jezreel Valley. The Israelites, the Bible tells us, had to be content with the mountains. They 'could not drive out the inhabitants of the valley, because they had chariots of iron'(Judges 1:19). These chariots – the 'iron' refers to their iron-rimmed wheels – were the state-of-the-art technology of the High Bronze Age, the battle tanks of their time. No lightly armed force of nomads and hill men, such as the Israelites comprised, could hope to stand against them in open battle.

During this extended lull in fighting, the Canaanites and the Israelites co-existed and even, on occasion, assisted each other in inter-city and inter-tribal conflicts. In the Jezreel Valley, however, the Canaanites took advantage of the interlude to consolidate their position. Here, we are told, the local commander, Sisera, a Canaanite prince who had oppressed the Israelites for 20 years, began to disarm them – 'was there a shield or spear seen among forty thousand in Israel?' (Judges 5:8) – and force them into bond-service.

As a result, revolt broke out in Galilee, inspired by a woman, the prophetess Deborah, 'the wife of Lapidoth ... she dwelt under the palm tree of Deborah ... in Mount Ephraim;

OPPOSITE: *The Israelites gather on Mount Tabor, while (in the foreground to the right) Sisera flees his chariot. Unstoppable on firm ground, the Canaanite chariots were vulnerable in the marshy Kishon Valley.*

'was there a shield or spear seen among forty thousand in Israel?'

JUDGES 5:8

and the children of Israel came up to her for judgement' (Judges 4:4–5). These 'Judges' were not legal officials but soldiers or tribal chieftains who provided leadership and settled disputes within and between tribes – at this time Israel was not yet the unified nation she was later to become under Saul. Deborah chose Barak, a military leader from the tribe of Isaachar, to command her army against the oppressive Canaanites.

Weapons of war

The backbone of the Canaanite armies was the war chariot. Invented in Mesopotamia more than a thousand years earlier, it had by this time reached its peak of sophistication. With two six-spoked wheels on one axle, and pulled by two specially trained horses, it was a fast-moving yet stable firing platform crewed by two armoured men – a driver and a fighting man armed with a bow. These were 'compound bows', made from a variety of materials – horn, sinew and wood – for extra power. A long-range, hand-held missile weapon, they were expensive and time-consuming to manufacture. The men who rode to war in these chariots – known as the *marianu* – were a social and military elite. Like medieval knights, they were aristocrats, holding land and privileges in return for military service. Also like knights, their strength lay in the single massed charge that would shatter an enemy's line. Once the enemy's line had been broken, the chariots would rampage among them, shooting down man after man at point blank range. Centuries later on the plains of North America, Colonel Bill Cody would train his horses to slow down beside buffalo to enable the rider to make an easy shot. Whether or not the horses and drivers of the Canaanite chariots were trained in a similar way for the *marianu*, the enemy could still be picked off easily, one by one.

Behind the chariots would come masses of armoured spearmen – more properly, 'pikemen', as they used their spears for thrusting only – to finish off survivors and the wounded. An army like this was a product of agricultural surplus – of a wealthy society that could spare men from the plough to become professional spearmen and charioteers, or makers of chariots and compound bows. Such a society could also devote precious land to the breeding of horses – stock that produces no meat, wool or milk.

Very different was the Israelite host, which could best be described as a tribal militia, an entirely infantry army composed of herdsmen, hill farmers and brigands. They were unarmoured light infantry, mustered by tribe and armed with a variety of weapons, from the *kophesh*, a curved cutlass-like copper sword designed for a slashing cut, down to adapted agricultural implements. Their main missile weapons were light wooden bows, stones and, of course, slings, but perhaps the most common was the javelin, a light throwing-spear that a fit young man could throw with force and accuracy. It would be a mistake to dismiss this Israelite host as a mere tribal mob. Subdivided by weapon and speciality, they had in the past proved formidable in the assault, capable of complicated manoeuvres and – crucially for the coming battle – very fast moving and sure-footed over rough ground.

Deborah's 'killing ground'

Having appointed Barak her commander, Deborah outlined to him a three-phase plan to defeat Sisera's army. Phase One involved luring Sisera out from the unassailable safety of his city walls. To do this Barak would assemble the fighting men of the tribes of Naphtali and Zebulun on Mount Tabor. By so doing he would pose a threat to the Canaanite lines of communication via the Jezreel Valley, forcing Sisera to act.

There are two ways of cutting an enemy's communication lines: one is to position troops astride them; the other is to take up a 'flanking position' to one side, from where you can interrupt them at will. Sitting astride Sisera's communications in the middle of the Jezreel Valley would have invited a battle on just the sort of ground that would favour Sisera's chariots. The Israelite force would be scattered and slaughtered. A flanking position on the top of Mount Tabor, on the other hand, would still pose a threat that Sisera would have to respond to, but from a commanding position on high ground where his chariots could not be deployed. With Sisera watching Mount Tabor, unable to attack and hoping to lure Barak down onto the plain, the stage was set for the second phase.

In Phase Two, a second Israelite force, gathered on Mount Ephraim, would advance up the Jezreel Valley as if to attack Sisera's own city of Harosheth or, just as worryingly, to bypass it and push on down as if to attack his coastal allies. Again, Sisera would have no choice but to respond to this new threat. He would abandon his blockade of Mount Tabor, turn about and march back to the Jezreel Valley. There, on the banks of the Kishon River, was the site Deborah had selected as her 'killing ground'.

In Phase Three, Sisera would find himself attacked on two sides on swampy ground where his chariots and heavy infantry would struggle. He would be attacked from the front by the Israelite forces he was marching to intercept, and from the rear by Barak's forces who, as soon as Sisera broke camp, would swarm down from Mount Tabor in pursuit of him.

The Israelites gather on Mount Tabor

Barak accepted the plan, but insisted that Deborah must come with him to Mount Tabor. Quite why is unclear. It may be that he wished to keep her under his eye and out of the fighting; or it may be that he felt unsure of being able to muster the men of the two tribes, Naphtali and Zebulun, without her charismatic presence. The tribes of Israel at this time were unruly and independent-minded – we know from the 'Song of Deborah' that not all the Israelites answered the call to arms. The men of Reuben are criticized for remaining aloof 'to hear the bleatings of the flocks' (Judges 5:16). Gilead, we are told 'abode beyond Jordan' and the men of Dan (intriguingly) remained in their ships . Whatever the reasoning, Deborah agreed to Barak's demand and accompanied him to Tabor, but she did so under protest. Barak's march, she told him, would bring him no honour, '… the Lord shall sell Sisera into the hand of a woman' (Judges 4:9). It must have seemed at the time that Deborah was claiming in advance the

> 'the Lord shall sell Sisera into the hand of a woman'
> JUDGES 4:9

Lines of communication

The lifelines of an army, all messages, all instructions, all supplies ('every bullet, every bayonet, every biscuit') must pass along their lines of communication. Armies trail them like a vacuum cleaner trails a flex – if they are cut, the army (like the vacuum cleaner) grinds to a halt. An army whose communications are cut will swiftly degenerate into a mob – indeed a bloodless way to achieve victory is to cut an army's communications, as Napoleon did to the Austrians at Ulm (1805), when 30,000 men surrendered with hardly a shot fired.

credit for any victory – later events, however, would give her words another, even more terrible significance.

So the men of Naphtali and Zebulun gathered on Mount Tabor, looking towards the Jezreel Valley. Having dominated the area for twenty years, Sisera must have had an extensive intelligence network. The Canaanite cities in the Jezreel Valley, Taanach pre eminent among them, would have been his main source of information, but according to Judges it was Heber the Kenite who informed Sisera of the threat. The Kenites were a nomadic tribe, who were neutral in the struggle between Canaanite and Israelite. Heber had pitched his tents away from the main body of his tribe 'unto the plain of Zaanaim which is by Kedesh' (Judges 4:11).

The waiting game

Sisera marched out of Harosheth with his entire army, numbered by Judges as 'even nine hundred chariots of iron, and all the people that were with him.' 'Nine hundred' tallies well with the 924 chariots that Pharaoh Thothmes III claimed to have taken from the Canaanite kings at his victory at Meggido – ten miles (16 km) away – some 300 years earlier. We may assume that both figures are exaggerated – ancient writers tended to cite impossibly large numbers simply to convey an impression of great strength. We may even go as far as to cross off a nought, bringing his chariot force down to a more manageable (and thus more believable) number. Even so, 90 massed chariots, backed by heavily armoured spearmen and supported by archers, is a formidable force, easily capable – on the plain – of sweeping aside Deborah and Barak's lightly armed tribesmen. They had done so many times before and would do so again – if the Israelites could be lured down from their mountain stronghold. Deborah and Barak, however, showed no sign of coming down, and so began a waiting game. With his lines of communication back to his base at Harosheth secure, and his army therefore well supplied, Sisera could afford to bide his time. Failing a surprise attack on his camp – a tactic the Israelites had employed before and against which he would have been on the alert – it was surely only a matter of time before hunger, disease or even dissension either broke up this tribal gathering or forced them down onto the level ground and their inevitable destruction.

So Sisera waited, blithely unaware that he was not the predator, but the prey. Above, on Mount Tabor, Deborah and Barak and their forces also bided their time.

Sisera's chariots clearly couldn't touch them, and he clearly lacked the specialist light or mountain troops he would need to evict them. From the summit of Mount Tabor it would have been perfectly possible, via signal beacons on the Hill of Moreh and Mount Gilboa, to communicate with the second Israelite force gathered in Ephraim. Everything was in place to spring the trap – to launch the men from Ephraim up the Jezreel Valley and threaten Sisera's rear. But still Deborah waited. What for?

Quagmire

It is here that another factor came into Deborah's planning, one which over the centuries has been the downfall of many a commander and many an army – weather. We can only speculate as to Deborah's powers as a prophetess, but it took no great powers of perception to predict the advent of the rainy season, which would turn the marshes of the Kishon River and its tributaries into a quagmire. Nor was the state of the ground the only danger – when Jesus talks of a man who 'built his house upon the sand' (Matthew 7:26), he was talking of those who built their homes on the slopes of long-dry wadis. As a

'Sisera waited, blithely unaware that he was not the predator, but the prey'

Galilean, Jesus must have seen himself how sudden rain could, within minutes, turn a dried-up watercourse into a raging, boiling torrent capable of sweeping away men, horses and even the 'iron chariots' themselves.

Phase Two of the plan began with the advance from Mount Ephraim of the Israelite force gathered there. On receiving what we can only assume was a long-distance signal from Deborah on Mount Tabor, they marched, under their unnamed commander, northwest up the Jezreel Valley. The valley was not unprotected, however – Sisera was an experienced enough soldier to keep his eye on the back door. At 'Taanach by the waters of Megiddo' (Judges 5:19) they were met by a Canaanite force drawn from that city and its surrounding villages. Whether the Israelites broke through and pushed on up the valley to threaten his base at Harosheth and, worse still, the cities on the coast, or whether the Canaanite commanders, under pressure at Taanach, sent frantic messages calling for reinforcements, we do not know. What we do know is that Sisera at once broke up his camp and prepared to march to their assistance. From the very outset of this campaign Sisera had lost the initiative – like an overmatched chess player, he did nothing throughout but react to his opponent's moves. It seems clear that the rains had already started – the fighting down by the waters of Taanach must have been a muddy, bloody slogging match – when Sisera set out. It was at this point – as the main Canaanite army set off in line of march back towards the scene of the fighting in the Jezreel Valley – that Deborah turned to Barak and uttered some of the most famous words in the Old Testament: 'Up; for this *is* the day in which the Lord hath delivered Sisera into thine hand; is not the Lord gone out before thee?' (Judges 4:14). It is inconceivable that Sisera's army did not have a rearguard, but it would surely have been overwhelmed as Barak's host

swept down from Mount Tabor and the surrounding Galilean
foothills. An army caught on the march is extremely vulnerable.
With no time to deploy from line-of-march into battle formation, its
units are devoured one by one, unable to support each other. Judging
by the slaughter that ensued, it seems probable that the men of
Ephraim had broken through the Canaanite forces further down
the valley and that Sisera was already deploying to fight them
when Barak's force swarmed over his flanks and rear.

It is not difficult to visualize the scene. Massed, on good ground,
Sisera's 'iron' chariots were a war-winner: strung out on the march
and – like Hitler's panzers before Moscow in the autumn
of 1941 – bogged to the axles, they were individual death traps.
Surrounded by superior numbers of lightly armed, fleet-footed
tribesmen, the chariot crews were hauled down from their lofty
positions in their vehicles to die among the slashing swords. The
heavy infantry will have fared little better, gathering back-to-back in
isolated clumps of men, their ranks thinned by a relentless rain of
arrows, stones and javelins, before the final, annihilating rush. This
was Little Big Horn by the Kishon River. Some survivors must have
made their way – under their officers no doubt – in a fighting retreat
back up the main valley towards Harosheth; others seem to have
attempted to cross the swollen Kishon and been swept away by the
torrent. Still others died where they stood or fell, or scattered in a
general *sauve qui peut* (save yourself who can).

Sisera's fate

Among the latter was Sisera. He fled on foot, alone it seems, in
the direction of Zanaaim, to the tents of his informant, Heber
the Kenite. He had no reason to doubt that he would find shelter
there, nor was he disappointed. He was met, as the Bible tells us, by
Heber's wife Jael, who gave him cool milk to drink, covered him with
a blanket and urged him to rest – if any pursuing Israelites came asking for him, she
would distract them. No doubt already contemplating his revenge, the exhausted Sisera
drifted into sleep. As he slept, Jael crept in and, taking a hammer and a tent-peg, drove it
through his temple. Although lauded in the Song of Deborah, Jael's murder of Sisera was
a gross violation of the Middle Eastern code of hospitality, and it raises a question about
her husband Heber's role in the campaign. Unless there was serious discord in the tents
of Heber, we are forced to conclude that Heber had been acting all along in collusion with
Deborah, feeding Sisera with the information *she* wanted him to receive, *when* she wanted
him to receive it.

So died Sisera – at the hands of a woman, as prophesied by Deborah – and so
died his army. There may be a certain grim satisfaction in reading of the destruction

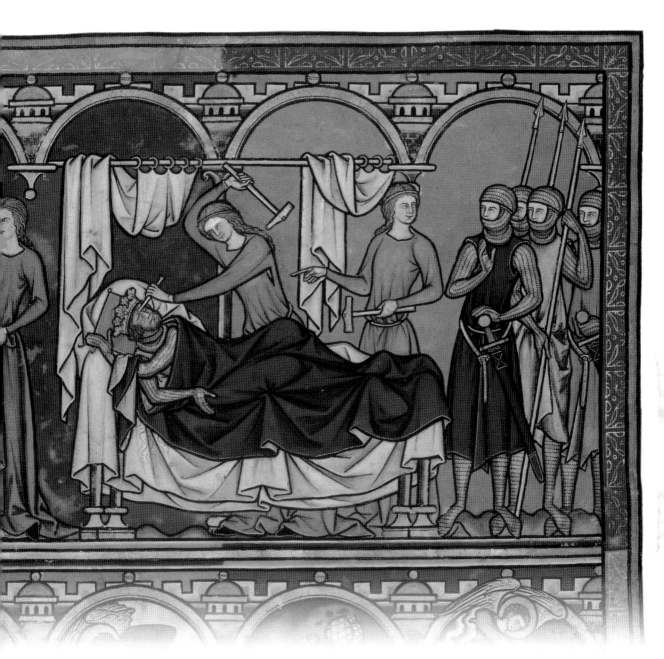

of an army, but we should never lose sight of the fact that the reality is hundreds, sometimes thousands, of dead soldiers. Although *The Song of Deborah* is a Biblical whoop of joy at an Israelite victory, there is still a certain poignancy in its portrayal of Sisera's mother awaiting her beloved son's return. As she looks out at her window and cries through the lattice, 'Why is his chariot *so* long in coming? Why tarry the wheels of his chariots?' (Judges 5:28), she might be the emblem of all the women through the ages who have waited for the return from battle of fathers and brothers, sons and lovers who would never be coming home.

'As he [Sisera] slept, Jael crept in and, taking a hammer and a tent-peg, drove it through his temple'

ABOVE: *A violation of the Middle Eastern code of hospitality – Jael is shown first offering Sisera a drink and shelter, but she then murders him in his sleep.*

The decline and fall of the chariot

As a result of the Battle of Mount Tabor, the Book of Judges tells us, '... the land had rest forty years' (Judges 5:31). It is to be hoped the Israelites enjoyed it – for the Philistines were coming. The Battle of Mount Tabor has to be seen against a background of the collapse of civilization as it had been known until then. The sophisticated 'chariot' civilizations of the High Bronze Age – Egypt, Minoan Crete, the Hittite Kingdom of Anatolia and its ally 'To-ro-ja' (Homer's Troy) – were being engulfed, one by one, by a combination of northern European tribesmen and 'Sea Peoples' (the Philistines among them). The armies of these peoples were characterized by lightly armed, sword-wielding infantry – a new kind of warfare was emerging, ending the dominance of the chariot. The Israelites themselves were part of this process – a process that began at Mount Tabor and would end with them occupying the whole land of Canaan. The consequences of this are with us to this day.

In the Biblical account of Sisera's defeat we have one of the first recorded instances of a commander falling for his enemy's deception plan, losing the initiative, underestimating his opponent, placing too much reliance on technology and falling victim to bad ground and adverse weather. It will not be the last.

'DO NOT INDULGE YOURSELF IN HOPELESS
PASSIONS FOR WHAT IS NOT THERE'
THUCYDIDES, QUOTING NICIAS

SYRACUSE
415–413 BC

Emerging from the Persian wars as the predominant naval power in the Mediterranean, Athens soon came to be regarded by other Greek city-states as a threat. The Delian League, set up by Athens among the city-states of the Aegean and Asia Minor as a naval alliance, soon took on the aspect of a naval empire. It was her westward ambitions, however, that led to war – first with Corinth and then with Sparta. It was the war of the whale and the elephant – Athenian seaborne raids on the Peloponnesian coast proved ineffective, while Spartan armies regularly ravaged Attica, but stood no chance of taking Athens herself, lying secure behind her walls.

In 418 BC Athens received an embassy from Segesta, a city in northwest Sicily, asking for help against a rival state and promising to fund a further joint project against the leading Sicilian power, Syracuse. Sicily seemed to offer Athens everything she needed: an abundant corn supply which – unlike her present source, the steppes of the Ukraine – could not be cut off; the spoils of a great city; opportunities to found new colonies; in short, the glittering prospect of an empire in the west, all funded by Segestan money.

After much debate, an expedition was fitted out, to be commanded by Athenian generals Nicias, Lamachus and one of the expedition's most fervent advocates, Alcibiades. Raised in the household of Pericles and a pupil of Socrates, Alcibiades was undoubtedly a man of genius, but he was also irreverent, ambitious and amoral. Shortly before the expedition sailed, in a shocking act of blasphemy, all the city's 'herms' (images of the god Hermes) were mutilated by unknown hands. Alcibiades's many enemies were quick to place the blame on him – at the very least it seemed a bad omen.

The Athenians set out

The expedition sailed in June 415 BC – 134 triremes and 130 transports carrying 27,000 officers and men. On their arrival at Rhegium in Italy (modern Reggio), they received intelligence that the promised Segestan money was a hoax. According to Thucydides, Nicias had been against the project from the start. 'Do not,' he had warned the Assembly when it was first debated 'indulge yourself in hopeless passions for what is not there.' His words were prophetic. Now he proposed a show of force followed by a return home. Again, however, the opinion of Alcibiades prevailed and the expedition sailed for Catana (Catania) in Sicily. No sooner had they reached Catana than a ship arrived from Athens to call Alcibiades home to stand trial on charges of sacrilege. Alcibiades set off on the return journey, but once on his way gave his captors the slip and fled to Sparta.

Syracuse, on the southeast coast of Sicily, was built on a promontory jutting out into the sea. It was served by two harbours – the Lesser Harbour to the north of the city and the Great Harbour to the south – making it almost impossible to cut off from the sea. It could be isolated from the mainland, however, if a besieging force could gain control of the Epipolae – a large plateau to the west of the city walls that lay between the city and the rest of the island.

Having lured the Syracusan army north by a ruse, the Athenians made a surprise landing to the south of the city, setting camp on the plains of Anapus, near the Temple of Zeus. The Syracusan army soon returned and deployed for battle in front of the Athenian camp. The Syracusans formed up in a 16-deep phalanx with their cavalry on their right. The Athenians had no cavalry, but their more experienced heavy infantry, in an eight-deep phalanx, made short work of the raw Syracusan troops. Only a rearguard action by the Syracusan cavalry saved their entire army from destruction.

A siege being impossible this late in the campaigning season, Nicias sailed back north to Catana where he went into winter quarters, and sent a letter to Athens requesting that a cavalry force be sent to him in time for the spring. For their part the Syracusans set about training their infantry and sending envoys to Corinth and Sparta to ask for aid. At Sparta they found a ready ally in Alcibiades, who outlined the Athenian plans and urged his hosts to help the Syracusans – the Spartans agreed to send an experienced general, Gylippus, to command the Syracusan army.

By May 414 BC Nicias and Lamachus, reinforced with cash and cavalry, were ready to start their summer campaign. The Syracusan commander Hermocrates had realized, belatedly it seems, the importance of the Epipolae plateau, but even as he was parading the troops he had allocated to its defence, Nicias and Lamachus made another surprise landing, this time to the north of the city. Before the Syracusans could respond, the Athenians had seized the Euryalus gate, the western key to the plateau. Too late, Diomilus led 600 Syra-cusans in an attempt to retake it, but arriving exhausted they were met by a well disposed Athenian force and slaughtered – only half of them made it back to the city's gates.

The next day the Athenians started work on a fort on the northern edge of the heights at a site known as Labdalum. With its fine views to the north, this was to be used as a look-out post, but its primary function was as a storehouse for cash and equipment – timber, stone, bricks, axes, shovels and picks – all the engineering stores needed for a siege. No sooner was the fort completed than they began work on another –the 'Round Tower' in the centre of the plateau. From here, Nicias intended to build walls south and north and seal off the city on its landward side – the siege of Syracuse had begun.

Walls and counter-walls

Seeing the Athenians building their wall southwards from the Round Tower, the Syracusans began a counter-wall running out at right angles from their city walls. The idea was to 'block off' the Athenian wall and prevent its further progress south. But the Athenians were ready for them. Catching the Syracusans off guard they stormed the half-finished Syracusan wall, demolished it and appropriated the materials for their own wall.

Undeterred, the Syracusans started a second counter-wall – this time further south, across the marshes, designed to prevent the Athenian wall from reaching the sea. Once again the Athenians reacted swiftly – Lamachus came down from the Epipolae with a strong force and, laying planks and doors across the marshes, attacked and captured the Syracusan works. Again the Syracusans were routed but at a cost to the Athenians – in the midst of the fighting Lamachus was killed.

Lamachus was a great loss to the Athenian expedition, but the Syracusan situation was now desperate. Soon the whole of the southern sector of their walls from the sea to the centre of the plateau was cut off, and there seemed no way to prevent the Athenians pushing their wall north and completing the encirclement of the city. Secret negotiations were opened with Nicias, but before they could bear fruit aid arrived in the form of the Spartan general Gylippus.

Arriving north of the Epipolae with a mixed force of Corinthian and Sicilian hoplites, Gylippus caught the Athenian garrison of the Euryalus fort by surprise. He occupied it and then marched up onto the plateau and linked up with the Syracusans. Quickly seeing that the Syracusans were in no condition to face the Athenians in open battle, he decided instead to storm the Labdalum and then begin work on a northern counter-wall.

Instead of marching immediately to disrupt the building of this wall, Nicias decided instead to seize a naval base on the southern side of the city, to ensure his sea communications. Accordingly, he occupied and fortified Plemmyrium, but as he consolidated himself in the south, Gylippus continued work on his northern counter-wall. The Athenians now tried to prevent the completion of this wall, and two battles followed. In the first the Syracusans were again routed, but in the second battle, as Thucydides tells us, 'The [Syracusan] cavalry charged and routed the Athenian left wing, which was opposed to them, with the result that the rest of the army also was beaten by the Syracusans and driven back headlong behind its fortifications. Next night the Syracusans achieved their object with their cross wall and carried it past the end of the Athenian fortifications. It was now no longer possible to stop them, and the Athenians, even if they were victorious in battle, had been deprived for the future of all chance of encircling the city.

A fatal error

The failure to prevent the Syracusans from blocking the northern extension of their wall – and thus to encircle the city entirely – was the major Athenian blunder of the campaign, and a fatal one. The whole northern half of the Epipolae was now *inside* the Syracusan defence system and their communications with the Sicilian interior were secure. Worse still, as Nicias wrote in a despondent letter to Athens that winter, 'There is now no longer any possibility of our being able to blockade the city, unless a strong force could be found to attack and capture this wall of theirs. The position therefore is that we, who thought we were the besiegers, have become the besieged, at least on land, since we cannot go far into the country because of their cavalry.' In his letter Nicias goes on to list his problems: rotting ships, exhausted crews, lack of reinforcements and the difficulties – when every sortie resulted in a fight – of gathering fuel, food and water. He ended, 'The time therefore has come for you to decide either to recall us, or else to send out another force, both naval and military, as big as the first, with large sums of money, and also someone to relieve me of the command, as a disease of the kidneys has made me unfit for service.'

'we, who thought we were the besiegers, have become the besieged'
NICIAS

The taking of Plemmyrium

Athens' response was to prepare a second expedition under Eurymedon and Demosthenes – arguably in defiance of the sound military maxim 'Never reinforce failure.' It was Gylippus who opened the next campaigning season, however, with an audacious plan to seize the Athenians' naval base at Plemmyrium. With the loss of the northern half of the Epipolae, the Athenians' sea communications were dependent on this southern port. Gylippus planned to feint with his fleet and attack with his army. The Syracusan fleet, split between the Great and Lesser Harbours, would unite off Plemmyrium and make as if to attack the base, then – while the Athenians were distracted by the sea fight, the Syracusan army would attack the base on its landward side. The sea fight went badly for the Syracusans – 11 ships were sunk and 3 captured, but even as the Athenian soldiers in the forts were cheering their sailors' success, Gylippus attacked by land. 'They were ... taken off their guard by Gylippus,' wrote Thucydides. 'First he captured the biggest one, and afterwards the other two also, the garrison of which did not wait for him, when they saw the biggest one taken so easily.'

The war of walls

'Walls' feature heavily in any description of the Peloponnesian War. It was Athens' Long Walls – between the city and her naval base at Piraeus – that rendered her immune to attack by the formidable Spartan armies. Failure fully to encircle a town or city, as at Syracuse, doomed many an ancient and medieval siege. To ensure a complete encirclement, besieging armies would often build two lines of walls. One wall, the wall of 'circumvallation', faced inwards to besiege the city; the other, the wall of 'contravallation', faced outwards to protect the besiegers from attack by a relieving force. At Syracuse both sides knew what was at stake in their 'war of walls' – not just here but throughout military history, two of the soldier's most effective weapons have been the pick and the shovel.

The loss of Plemmyrium was catastrophic for the Athenians – inside the forts were all their supplies of corn, naval equipment and masts for triremes. Thucydides sees it as the turning point of the campaign. 'This capture of Plemmyrium was indeed the greatest and principal cause of the deterioration of the Athenian army. Convoys with supplies were no longer safe even at the entrance to the harbour, since the Syracusans had ships waiting to intercept them, and it was now necessary to fight if supplies were to be brought in at all. In other respects, too, this event had produced a feeling of bewilderment in the army and a decline in morale.'

Skirmishes at sea

The Athenians were now forced back to their original naval base in the Great Harbour, where their superior seamanship would be much less of an advantage than in open waters. Both sides now began consolidating their naval bases by driving piles into the harbour bed and mounting raids to disrupt each other's building operations.

Aware that Demosthenes's new armada was sailing from Athens, the Syracusans decided to mount a new offensive before it could arrive. This time Gylippus reversed the plan by which he had captured Plemmyrium, carrying out a feint attack by land to

ABOVE: *Syracuse besieged – on the high ground to the north of the city, the Athenian double walls can clearly be seen (K–K), as can the Round Tower, the Syracusan counter-wall (N) and the Great Harbour and Lesser Harbours.*

distract the defenders from the main attack that would come by sea. Knowing that the Athenians' manoeuvrability would be limited by the narrow waters of the Great Harbour, the Syracusans strengthened the prows of their triremes for what they realized would inevitably be a head-on fight. The forces were almost evenly matched – 75 Athenian triremes against 80 Syracusan.

The sea fight lasted three days. On the first day the Syracusans contented themselves with skirmishing to exhaust the Athenian crews. After a lull on the second day, the Syracusans decided, on the third, to employ a ruse, withdrawing their ships to harbour

as though they had had enough. Satisfied that the battle was over, the Athenians then withdrew their own ships and, once ashore, began preparing their meals. The Syracusans had already made their preparations, moving all the market traders and food vendors down to the sea so that their men could eat quickly and be ready for action while the Athenians were still cooking. 'Suddenly,' says Thucydides 'the Syracusans manned their ships and sailed out to attack for the second time. The Athenians, in great confusion and most of them still having not eaten, got aboard in no sort of order and with considerable difficulty managed to put out against the enemy.' The Syracusans, he wrote, were ready for them and 'met their attack prow to prow, as they had intended, and with the specially constructed beaks of their ships stove in the Athenian bows to a considerable distance; the javelin-throwers on the decks also did a lot of damage to the Athenians, but much more harm still was done by the Syracusans who went about in small boats, slipped in under the oars of the Athenian ships and sailing close in to the sides hurled their weapons in upon the sailors.' At length the beleaguered Athenians were forced to retreat to the safety of their naval defences – although they lost only seven ships, the defeat was to prove damaging to morale and handed supremacy at sea to their opponents.

A double-edged sword

Still, the Athenians had one last throw of the dice. In July 413 BC Demosthenes's armada arrived: 73 triremes containing 15,000 fresh men – hoplites and light infantry armed with slings, bows and javelins – sailed into the Great Harbour. Seeing Nicias's poor state of health, Demosthenes now took command. He understood at once that the Athenian position was hopeless unless Gylippus's counter-wall across the north of the Epipolae could be destroyed and the complete encirclement of the city achieved. He made two attempts. The first involved a full-scale assault on the wall with infantry storming parties and battering rams, but the Syracusans under Gylippus beat off all these attacks and even succeeded in setting fire to the Athenian war machines. Demosthenes now determined on a plan he had been nursing for some time – a night attack round the end of the counter-wall to retake the Euryalus fort and ascend the Epipolae plateau by the same route they had used when the first expedition had landed.

At first the attack went well – Euryalus was surprised, and Demosthenes and his men pushed up onto the high ground. 'The Athenians immediately pressed forward,' says Thucydides, 'so as not to lose their present impetus before they had reached their objectives. Others from the very beginning of the action were occupying the Syracusan counter-wall, the garrison of which put up no resistance, and were tearing down the battlements.' Victory seemed at hand until the Boeotians, Syracusan allies, counter-attacked a part of the Athenian force and put it to flight. These fell back upon the main body and confusion resulted. Thucydides, himself a soldier, knew that the confusion caused among the enemy by a night attack can be a two-edged weapon. 'In a battle by night (and this was the only one that took place between great armies in this war), how could anyone be sure of what happened exactly? ... Some of the Athenians were already defeated, some had not been defeated at all and were coming up fresh to the attack ... After the rout that had taken place, everything in front of them was now in disorder, and the noise made it difficult to tell who was who.' Soon the Syracusans were driving the Athenians, in confusion and with great slaughter, back down the narrow track that led up from Euryalus. Once on the plain those who knew the terrain made their way back to the Athenian camp – many more, new to the island, were rounded up and slaughtered by the Syracusan cavalry.

Bad omen

The Athenians' last attempt to take Syracuse had failed – what remained, Demosthenes decided, was to save the army and the fleet, extract them and get them back to Athens. Nicias, however, was in touch with factions within the city who claimed they wished to deliver the city to the Athenians and who now urged him not to abandon the siege. In almost every Greek city-state there were certain groups who could be relied upon to co-operate with a potential aggressor, if only to change the political dynamic. So, too, at Syracuse there was a pro-Athenian party, but it is difficult to resist the conclusion that these messages to Nicias were a 'blind' designed to delay the Athenians' departure – for Gylippus and the Syracusans were now intent not only on defending the city, but on annihilating the Athenian expeditionary force. News of further Syracusan reinforcements made even Nicias realize that withdrawal was inevitable, but just as the Athenian fleet was about to sail for home there was an eclipse of the full moon. The soldiers and sailors of the expedition – with the concurrence of Nicias – decided that this was a bad omen. Soothsayers predicted that it would not be propitious to sail until 'thrice nine days' had passed – time that Gylippus put to good use. Although outnumbered in ships he launched his fleet once more against the Athenian naval base in the Great Harbour. The Athenians came out to fight, relying on their numbers and the skill of their sailors. Attempting a flanking manoeuvre, Athenian general Eurymedon was isolated, surrounded and killed, and the Athenians' centre was broken. Their ships were driven back to the shore and the crews only saved by the soldiers who ran down to the shore to help them.

Trapped in the Great Harbour

Following this defeat, the only hope of escape for the Athenians lay in one last attempt at a breakout through the Great Harbour – loading every man they could on the ships and forcing a way out through what was now a Syracusan blockade. Gylippus knew this too and blocked the exit to the Great Harbour with a line of ships chained together. For the Athenians it was literally do or die. The Athenian leaders steered their ships head-on towards the boom formed by the Syracusan vessels – Nicias remained on shore with those of the land forces who could not be embarked, having claimed that 'honour' as his right. The Syracusan centre was held by their Corinthian allies, who were thrust back by the Athenians almost onto the blockading ships, but before the Athenian sailors and marines could hack a way through, the Syracusan ships closed in on their flanks. 'Soon,' wrote Thucydides, 'the fighting was not only in front of the barrier but all over the harbour. And hard fighting it was – more so than in any of the previous battles... Many ships crowded in upon each other in a small area – indeed, never before had so many ships fought together in so narrow a space – there were almost 200 of them on the two sides. Consequently there were not many attacks made with the ram amidships, since there was no backing water and no chance of breaking the line; collisions were much more frequent, ship crashing into ship in their efforts to escape from or to attack some other vessel. All the time that one ship was bearing down upon another,

'ship crashing into ship in their efforts to escape'
THUCYDIDES

javelins, arrows and stones were shot or hurled on to it without cessation by the men on the decks; and once the ships met, the soldiers fought hand to hand, each trying to board the enemy.'

Finally the Athenians broke – the Syracusans and their allies drove their ships back to land with the loss of 50 ships to their own 26. On land, those Athenian soldiers guarding the naval base, helpless spectators of the sea fight 'cried aloud and groaned in pain for what had happened, some going down to give help to the ships ... while others (and these were now in the majority) began to think of themselves and how they could get away safe.'

The Athenian leaders, seeing they still had the advantage of numbers at sea, resolved on a second attempt at a breakout from the harbour, but the crews had had enough. They refused to embark, demanding instead an escape overland. Again Athenian action was delayed by misinformation – in order to allow time for the Syracusans to celebrate their victory, their leader, Hermocrates, spread a false rumour that the Athenians' avenue of retreat was blocked. It wasn't until three days later, then, that the Athenians, in two great divisions under Nicias and Demosthenes, having abandoned their sick and wounded, began a march north across plains teeming with Syracusan cavalry. Progress was slow, and on the second day the two divisions became separated. Nicias's division, leading, pushed on doggedly towards the coastal road under constant cavalry attacks, while Demosthenes's division soon found itself surrounded in a walled enclosure. He and his 6,000 men fought on until, on receiving a guarantee that their lives would be spared, they surrendered. Nicias's band fought on for another three miles. On reaching the River Assinarus , the men, tortured by thirst, broke ranks and waded in. They, too, were surrounded and slaughtered, only 1,000 surviving to surrender with Nicias.

The writing on the wall

The failure at Syracuse was Athens' crowning disaster – only 7,000 men survived out of the force of nearly 50,000 that she had sent against the city. The prisoners were sold into slavery or set to work in the city's quarries, where torture, sickness and exposure to the elements took a terrible toll. Nicias was – against the wishes of Gylippus – put to death; the factions in Syracuse who had been in secret communication with him feared he knew too much. Demosthenes shared his fate.

Thucydides says of the Athenians, 'They were utterly and entirely defeated; their sufferings were on an enormous scale; their losses were, as they say, total; army, navy, everything was destroyed, and, out of many, only few returned.'

Her naval power shattered, Athens fought on for another nine years, but Sparta, now financed by the Persians and joined by a number of Athens' former allies, began to make a serious effort at sea. Having made the Spartan queen pregnant, Alcibiades re-entered the war on the Athenian side, but withdrew again after his lieutenant was defeated at sea in 407 BC. When he was mysteriously murdered a few years after the war, the list of suspects was a long one. After the Spartan admiral Lysander defeated Athens' last fleet at Aegos-potami in 405 BC, the writing was on the wall for Athens – by 404 BC the Acropolis had a Spartan garrison.

CANNAE
216 BC

When King Pyrrhus of Epirus, a relation of Alexander the Great, famous for his costly 'Pyrrhic' victories, abandoned his invasion of Italy, he declared, 'What a battlefield I am leaving for Carthage and Rome.' They were prophetic words, for by the second century BC, with the decline of the Greek and Hellenistic states, it was perhaps inevitable that these two powers should vie for supremacy in the western Mediterranean.

Originally a Phoenician colony near modern Tunis, Carthage was a maritime empire based on trade and the power of its fleet; Rome had used the power of her citizen army to subdue and later absorb her Italian neighbours into a powerful Latin confederacy with Rome as senior partner. The first clash came in Sicily, where opponents of the king of Syracuse called upon both Rome and Carthage for assistance. Both powers responded, and the resulting confrontation sparked the First Punic War (264–241 BC) from which Rome emerged victorious.

Hannibal's destiny

Ejected from her former zones of influence in Sicily, Corsica and Sardinia, Carthage set about acquiring a new empire in Spain under the command of one of her more successful generals, Hamilcar Barca, and later his son Hannibal. When Hannibal was nine years old, according to the Roman historian Livy, 'Hamilcar, who was preparing to offer sacrifice ... led the boy to the altar, and made him solemnly swear, with his hand upon the sacred victim, that as soon as he was old enough he would be the enemy of the Roman people.' Grown to manhood, Hannibal continued his father's work in Spain, acquiring in the process the military experience that, combined with his innate qualities, was to place him among the great military commanders of history. He also proved true to his oath. By an attack on Rome's Spanish ally Saguntum, he brought about the war with Rome that he had long sought, and in 218 BC, in perhaps the most famous march in military history, Hannibal overcame hostile tribes, weather and terrain to cross the Alps into northern Italy. Here, the Gauls, only partially subdued by Rome, rallied to his cause and swelled his depleted ranks. Only a handful of the elephants with which his name is inextricably linked in popular memory survived the march, and they were in reality only a negligible factor in the fighting that was to follow.

Experienced in Hellenistic warfare, Hannibal had also studied the Roman system and at the Trebia River in 218 BC and Lake Trasimene the following year, he inflicted severe defeats on the Romans and their allies. Hannibal's aim was not to conquer Italy but to break Rome's Latin confederacy and impose on her the sort of unfavourable peace that she had inflicted on Carthage at the end of the previous war. Hannibal wanted to present himself to non-Roman Italians as a liberator. To this end, troops allied to Rome who had been captured in battle were treated with the utmost consideration and sent home

PREVIOUS PAGE: *The Battle of Cannae. Hannibal's plan was a calculated risk, based on a careful study of Roman tactics. Everything depended on whether his centre could hold for long enough to draw the enemy into his trap.*

without ransom. Since Allied contingents made up some 50 per cent of Rome's armies, this strategy would have been the source of a permanent weakening of Rome's power.

Two consuls, two opponents

After his victory at Trasimene, Hannibal moved south to Italy's Adriatic coast and captured a Roman supply base at Cannae on the River Aufidus (present-day Ofanto). Hannibal's presence here, in grain-rich Apulia, was a threat to Rome's food supplies. The terrain in this part of Apulia was well suited to the use of cavalry, the main arm of Hannibal's force, and he hoped to lure the Romans – who, under their general, Fabius, had adopted the 'Fabian' strategy of avoiding open battle – into marching against him with their main field army.

Hannibal was fortunate in at least one of his two opponents in this campaign. For the campaigning season of 216 BC the Roman army was led by two consuls, Aemilius Paullus and Gaius Terentius Varro, who, in keeping with traditional Roman practice, commanded on alternate days. This strange system of command had its origin in the politics of the Roman Republic. As a political safeguard – to prevent commanders becoming too

Double envelopment

Turning or 'enveloping' an enemy's flank is one of the quickest ways to defeat him. Troops attacked in the flank, especially if 'pinned' by a frontal attack, cannot turn to confront this new threat in any numbers and an enemy's whole battle line can quickly be 'rolled up'. Hannibal's tactic – a 'double-envelopment' followed by attack from the rear – was the prelude for a battle of annihilation, and has been the 'Holy Grail' for military commanders ever since. It particularly influenced German military thinking, inspiring Helmuth von Moltke's victories at Koeniggratz in the Austro-Prussian War and Sedan in the Franco-Prussian War – as well as the German general staff's Schlieffen Plan in World War I, and the great encirclement battles of World War II.

powerful, subverting the army and using it against the state – it was an excellent device; as a system of command it was pregnant with disaster. It was especially so in this case, for Paullus, mindful of lessons already learned against Hannibal, favoured a cautious strategy against this master tactician, whereas Varro, a rising man of the merchant class, was intent on a war-winning conflict to make his political career.

Once Hannibal's whereabouts were known, the Romans marched to the Aufidus and there, about three miles (4.8 km) apart, the two armies faced each other. The Roman historians Livy and Tacitus, and the Greek Polybius, all tended to support the 'patrician' or aristocratic class to which Paullus belonged and were hostile to the 'new man' Varro, so their judgements on him should be viewed with a certain caution. Nevertheless it does seem that Paullus's warnings about the risks involved in fighting Hannibal on ground of his own choosing were ignored, and on the fourth day, when it was Varro's turn to command, he marched the whole army out to give Hannibal the battle he wanted.

Contrasting forces

The two armies that faced each other on the banks of the Aufidus were very different.
The backbone and building block of the Roman army was the legionary, still at this time
a citizen soldier. He was equipped with an oval or rectangular shield, body armour and
helmet, and armed with javelins and the short stabbing-and-slashing sword, the *gladius
hispaniensis*. As its name indicates, the sword was of Spanish origin and was carried by
many in Hannibal's army too. Poorer citizens formed the skirmishers or *velites*, lightly
armed javelin throwers who operated in advance of the army. The heavier-armed infantry
formed the bulk of the legion and were organized into maniples (units of 60–120 men)
who, for battle, were arrayed in a chequerboard formation. On paper this looks like a
rather static, even passive, formation, but it was
flexible, capable of swift manoeuvre and in battle
produced wave after wave of crashing attacks – each
wave capable of breaking off, falling back, splitting
up and making way for a fresh one. This military
system had served Rome well and proved such a battle winner that it almost obviated the
need for skilful generalship. The Allied infantry were armed and organized on similar lines.

> ‘the line presented a strange
> and terrifying appearance’
>
> POLYBIUS

   Roman and Allied cavalry were equipped Greek-style, with helmet, breastplate mail
shirt, round shield and spear. The army of the two consuls comprised approximately
80,000 infantry and 6,000 cavalry.

   By contrast, Hannibal's mercenary army, some 40,000 infantry and 10,000 cavalry, was
heterogenous and colourful. His heavy infantry was African – Libyan mercenaries armed,
since Hannibal's victories in the north, in Roman style with Roman weapons. The greater
part of his infantry, however, were Gauls and Spaniards, barbarian tribesmen fighting in
their own war bands under their own leaders. The Greek historian Polybius describes
them thus: 'The shields used by the Spaniards and Celts were very similar to one another,
but their swords were quite different. The point of the Spanish sword was no less effective
for wounding than the edge, whereas the Gallic sword was useful only for slashing and
required a wide sweep for that purpose.' Hannibal, he says, placed these troops in
alternate companies: 'the Celts naked, the Spaniards with their short linen tunics
bordered with purple – their national dress – so that the line presented a strange and
terrifying appearance.'

   It was the practice of a number of 'barbarian' peoples to fight naked – an order of
dress (or lack of it) that would make men fighting in uniform feel more, rather than less,
vulnerable. There may have been religious or ritualistic reasons for the practice, but it had
certain practical advantages. A naked foot has a greater grip on muddy and blood-stained
soil and naked limbs enjoy greater ease and freedom of movement. Moreover, the Maoris,
who also fought naked, told the British that they had observed that among their wounded
the naked often recovered where clothed men did not. The reason for this is simple.
A sword, spear, bayonet or missile driven through dirty clothing carries infection into
the body of its victim, whereas a naked man's wounds are therefore inevitably cleaner
and, if they are not fatal, more likely to heal.

The Carthaginian cavalry was divided into two types. The Gaulish and Spanish cavalry were Hannibal's 'heavies', armed in a similar fashion to the Romans and their Allies. More than half of his cavalry, though, were Numidians, tribesmen from North Africa. The Numidians were the finest – practically the *only* – light cavalry in the world. Their value to Hannibal for scouting, screening, harassing and foraging, bread-and-butter cavalry work, was incalculable. Unable to stand up against heavier cavalry in an open fight, their tactics consisted of charges, feigned retreats, swift rallies and rapid envelopments, all accompanied by showers of javelins. They were the nearest fighting force the ancient world produced to the Plains Indians of the American West.

A plan of annihilation

Varro arrayed his legions in the traditional Roman manner, with his Roman infantry massed in the centre. Covering his right flank, with *their* flank covered by the river, he placed his Roman cavalry. His left flank was covered by the Allied cavalry, with their flank open. It was the usual Roman formation, with one crucial difference. In order to gain greater depth in the attack, he ordered the maniples to form up closer together than usual, thus reducing their frontage. 'The depth of each was several times its width,' comments Polybius. Paullus commanded the right wing of the army, Varro the left, and in the centre were the previous year's consuls, Marcus Atilius Regulus and Gnaeus Servilius.

Varro's plan seems to have been to bulldoze through the Carthaginian centre, where Hannibal was very much weaker in infantry. Both previous battles, at Trebia and Lake Trasimene, though ultimately Roman defeats, had shown that, man-for-man, their infantry was superior. If this central attack was pressed home with sufficient speed and vigour, he probably felt that nothing that occurred on his flanks could be of any importance. It would perhaps be unfair to dismiss Varro as a bungler. He cannot have been unaware of the striking power of the Carthaginian cavalry – *his* calculation was that the Roman infantry would have ripped open Hannibal's battle line before that power could be brought to bear. By massing his maniples in depth this way, however, Varro sacrificed the very flexibility and power to manoeuvre that was the strength of the manipular system. In effect, the Roman infantry had reverted to the Greek phalanx, with all that formation's disadvantages.

The other problem was that Varro's planned central attack was exactly what Hannibal was expecting – and in that expectation the Carthaginian had planned a battle of annihilation. Hannibal now deployed his own troops accordingly. On his left, by the river, facing the Roman cavalry, he placed his Gaulish and Spanish cavalry. Next in line were half of his elite Libyan heavy infantry. His centre was formed by the Gauls and Spanish infantry – formidable fighters, but savage, undisciplined and unreliable.

To *their* right he placed the other half of his Libyan heavy infantry, and on his right flank, facing the Allied cavalry, he deployed his finest Numidian light cavalry. While Varro had placed his strongest forces in the centre, Hannibal had done the opposite. His strongest elements, his cavalry and his Libyan infantry, were on his flanks. What were potentially his weakest troops, the wild and unpredictable Gaulish and Spanish infantry,

were positioned in the centre and pushed slightly forward in a crescent-shaped bulge, protruding towards the enemy, so as actually to *invite* Varro to make a central push. It is clear from Hannibal's deployment that his plan was to lure the Roman infantry forward and encircle them. His centre, the Gaulish and Spanish infantry, would engage the Roman infantry and then give ground. Their convex formation would gradually, under Roman pressure, become *concave*. As the Romans pushed forward, they would expose both of their flanks to the heavy Libyan infantry who would turn inward and attack. The cavalry would drive off their opposite numbers and complete the encirclement.

The whole plan depended on whether the Gauls and Spanish in the centre could give ground without breaking. If they did break, Varro's plan would succeed and Hannibal's army would be split in two. It was a finely calculated risk, but Hannibal knew his troops well enough to have confidence in the outcome. To reassure them that they were not just battle fodder being sacrificed in the cause of a greater plan, Hannibal and his brother Mago took up their battle stations in their midst. Hasdrubal, another brother,

ABOVE: *Hamilcar makes his son Hannibal swear undying enmity to Rome and its people. Hannibal terrorized Italy for 16 years, but his strategy – to break up Rome's Latin confederacy – was destined to fail.*

commanded the Carthaginian left, Hanno the right. The Romans faced south, the Carthaginians north, so neither side was facing the morning sun. However a local wind, known as the Volturnus, blew from behind the Carthaginians, carrying clouds of dust towards the Romans and therefore obscuring their vision.

Hannibal's trap

After initial skirmishing, the battle began with the clash of the cavalry – Varro's Romans against Hannibal's Gauls and Spanish. These were the heaviest of Hannibal's cavalry and he had placed them here on purpose, where there was little room for manoeuvre or for charge and counter-charge, and weight was everything. According to Polybius, 'There was none of the usual formal advance and withdrawal about this encounter; once the two forces had met they dismounted and fought on foot man-to-man.' After a fierce fight, the Roman cavalry began to give ground and then broke and fled, the Gauls and Spanish pursuing mercilessly. By now the Roman centre had engaged Hannibal's. The Gauls and Spanish fought hard but slowly – as Hannibal intended – their line, which had curved forward, began to curve back. Varro's decision to narrow his infantry's frontage was exacerbated now, as the Roman infantry began to crowd in towards the centre where victory appeared imminent. In Polybius's words, 'Because the Romans were pursuing the Celts and pressing inward against that part of the front which was giving way, they penetrated the enemy's line so deeply that they then had both contingents of the African infantry on their flanks.' Almost untouched by the Roman advance, these, Hannibal's heaviest-armed infantry, now wheeled inwards. As Polybius explains, 'The African infantry on the right wing turned inwards so as to face left, and then charged the enemy's flank beginning from the right, while those of the left wing likewise turned inwards and attacked in similar fashion.' The Romans, tired now, found themselves trapped between two divisions of fresh, unblooded African infantry, with the unbroken

'Once the two forces had met they dismounted and fought on foot man-to-man'
POLYBIUS

'their tactic was to charge, harass, threaten, throw javelins, retire and charge again'

Gauls and Spanish to their front. Bunched together in the large phalanx that Varro had created, the maniples could not wheel as units to face this new threat, only individuals were able turn and fight as best they could. Gradually the pressure on the Gauls and Spanish to the front eased.

On Hannibal's right his Numidian cavalry had been unable to drive off the heavier Allied cavalry, but had kept them occupied with continual charges and counter-charges. While they did so, Hasdrubal (commander of the cavalry on the other flank), having pursued the Roman cavalry off the field and ridden round the rear of the Roman army, threw his cavalry into the fight on the right. Outnumbered now, the Allied cavalry also broke and fled. Rallying pursuing cavalry was a notoriously difficult business, and the fact that Hasdrubal was able to halt at least of some of his triumphant Gaulish and Spanish cavalry and take them into the fight on the other side of the battlefield is a testament to his leadership skills and the discipline that prevailed in Hannibal's army. Either that or Hasdrubal had started the battle with sufficient men to keep some squadrons under his hand and uncommitted.

Whatever the reason, the destruction of both the Romans' cavalry wings left the infantry in the centre in a desperate plight. Sending the Numidians off in pursuit, to ensure that the Allied cavalry did not rally and try to re-enter the battle, Hasdrubal now attacked the Romans in the rear with repeated charges from different directions. Cavalry, however heavy, were normally no match for Roman infantry – their tactic was to charge, harass, threaten, throw javelins, retire and charge again. However, by forcing men at the rear of Varro's army to turn and organize a front against them, they brought the whole army to a halt and spread panic among its ranks.

'All killed where they stood'

The Roman infantry were now completely surrounded – Gauls and Spanish infantry to their front, Libyan heavy infantry on either flank and Gaulish and Spanish heavy cavalry attacking their rear. For the men at the edges of the Roman mass, the fighting was desperate, bloody and confused; for those in the centre, crowded together, helpless spectators, watching victory turn to disaster, it was bewildering and demoralizing. Leaders began to fall. Paullus was killed, Polybius tells us 'in the thick of fighting after receiving several wounds.' In the centre the previous years' consuls, Regulus and Servilius, died among their infantry. Varro managed to attach himself to a party of cavalry and made his escape with them.

Leaderless, disorganized and surrounded on all sides, the Roman infantry fought on. 'So long as they could keep an unbroken front,' wrote Polybius, 'and turn to meet successive attacks of the encircling enemy, they were able to hold out. But as their outer ranks were continually cut down and the survivors were forced to pull back and huddle together, they were finally all killed where they stood.'

Ancient and medieval writers should be treated with great suspicion when they discuss numbers. Figures were often plucked out of the air to signify 'a mighty host' or exaggerated upwards or downwards to make victory more spectacular, defeat more catastrophic. For Roman losses we may choose between Polybius's 70,000 and Livy's later, more conservative, 50,000 killed. Among them, as well as Paullus and the two ex-consuls, died 29 military tribunes and 80 men of senatorial rank.

Flawed success

Yet Rome, neither for the first nor the last time, proved resilient in defeat. When news of the disaster reached the city, the authorities banned all public displays of grief and set about raising new armies. They contemptuously refused Hannibal's offer to ransom some 7,000 Roman prisoners, regarding them as men who had failed in their duty to the Republic. Instead they preferred to arm 8,000 slave volunteers, bought from their owners out of the public purse. When Varro returned to the city, he was met, according to Livy 'by men of all conditions, who came in crowds to participate in the thanks publicly bestowed upon him 'for not having despaired of the commonwealth'. In such circumstances a Carthaginian general would have been crucified.

'You know how to win a fight; you do not know how to use your victory'
MAHARBAL

Hannibal has been much criticized for not capitalizing on his victory by marching immediately on Rome, despite the urgings of his senior commanders. Livy has one of his cavalry commanders, Maharbal, telling him that in five days they could dine in triumph on the Capitol and, when Hannibal still refused to march, adding, 'Assuredly no one man has been blessed with all God's gifts. You know how to win a fight; you do not know how to use your victory.' Hannibal, however, knew that attacking Rome's city walls was a hopeless task for a battle-weary army not in possession of a siege train. He preferred to wait, let the news of the city's humiliation sink in among her allies, and watch as Rome's Latin confederacy unravelled. There were some defections – Tarentum in the south, as well as cities in Samnium, Apulia and Campania, notably Capua. But the three crucial Allied states around Rome – Latium, Umbria and Etruria – remained loyal. Ultimately Hannibal's strategy was flawed, and no amount of battlefield victories could compensate for that. Hannibal would be free to rampage round Italy for another 14 years as his army dwindled and the Romans and their allies grew in strength. An attempt by Hannibal's brother, Hasdrubal, to reinforce him from across the Alps was halted at the Metaurus River in 207 BC– the first Hannibal knew of it was when a Roman cavalry patrol threw his brother's head into his camp. Recalled to Africa in 202 BC to defend Carthage from a Roman counter-stroke under Publius Cornelius Scipio, a veteran of Cannae, Hannibal met defeat at Zama, after which both he, and ultimately his city, were doomed.

TEUTOBURGER
WALD

AD 9

'A SENSE OF SECURITY IS VERY OFTEN
THE BEGINNING OF DISASTER'

VELLEIUS PATERCULUS

'**On the open ground were whitening bones,** scattered where men had fled, heaped up where they had stood and fought back. Fragments of spears and of horses' limbs lay there – also human heads fastened to tree trunks. In groves nearby were the outlandish altars at which the Germans had massacred the Roman colonels and senior company-commanders.' Thus the Roman historian Tacitus describes how, in AD 15, a Roman army under Germanicus, nephew of Emperor Tiberius, came upon the spot where, six years previously, three Roman legions, some 20,000 men, had been massacred by the barbarians they had been accustomed to slaughter like cattle.

The threat from the north

By AD 9, in the reign of Tiberius's predecessor Augustus, the Rhine and the Danube formed the northern frontier of the Roman Empire. Behind it lay peaceful Roman provinces; beyond, hostile German tribes. These two rivers form two sides of a vast triangle, a long and difficult border to defend, with a huge salient (or bulge) pushing into Roman territory. Operating on 'interior lines', that is *inside* the triangle, the Germanic tribes had only a short distance to travel in order to threaten the Roman border wherever they pleased. The Romans, forced to work on 'exterior lines', that is *outside* the triangle, had much greater distances to travel to respond to any threat. The only answer for the Romans was to deploy two large armies, one to cover each river, which was very expensive.

In order to simplify his border Augustus planned to push it some 200 to 250 miles (320–400 km) to the east, as far as the River Elbe, eliminating the salient and creating one border that stretched from Hamburg to Vienna. Some progress had been made toward this goal by Drusus, who, having established winter bases for the Rhine army at Mainz and

> '*he was slow in mind as he was in body, and more accustomed to the leisure of the camp than service in war*'
> DIO CASSIUS

Xanten, campaigned beyond the Rhine as far as the River Weser. After Drusus' death, the work had been continued by his brother Tiberius (later emperor), but each incursion had been followed by a return to winter quarters in the Rhine bases.

Tiberius's plans for a double thrust into Germany by both the Rhine and Danube armies were frustrated by rebellions elsewhere in the empire, and in AD 6 command on the Rhine was given to Publius Quintilius Varus. Married to a great-niece of Augustus, he was, according to the Roman historian Dio Cassius, 'a man of mild character and of a quiet disposition, somewhat slow in mind as he was in body, and more accustomed to the leisure of the camp than actual service in war.' If the campaigns of Drusus and Tiberius had not yet resulted in the conquest of Western Germany, they had spread the

OPPOSITE: *One-time collaborator with Rome, Arminius turns on Varus and slaughters his legionaries in a battle of annihilation. In the thick forests and on narrow tracks the Romans could not deploy their usually invincible battle-line.*

terror of the name of Rome among the German tribes, and with Gaul now a peaceful Roman province and all seemingly quiet across the Rhine, Varus may have seemed an ideal candidate for the job. There were signs by this time that the Germans immediately beyond the Rhine had largely reconciled themselves to the Roman presence which, however irksome, brought them considerable benefits in the form of trade, although the payment of tribute to Rome in gold or silver remained a grievance among the German tribes. Varus had experienced this before as governor of Syria, but seems to have under-estimated the underlying discontent among a people very different from the Syrians, in what he still regarded as a peace-time posting. According to Velleius Paterculus he [Varus] 'entertained a notion that the Germans were men only in limbs and voice, and that they, who could not be subdued by the sword, could be soothed by the law.'

The enemy within

He had some grounds for this delusion – some German leaders had collaborated actively with the creeping Roman domination of German lands. Prominent among them was Segestes, a chief of the Cherusci and a loyal ally of Rome. Segestes had a daughter, Thusnelda, whose hand in marriage was sought by Arminius, a young Cheruscan nobleman – and Segestes's nephew. Arminius, too, it seems had been a long-term collaborator. He had served with Tiberius on his Danubian campaigns, leading a contingent of his own tribe. He had had plenty of opportunity to study at close hand the Roman way of waging war. Having distinguished himself in their service, he had been granted Roman citizenship and equestrian rank, but in his heart he continued to hate Rome and was determined to unite the currently leaderless Germans in resisting any further incursions. Segestes, whether sensing Arminius's intentions or for other reasons, refused his nephew's suit for Thusnelda's hand. The lady, however, had her own ideas and eloped with Arminius. Aged 26, Arminius was attached to Varus's staff and soon became one of his most trusted advisors. However, he had already conceived the plan of uniting the German tribes under his own leadership and using Varus's forthcoming summer campaign to lure him into a trap where his army could be annihilated. According to Velleius, Arminius had concluded 'that nobody can be more quickly destroyed than he who fears nothing ... a sense of security is very often the beginning of disaster.'

> 'nobody can be more quickly destroyed than he who fears nothing'
> VELLEIUS PATERCULUS

The German advantage

In the spring of AD 9 Varus set out on his summer campaign. He took with him three of his five legions, the 17th, 18th and 19th. The bulk of his force, and the mainstay of any Roman army, were his legionaries. They were equipped with helmet, chain mail or scale body armour, an oval or rectangular shield, the *pilum* (javelin) and the *gladius* – a short, straight sword of Spanish origin, ideal for both stabbing and slashing. Each legion, including its small cavalry contingent, totalled about 5,000 men. There were also six cohorts (about 3,000 men) of auxiliary infantry – similarly armed troops of non-Roman origin. The force also included other auxiliary troops – mostly local, Allied German infantry and cavalry employed as scouts and skirmishers. With the women and children and the baggage train, the whole probably amounted to some 20,000 souls.

About German numbers we can only speculate, other than to say that Arminius's army, drawn mostly from his own Cherusci tribesmen, would have enjoyed a potentially overwhelming superiority in numbers. In the open field such an advantage would have been nullified by the Romans' superior weaponry, military system, and command and control. In general, barbarian armies became more unruly and less effective as their numbers swelled. However, in the thick forests of western Germany, in conditions that approximated to jungle fighting, many of the Romans' advantages would count for nothing.

For the Germans' equipment we can do no better than turn once more to Tacitus. In his *Germania*, a guide to the peoples who had come to fascinate and terrify the Romans, he describes their weaponry thus: 'Only a few of them have swords or large lances; they carry spears – called *frameae* in their own language – with short and narrow blades, but so

> '**Many such survivors from the battlefield have ended their lives by hanging themselves**'
> TACITUS

sharp and easy to handle that they can be used as required, either at close quarters or in long-range fighting. Their horsemen are content with a shield and a spear; but the foot soldiers also rain javelins on their foes: each of them carries several, and they hurl them to immense distances, being naked or lightly clad in short cloaks... Few have breastplates, and only one here and there a helmet of metal and hide.' Of their tactics Tacitus tells us: 'The battle-line is made up of wedge-shaped formations. To give ground, provided that you return to the attack, is considered good tactics rather than cowardice. They bring back the bodies of the fallen even when a battle hangs in the balance. To throw away one's shield is the supreme disgrace, and the man who has thus dishonoured himself is debarred from attendance at sacrifice or assembly. Many such survivors from the battle-field have ended their lives by hanging themselves.'

Cunning and deceipt

Varus's 'campaign' was really rather more of a military progress – 'showing the flag' in later military parlance. It was to be a demonstration of force to reassure allies and cow the disaffected, to settle disputes and dispense judgements among the tribes, as well as to act as a reconnaissance in force through territory marked to be incorporated into Varus's new province. During this semi-royal progress, disturbing rumours reached Varus from – if he but knew it – his true ally Segestes. Almost inevitably, word of Arminius's grand plan had leaked out. Segestes warned Varus that treason was afoot and urged him to place Arminius and his confederates in chains. Such was the ascendancy, that Arminius had achieved over Varus, however, that Segestes's warnings were put down to jealousy of Arminius and a desire to settle his old quarrel with his nephew.

Father of a nation

There was a tendency among the British and American historians of the 19th century to see, in the Germans' robust rejection of Roman rule, the origin – transmitted via the Anglo-Saxons – of their own spirit of freedom, democracy and independence. The huge monument erected in the Teutoburger Wald in 1875 became a place of pilgrimage for Germans, who saw Arminius as the founding father of a strong, united Germany, unsullied by 'decadent' Latin culture. As a united Germany came to trouble the peace of Europe and the world in the late 19th and 20th centuries, however, non-German historians in particular began to take a dimmer view.

Varus was just about to move from summer to winter quarters when he received news, via Arminius, of the rising of a neighbouring tribe. Segestes had already warned Varus of the danger of treachery from Arminius, but Varus had convinced himself that Arminius was a steadfast ally of Rome. He decided to march via the disaffected area, and settle what he assumed to be a minor local difficulty en route to winter quarters. Such was his confidence that he neglected to send the women and children back to Aliso or even to take any extra precautions on the march. Arminius took his leave from the army on the pretext of raising men of his own tribe to assist Varus in quelling the revolt. He left Varus to follow on around the northern edge of a long line of hills running east-to-west, known as the Wiehengebirge. Unknown to Varus, Arminius had gone on ahead to put his final preperations in place for the forthcoming battle of annihilation.

Arminius had carefully selected an ambush site near the present-day village of Schwagstorf at the base of the Kalkriese hill. Here, the track that Arminius knew Varus must follow took a turn to the north for two miles and passed between the hill and a great bog – very difficult terrain indeed for a large, baggage-laden army to pass through, let alone deploy and fight in. The Romans' natural advantages on an open battlefield would be nullified and the ground would favour fast-moving, lighter-armed troops fighting in a manner, and on a type of terrain, familiar to them. It seems, too, that Arminius altered the ground around the base of the hill, obscuring the true track so as to funnel the Romans into a narrow, marshy defile. To give his own men every possible advantage, Arminius created here an earthen wall that was well camouflaged with sections of turf. The German tribesmen were thus able to attack the Roman forces from the cover of the wall. This careful preparation of the battleground must have been the product of many weeks – even months – of intensive labour; proof if it were needed that Arminius's treachery in the setting up of this deadly ambush was clearly pre-meditated and, moreover, had long been contemplated.

'German warriors unleashed volley after volley of Javelins, a blizzard in which every snowflake was tipped with razor-sharp iron'

The Romans march headlong into the trap

Archaeologists have identified signs of a Roman 'marching camp' some eight miles (12.8 km) to the east of the Kalkriese ambush sight. This is most likely the camp from which Arminius and his men rode on the evening before the battle, and from which Varus and his army marched out the following morning. Varus's auxiliary scouts must have ridden ahead and reported all clear. Either they were fooled by Arminius's camouflage or, more likely, being themselves German tribesmen, they were co-operating with him. As a result, the Roman column marched on unaware, right into Arminius's killing ground. According to Dio Cassius it was when 'the Romans were not proceeding in any regular order, but were mixed in helter-skelter with the wagons and the unarmed,' that Arminius attacked. From behind their cover the German warriors unleashed volley after volley of javelins – a blizzard in which every snowflake was tipped with razor-sharp iron. The effect of this against men, horses and mules, women, children and camp followers, strung out, unsuspecting, on the march, must have been devastating. As the fighting men unslung their shields, drew their weapons and tried to form into some sort of fighting line, the panic among the non-combatants must have increased the disorder.

The German auxiliaries, who had provided the greater part of Varus's light troops, seem to have deserted at the start of the fighting, many of them probably joining the German side. The lack of German weapon finds on the Kalkriese site has led archaeologists to speculate that many of Arminius's men were Cherusci auxiliaries – only days earlier under Varus's command – armed with Roman weapons.

The front and centre of the Roman column, now hastily converted into a makeshift battle line, must have been a scene of chaos, compounded by pressure from behind as the rear of Varus's column pushed forward into the killing zone. With plenty of time to prepare the ground, the Germans' lateral communications would have been excellent, with prepared pathways allowing them to range up and down the length of the Roman column, attacking it wherever it seemed weakest or most confused. After the javelin storm came the assault – a succession of charges by groups of warriors armed with spears, lances and swords, slashing their way into Roman ranks already encumbered by the dead and dying. Once again the advantage lay with the Germans. There was no room for the Romans to deploy into their usual battle formations – formations that on open ground would have enabled them to face such an onslaught with confidence. Describing an incident in a later campaign against the same enemy, Tacitus gives us an idea of what the fighting on the track was like: 'Everything was against the Romans. The waterlogged ground was too soft for a firm stand and too slippery for movement. Besides, they wore heavy armour and could not throw their javelins standing in the water. The Cherusci, on the other hand, were used to fighting in marshes. They were big men, too, whose thrusts with their great lances had a formidable range.'

No doubt the Germans had concentrated their initial 'fire' on the Roman commanders – tribunes and centurions, conspicuous enough in their decorated armour. Nor could those commanders who were still alive and unwounded perform their usual function. Pinned on a narrow track, Roman lateral communications were almost non-existent.

Unable to leave the track, any officer needing to ride up or down the line would have been forced to drive his horse through masses of armed men and mobs of panicking camp followers. With command and control, the supreme advantage of Roman armies over their barbarian foes, broken down, units fought where they stood. Roman soldiers – knowing that, in Kipling's words, 'it's ruin to run from a fight' – rallied where they could and fought on doggedly, hoping, and no doubt praying, that discipline alone would carry them through against an enemy they had hitherto regarded with contempt.

A running battle

Discipline seems to have at least averted disaster on that first day. The 'battle' of the Teutoburger Wald seems to have been rather a running fight that went on for several days, for even in these unfavourable conditions, three Roman legions were a formidable opponent. There is even a suggestion from archaeological finds that some Roman troops tried to storm the Kalkriese hill before being driven back down onto the track. By nightfall of the first day, although the Romans had taken heavy casualties, the line had held and some sort of fortified camp seems to have been improvised. The following day, Dio Cassius tells us, the Romans burned their wagons and then proceeded 'in a little better order', but the ground over which they stumbled was no less unforgiving, and Arminius's warriors no less relentless. The column's progress was hampered by constant harassing attacks. Even the weather now turned against them – it was as if the very gods of the north now aligned with Arminius to punish the intruder. According to Dio, soon after the second day's march began, a heavy downpour of rain prevented them 'from going forward and even from standing securely, and moreover deprived them of the use of their weapons. For they could not handle their bows or their javelins with any success, nor for that matter their shields, which were thoroughly soaked.' Now Arminius launched a full-scale assault. This time his warriors slashed through the weakened Roman lines in several places.

Desertion and suicide

Desertion by their allies had been bad enough, but soon Varus's men found themselves abandoned by their own cavalry. Velleius Paterculus tells us that the Roman cavalry commander 'Vala Numonius ... who in the rest of his life had been an inoffensive and an honourable man ... set a fearful example in that he left the infantry unprotected by the cavalry and in flight tried to reach the Rhine with his squadrons of horse. But fortune avenged his act, for he did not survive those whom he had abandoned, but died in the act of deserting them.'

Varus and his senior officers, according to Dio Cassius, 'fearing that they should either be killed or captured by their bitterest foes (for they had already been wounded), made bold to do a thing that was terrible yet unavoidable; they took their own lives.' All very Roman, and, by the standards of their society, the appropriate action to take, but, no less than Numonius's flight, it constituted an abandonment of the men still fighting, who looked to them for leadership. Now the army fell apart. It is not difficult to picture the scenes – small groups of men fighting on under their few remaining commanders until overwhelmed, killed or made captive; others scattering and fleeing to be hunted down like deer by the exultant tribesmen. A small number escaped – we hear from Tacitus of survivors of the massacre who were on hand six years later to point out to Germanicus where the generals had fallen and where the Imperial Eagles had been captured.

Almost all of Varus's command – some 20,000 men, women and children – were killed or captured. We can only guess at German losses, however, but given the advantages they had taken such pains to ensure for themselves, they must have been far fewer.

Of those captured alive the majority were slaughtered – crucified, buried alive or hanged – as sacrifices to the Germans' gods. The few senior

> 'Of those captured alive the majority were slaughtered as sacrifices to the Germans' gods'

officers, including one legate, who fell alive into the hands of the enemy were put to death with every refinement of cruelty. It was no more than they would have expected – it was not the *Roman* practice to show mercy to a conquered foe. The skulls and bones of these unfortunates were used to decorate the shrines and groves set up by the victors on the scene of their triumph.

Arminius tried to follow up his victory with an attack on the Roman fortress of Aliso (Haltern on the River Lippe), but the fort's commander, Lucius Caedicius, managed to hold firm and later break out by night, taking the garrison and its women and children safely to Vetera (Wesel) on the Rhine. Arminius and his army then withdrew into their forests. Arminius sent Varus's mutilated head to King Maroboduus, leader of the Germanic tribes along the Danube, who sympathized, and even on occasion co-ordinated their offensives, with their cousins along the Rhine.

'Give me back my legions!'

Having recently agreed a peace with the emperor's stepson Tiberius, and being reluctant to jeopardize it, Maroboduus sent the head of Varus to Caesar, who gave it an honourable burial. Varus was not forgiven, even though he had not been alone in misreading the situation on the far side of the Rhine. According to Augustus's biographer Suetonius, the disaster 'nearly wrecked the empire.' Certainly it shattered the myth of Roman invincibility, unsettled Rome's allies and encouraged her many enemies. The loss of three legions was, in itself, a serious one. According to Suetonius, Augustus 'took the disaster so deeply to heart that he left his hair and beard untrimmed for months; he would often beat his head on a door, shouting "Quintilius Varus, give me back my legions!" and always kept the anniversary as a day of deep mourning.'

The battle in the Teutoburger forest convinced Augustus, and his successors, to keep the Rhine and Danube as the empire's frontiers and so, by and large, they remained. The German tribes continued to be a threat to the Roman Empire, and although many Germans crossed over into Roman territory and, as soldiers, served Rome loyally and well, it was Germanic tribesmen who would ultimately bring about the fall of Rome and the destruction of the western Roman Empire.

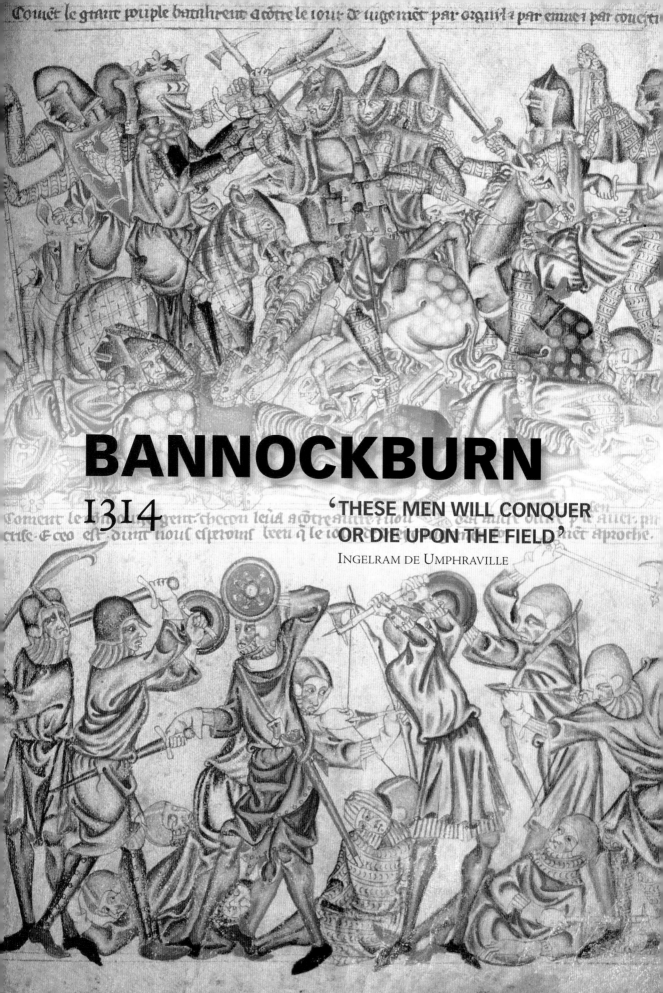

BANNOCKBURN

1314

'THESE MEN WILL CONQUER
OR DIE UPON THE FIELD'

Ingelram de Umphraville

By 1314 Robert the Bruce had consolidated his hold on the Scottish throne and successfully resisted the English King Edward I's claims of paramountcy. Edward is remembered by the English as a crusader and lawgiver, the 'English Justinian', and by the Scots as a bloodthirsty tyrant – but there is truth in both portraits. Edward, the 'Hammer of the Scots', had been marching north to contest Bruce's claim once more when he died, in July 1307. With the accession of his son, the second Edward – who was feckless, reputedly homosexual and in no way the man his father had been – fortune's wheel seemed to have turned in favour of the northern kingdom.

Edward II was content to let affairs in Scotland wait while he consolidated his own rule at home. During this respite, Bruce took ruthless action against his own rivals in Scotland. The Balliol-Comyn faction were harried out of their castles and off their lands, many fleeing to England to seek service with Edward. A few English garrisons remained, notably the strategically vital Stirling Castle to which, in 1313, Bruce's brother Edward laid siege. By the summer of that year a truce had been agreed – if by midsummer's day 1314 an English force had not relieved the castle, it would be surrendered.

Edward rides north

For the relief of Stirling Castle, and the reconquest of Scotland, Edward II assembled at Berwick one of the largest armies the English had ever put in the field, estimated at 2,000 mounted knights, 15,000 foot soldiers and 5,000 archers. The army Bruce was able to muster to meet this threat was considerably smaller – it may have been as few as 500 horse and 7,000 foot – but it was experienced and battle-hardened and had, in Bruce, one of the supreme military commanders of the age. In 1307 he had, at Loudon Hill near present-day Kilmarnock in Ayrshire, defeated a larger English force under Aymer de Valence – now riding north at Edward's

> ' Edward II assembled one of the largest armies the English had ever put in the field '

side. Bruce knew that with his shortage of cavalry he could not match the English on horseback – his army must fight on foot. On Edward's route to Stirling Castle there was a site known as New Park – a flat field surrounded on three sides by woods and marshes. The site would be advantageous to the Scots in that it would serve to channel the English attack into the centre, but here the ground would have to be 'improved', in favour of Bruce's forces naturally, and to disrupt the advance of Edward's heavily armoured horsemen.

OPPOSITE: *A typical 14th-century battle scene, from the* Holkham Bible Picture Book, *1327. If the foot soldiers lacked the glamour of the mounted knights, it was nonetheless by them that medieval battles were won.*

Countering the cavalry

The strength of such cavalry lay in the speed and impact of the charge. Unlike the cavalry forces that fought in ancient conflicts, where men rode without stirrups, threw javelins and sometimes, as seen at Cannae, dismounted to fight on foot, the medieval knight was well anchored in a high-cantled saddle. He could crash at a gallop into formed ranks of men without risk of being unseated. It is a myth that knights had to be winched into their saddles. The roughly 23 kilos (50 lb) of armour they wore is the same weight as a modern infantryman carries on his back, and was distributed evenly over his whole body – many accomplished knights, Henry V for example, could vault into the saddle over their horse's rump. Nor is it true that a knight once unhorsed was as helpless a tortoise on its back – unless he was wounded or winded by the fall.

If Bruce could contrive to break the momentum of the English charge, however, much of their offensive power would be lost. If Bruce's dismounted spearmen could withstand the initial shock of contact with Edward's horse, he knew from his experience at Loudon that they could win the day. The chronicler Geoffrey le Baker says 'The Scots ... dug extended ditches three feet deep and three feet wide from the right to the left flanks of the army, filling them with a brittle plait of twigs, reeds and sticks, that is a 'trellis,' and covering them with grass and weeds. Infantry might be aware of a safe passage through these, but heavy cavalry would not be able to pass over them.'

The English attempt a pre-emptive manoeuvre

Bruce arrayed his army in four divisions under the command (from Scots left to Scots right) of himself, James Douglas, his brother Edward Bruce and Thomas Randolph, earl of Moray. It was the afternoon of 23rd June and the English attack was expected that day, but the English host had not appeared. The reason soon became apparent – Edward was trying to slip a force round the Scots' right flank to achieve a relief of Stirling Castle *before* fighting the main battle.

If he could manage to do this, he probably reasoned, it would, under the terms of medieval warfare, free Stirling's commander Sir Philip Mowbray from his promise of surrender and enable him, without loss of honour, to sally out of the castle and attack the Scots' left. To this end, a force of 800 men under Sir Robert de Clifford and Sir Henry Beaumont detached itself from Edward's array and set off past the Scots' right, separated from it by the woods, and heading towards Stirling. As they did so, however, Sir Thomas Randolph took 500 of his men from the right-hand Scots division through the woods to forestall them. It speaks volumes for the high morale and determination of this Scots army that Randolph's 500 men were willing to take on De Clifford's 800.

'the English horse threw spears, darts, knives and finally even swords, axes and maces into the Scottish ranks'

High morale or not, they soon found themselves surrounded by superior numbers of armoured cavalry. Formed in a circle with levelled spears, Randolph's men beat off

repeated attacks by the English horse who, frustrated in their attempts to break the spear line, threw spears, darts, knives and finally even swords, axes and maces into the Scottish ranks. Seeing Randolph's men embattled and in danger, eventually, of being worn down, James Douglas rode over to Bruce and asked permission to take a force to their relief. Initially reluctant to weaken further his battle line in the presence of Edward's main force, Bruce eventually relented, and Douglas led his men off.

'I have broken my good axe'

Perhaps believing that this was the beginning of a general retreat, the English vanguard – led by Gilbert de Clare, earl of Gloucester, and Henry de Bohun – charged in what they thought was pursuit. However, what confronted them, seemingly to their surprise, was not

ABOVE: *Robert the Bruce, about to bring his 'good axe' down on the head of Henry de Bohun in front of both armies. The hand-to-hand encounter raised Scottish spirits and demoralized the English.*

Douglas's relieving force but the remnant of the main Scottish body, led by Bruce himself. Bruce was easily recognizable from the crown on his helmet and it was at this point that De Bohun decided on a solitary action that – if successful – could have decided the issue of the war at a stroke. He charged at Bruce, intending to kill him. Bruce was not mounted on his battle charger. These horses – known as 'destriers' because they were led by a squire on the 'dexter', or right-hand side of the knight, to be ready when needed – were far too precious and highly trained for general use, for which a smaller horse, or 'palfrey', was preferred. Bruce, then, was at a disadvantage, but he reacted coolly, awaiting his heavier-mounted opponent and, at the last minute, turning his mount to one side. As De Bohun's lance missed him by inches and the knight was carried past by the momentum of his charge, Bruce rose in his stirrups and brought his axe crashing down on his noble opponent's head with such force that the handle broke. De Bohun was killed instantly in front of both armies, inspiring the Scots and dismaying the English.

> 'Bruce brought his axe crashing down on his noble opponent's head'

Medieval infantry

The armoured knight, mounted on his charger, is the dominating image of medieval warfare, but he did not necessarily dominate the battlefield. Bannockburn is an early example of a phenomenon we see throughout the period – of large, cavalry-based armies being defeated by smaller infantry forces. In most cases the infantry chose the site of the battle and arrived early, in time to ready the ground, leaving their opponents just one avenue of attack. The infantry formed up for battle in a succession of thick lines, usually two lines and a reserve, designed to absorb the initial shock of the cavalry onslaught. Channelled onto unsuitable ground, their attacks uncoordinated and all impetus lost, cavalry could prove as vulnerable, as one English poet put it, as hares in a trap.

Breaking formation, the Scots surged forward, driving Gloucester's men before them. The impromptu attack of the English vanguard defeated, Bruce rode back to be rebuked by the Scottish leaders for so exposing himself. 'I have broken my good axe!' was his only reply.

Meanwhile, Douglas's force had arrived on the field of Randolph's struggle with De Clifford. Both sides were exhausted, having fought for hours in the broiling sun and, according to some chroniclers, at the very sight of Douglas's fresh troops, the English began to fall back. Douglas, it is said, noble in character as well as in name, halted his force so as not to rob Randolph of credit for the victory. 'It would be a sin for him to lose his well-earned honour.'

Edward had never intended to fight that day, and the two small battles that had taken place had ended in Scottish victories. Morale in the English camp was low, not helped by its situation in low, marshy ground. The English nobles went about assuring their men that the issue of the next day, when their main force engaged the Scots, would be very different. At the same time Bruce was touring the Scottish camp warning his exultant men of the dangers of overconfidence, but reminding them of the justice of their cause and the need for strict discipline the following day – no one was to stop for loot until the day was truly won. It must have been reassuring for the Scots to learn that this was their commander's main worry – it is the victors, after all, who get to plunder the dead.

Honour and chivalry

The following morning Bruce formed his army in three lines – two main battle lines and a reserve. The whole army would fight on foot and, to indicate that there would be no question of flight, Bruce and his staff dismounted. According to the anonymous author of the *Vita Edwardi Secundi* (*Life of Edward II*), the Scots host was equipped with light armour and 'had axes at their sides and carried lances in their hands.' After knighting James Douglas and another knight who had distinguished himself in the previous day's fighting, Bruce led the army in prayer.

Seeing the entire Scots army fall to their knees in prayer, not in itself an unusual sight in those times, Edward said, possibly in jest, 'They kneel down – they beg for mercy!' Ingelram de Umphraville – a Scottish knight, but an enemy of Bruce – replied 'Yes, but they ask it from God, not from us – these men will conquer, or die upon the field.'

In fact, Bruce's choice of formation had caused Edward to confer with his senior commanders about the best way to deal with the Scots. De Umphraville, a renowned man of war who had recently returned from the Holy Land, suggested that the English feign retreat, falling back behind their camp, thus inducing the Scots to break ranks and loot it – Bruce's fear of the night before. Once they had done so, he argued, the more numerous English could attack and hew down their disordered ranks. Edward would have none of it – as with Douglas, holding short of rescuing Randolph, honour was a powerful factor in medieval military decision-making. It was not the ruse but the idea of a retrograde step that Edward considered shameful. Honour may have played its

> '**these men will conquer, or die upon the field**'
>
> INGELRAM DE UMPHRAVILLE

part, too, in his decision not to deploy the one sure war-winning weapon the English possessed – their longbowmen. These had methodically massacred William Wallace's schiltrons, hedgehog-like spear formations, at Falkirk, allowing the knights of Edward I father's to ride over the remnant. At Bannockburn, their constricted frontage made it more difficult for the English to deploy their archers – in truth, the best battlefield asset they possessed. There may, however, have been another reason why they were held back. This was to be the decisive clash between two kings and two kingdoms – archers, however effective, were mere professional soldiers. It is likely that Edward and his nobles were reluctant to share the glory of what must surely be a notable victory, one that would be remembered in songs and chronicles for years to come, with men who were, by origin, peasants. This victory would be won by the might of English chivalry, by noblemen performing noble feats of arms against men of their own caste – enemies, it is true, but men they both knew and respected.

The English charge repeatedly

The English host, a mass of armoured cavalry, advanced slowly, first at a walk, then at a trot and finally at a gallop. The evidence of the chronicles is confused, but there is more than a hint that the Scots made a partial advance to meet them 'like a thick-set hedge' according to the *Vita*. As Bruce had intended, the broken ground – pits, ditches and trenches – slowed the English here and there, but not enough to prevent them crashing into the ranks of his spearmen. This was not one charge but a succession of charges, as the English horse, led by the rival earls of Gloucester and Hereford, made repeated attempts to plunge through the Scottish mass, only to see men and horses spitted on Scottish lances.

Bruce's lines held, though, and groups of Edward's cavalry fell back and charged again repeatedly all along the battle line. Even if the first charge did not sweep away a dismounted enemy, the constant pressure of charge after charge could be expected to wear them down to breaking point. The chronicler John de Trokelowe paints a vivid picture of the fighting: 'The crash of the lances, the ringing of the swords, the noise of hasty blows, the groan of the dying, the lamentations of the wounded, being heard in this conflict seemed to split the air. For a long time it was fought at the front of the lines with the ringing of many swords and both armies fighting strongly against each other.' The fight seemed evenly matched for some time, but then the exhausted English horse began to waver. With levelled lances the Scots began to push steadily forward.

Seeing this, some of the English archers attempted to deploy, forming up on the English right flank and opening a deadly fire that was soon creating gaps in the massed Scottish ranks. Forewarned by bitter experience, Bruce had set aside a small mounted force, under Sir Robert Keith, for just such a contingency. Edging round the marsh, Keith's men were soon slashing among the archers, scattering and slaughtering the lightly armoured footmen. Observing the fate of their comrades, the rest of the archers remained crowded at the rear and contented themselves with sending a desultory shower of arrows over the heads of their own troops. They caused few casualties, and these most likely shared equally among the combatants of both sides.

> 'the cry went up along the Scots line 'On them, on them! They fail, they fail!'

The English line breaks

Now the English main body was being driven back in disorder and the cry went up along the Scots line 'On them, on them! They fail, they fail!' Finally the English line broke, and it was now that the broken ground really began to take effect. In the words of the *Lanercost Chronicle*, 'Another misfortune which happened to the English was that, although they at first had crossed a great ditch called Bannockburn, into which the tide flows, and now in confusion wanted to re-cross it, in the press many nobles and others fell into it with their horses. And while some escaped from it with much difficulty, many were never able to remove themselves from the ditch. Thus Bannockburn was in the speech of Englishmen for many years after.'

At this point, several chroniclers report that the Scots 'small folk' – interpreted as camp followers and local peasantry, though it has been suggested that they may in fact have been a force of lightly armed highlanders – joined in the fight, cutting down English stragglers and helping in the capture of English knights for ransom.

Among the knights foundering in the marshy ground was the earl of Gloucester. This young nobleman, no doubt angered by the previous day's check, had been all morning in the thick of the fighting. In the words of John de Trokelowe, 'Whomever he struck with his sharp blade, he cut off a head or some other limb. Finally thirsting so for their deaths, the equilibrium of the entire battle was turned around to such a degree that the points of the lances being applied to each part of his own body stabbing several places, he was knocked to the ground, and his head was struck on all sides by the clubs of the enemy, until he breathed out his soul under the horse's feet.' Gloucester had neglected to wear a surcoat over his armour – otherwise his opponents would surely have spared his life for the enormous ransom his family could have been expected to pay.

Whatever his perceived weaknesses, there is no evidence that Edward lacked personal courage. It was two members of his personal retinue, Aymer de Valence, earl of Pembroke, and Sir Giles de Argentine who, seeing that all was lost, persuaded him to quit the field. Argentine, a noted crusader,

> '**O day of vengeance and misfortune! Odious and accursed day!**'
> WILLIAM OF MALMESBURY

actually grabbed Edward's bridle, turned his horse and bade him farewell. 'It is not my custom to fly!' the knight added and, shouting his battle cry of 'Argentine! Argentine!', charged onto the Scottish spears. Bruce, who knew De Argentine well, later had his body interred in the Church of St Giles in Edinburgh.

Edward fled first to Stirling Castle, but was denied admittance, its governor, Sir Philip Mowbray, reminding him that he was obliged to surrender the next day. The king then rode through Torwood, hotly pursued by James Douglas and, soon, Sir Laurence Abernethy, a Scottish knight who had been bringing his men to fight for Edward but, hearing of the battle's outcome, had changed sides. They pursued Edward as far as the mighty fortress of Dunbar Castle, which looms over the town and its port below, where the king found refuge with the earl of March. From Dunbar, Edward was able to sail to England in a fishing boat.

Passing into legend

The Battle of Bannockburn passed almost immediately out of history and into legend, where it remains. Accurate figures for those engaged, killed and wounded are, therefore, even more difficult to come by than is usually the case. John Barbour gives a – probably exaggerated – figure of 30,000 for the English dead. What is certain is that the casualties were in the thousands and included 200 English knights and 700 squires – Edward's army had effectively ceased to exist. Some idea of the extent of the disaster can be gained from the lament of William of Malmesbury: 'O day of vengeance and misfortune! Odious and accursed day! Unworthy to be included in the circle of the year, which tarnished the glory of England, and enriched the Scots with plunder of the precious stuffs of our nation to the extent of two hundred thousand pounds; how many illustrious nobles and valiant youths, what numbers of excellent horses and beautiful arms, precious vestments and golden vessels, were carried off in one cruel day!' Scots casualties were far fewer, with only two knights – Sir William Vipont and Sir Walter Ross – having perished.

The making of Scotland

Bannockburn was a stunning victory by an army inferior to its enemy in numbers and equipment, its only advantages being in morale, determination and the quality of its leadership. The battle ensured the survival of Scotland as an independent kingdom, which even the English crown was, at length, obliged to recognize. Arriving safely home, unlike his army, Edward's problems were far from over. Defeat in Scotland tarnished his image as a military leader, on which so much of medieval kingship depended. His reign would end in his deposition by his wife and her lover, and his hideous murder carried out, it was said, with a red-hot poker.

The defeat caused shockwaves throughout England, and its causes were much debated in military circles. We can see that Bruce's eye for and use of ground together with outstanding qualities both as a general and a leader of men, were major factors in the Scottish victory. The Scots formation of massed spears in successive thick lines proved most effective against massed cavalry, something which should not have come as a surprise to the English since the Flemings had won a similar victory against the might of French chivalry at Courtrai in 1302. Perhaps the greatest mistake on the part of the English was their failure to deploy what we would now call a combined-arms force and give full play to the strongest piece on the board – the longbowman. Under Edward's son, the third king to bear that name, the English were soon to embark upon the longest war in history. The lessons learned at Bannockburn would not be forgotten.

'IN THE NAME OF GOD AND ST DENIS!'
FRENCH MARSHAL

CRÉCY

1346

The origins of the series of wars between England

and France, known to history as the 'Hundred Years' War', lie some 200 years earlier when, by marriage, the king of England also became duke of Aquitaine. Thus the king of one country, England, became the nominal vassal of another country, France. Medieval kings' relations with their vassals were often troubled, to say the least, and the French kings were no exception. Much of their time was spent in dispute, or even at war with their own over-mighty subjects. If the French king was able, ultimately, to maintain his authority over most of his counts and dukes, it was a very different story with the duke of Aquitaine.

Aquitaine consisted of most of the western half of France, from the English Channel to the Pyrenees. Its people and nobles owed allegiance to their duke, the king of England, who could throw the whole strength of that kingdom into the scale in any conflict. The situation was galling to both parties. If it was hard for the French king to stomach another king owning half of his kingdom, it was equally hard for an English king to be required to do homage to another king for half of *his* kingdom. As a result, war between England and France was nothing new when, in 1327, Edward III – son of Edward II, defeated at Bannockburn – came to the English throne. Competing interests in the Low Countries, as well as French support for Scotland, had already brought the two kingdoms to the brink of war.

Tensions were further raised when the death of Charles IV of France gave the English king a claim on the French crown. As Charles's nephew, Edward III was considered by the English, and even by many French, as the rightful heir to the French throne. However, the French barons chose Philippe de Valois, Charles's cousin, as their king. They rejected Edward because, although he was French-speaking and of French descent, he was also the king of England and a foreigner. Edward's claim on the French throne may not have been the cause of his going to war with France in 1337, but it was a useful pretext.

Edward invades

In 1346 Edward invaded northern France, marching his army from the Cherbourg Peninsula northwards towards Paris, ravaging all the way. He crossed the Seine at Poissy, intending to march north and join with his Flemish allies at Amiens, but by now King Philippe of France had taken the field with 60,000 men – almost three times Edward's number. The French army blocked all Edward's attempts to cross the River Somme until a French prisoner, bribed with gold, guided Edward to a ford named Blanchetaque ('white spot'). It was an opposed crossing – Philippe had posted 3,500 men-at-arms there, as well as a contingent of Genoese crossbowmen – but the English army fought its way

---

PREVIOUS PAGE: *The defeat of Philippe IV's French troops by the English army of Edward III at the Battle of Crécy. Edward's was a semi-professional army against which courage alone could not prevail.*

across and continued its northward march. The English were in a bad way: supplies were low, boots were worn out and sickness was taking its toll on men and horses – and Philippe's army was close on their heels.

On 23rd August – the day after Blanchetaque – Edward was at bay. He turned and made a stand near the market town of Crécy-en-Ponthieu. He chose his position well on a ridge to the northwest of the town, his right flank protected by the River Maye and his left, 2,000 yards (1828 m) away, by the village of Wadicourt. In the centre, the ground was terraced, allowing him to hold what was an extensive position given the size of his army of approximately 12,000–13,000 men.

A 'great and bloody battle' is foretold

Edward formed his army for battle in three divisions. The vanguard was commanded by his teenage son Edward, the Black Prince – the name, which may refer to the black armour that he wore, was not used in his own time. The vanguard was posted at the place of honour on the army's right. The prince was only nominally in command, actual command being exercised by the earls of Warwick and Oxford, with the king's friend Godfrey Harcourt acting as the boy's tutor and bodyguard. This division was deployed part way down the slope, with its left flank resting on one of the terraces. The rearguard, commanded by the experienced earl of Northampton, took the left, slightly higher up the slope, and to the left of the terrace on which the prince's right rested. The centre, the reserve which the king commanded personally, was posted in the centre near a windmill, approximately 700 yards (640 m) to the rear and to the left of the prince's division. From here Edward could reinforce his left or right, as occasion demanded. The baggage was positioned to the rear of the army, with the wagons deployed as a defensive perimeter – Edward intended to fight on foot. From the front of the English line the ground sloped down gently to the River Maye – the area later renamed the Vallée au Clercs.

The English lines consisted of groups of men-at-arms on foot, interspersed with wedges or 'herces' of longbow archers. The army arrayed and reviewed, there was time for the cooks to prepare a meal and for the soldiers to eat and rest. As they did so, a brief but fierce storm arose, with thunder and lightning, and flocks of crows flew over both armies – the resting English and the still-marching French. Experienced knights said this portended a great and bloody battle.

If the two armies about to engage were similar in appearance, they were very different in nature. The French army was the classic feudal host, composed of masses of mounted, armoured knights, serving unpaid under the terms on which they held land from the king. They were a military caste, formidable fighting men, but proud, independent-minded and impatient of discipline. Recruited by an early form of *levée en masse* (mass conscription), the foot were variously armed, equally undisciplined and generally of little use in the open field. An element of professionalism was provided by the Genoese mercenary crossbowmen, under their leaders Ottone Dorian and Carlo Grimaldi, who had taken a toll among the English archers as they had crowded together to wade across the Blanchetaque ford.

Although the English army was, apart from its longbow archers, equipped in a similar way to the French, they had been recruited on a very different basis. Nearly every man in the army, from the highest to the lowest, was 'indentured', which is to say he served for pay under a nominated captain. As medieval historian Carl Stephenson put it, 'The English army ... had definitely ceased to be feudal. Rather it was a mercenary force, in which the mounted noble, as well as the yeoman archer, humbly served at the King's wage.' This difference had implications for discipline in the two armies, which would prove crucial in the hours to come.

The longbow

With an effective range of 200 yards (183 m) and a much higher rate of fire than the crossbow, the longbow proved a consistent battle-winner for the English. So why did the French not adopt it? The answer lies in the fact that both longbows and longbowmen took a long time to produce. The longbow archer's training began almost as soon as he could stand, the skills being passed from father to son – no nation could suddenly decide to equip its army in this way. In all likelihood the French would not have done so even if it had been possible. The longbow was a peasant's weapon and, more wedded than their ancient enemy to the feudal system, the French would have been reluctant to place such a weapon in the hands of those who might well be tempted to use it against their feudal masters.

Premature attack

At about the hour of vespers (4 p.m.) the French appeared, approaching from the southeast, and the English army stood-to. The French had been marching all day and King Philippe wanted to halt for the night. His advisors agreed – the army was disordered, tired and hungry. The chronicler Jean Froissart, who had talked to men who had fought on both sides, described what followed as the king's two marshals tried to halt the army: 'One of them rode forward and the other rode back, shouting to the standard bearers: "Halt banners on the King's orders, in the name of God and St Denis!" At this command the leaders halted, but those behind continued to advance, saying they would not stop until they had caught up with the front ranks. And when the leaders saw the others coming they went on also. So pride and vanity took charge of events. Each wanted to outshine his companions. Neither the King nor his Marshals could restrain them any longer, for there were too many great lords among them, all determined to show their power.'

Confident in their numbers – about three times those of the English – and eager to get to grips with the enemy, the French host surged forward. Close behind them followed a large mass of French foot – the provincial levies. Froissart tells us: 'They crowded the roads between Abbeville and Crécy, and when they came within ten miles of the enemy they drew their swords and shouted "Kill! Kill!" Yet they hadn't seen a soul.'

In their haste to attack they pushed before them the Genoese crossbowmen who, descending into the Maye Valley, were forced to halt three times to reorder their ranks. Behind them the French knights set about what we would call 'improvising an attack off the line-of-march', though their attempts to shake out into battle order were as confused as the day's march had been.

The Genoese come under fire

When they were about 300 yards (274 m) from the English line, the crossbowmen halted and opened fire. The English archers watched as the first 'volley' of crossbow bolts, deadly enough at the right range, nevertheless thudded uselessly into the earth short of the English position. The Genoese reloaded their weapons and advanced once more. At this time, according to Jean Froissart, 'The English archers took one pace forward and poured out their arrows on the Genoese so thickly and evenly that they fell like snow. When they felt those arrows piercing their arms, their heads, their faces, the Genoese, who had never met such archers before, were thrown into confusion. Many cut their bowstrings and some threw down their crossbows.'

'The English archers poured out their arrows on the Genoese so thickly and evenly that they fell like snow'
JEAN FROISSART

This was payback for Blanchetaque. Both of the Genoese leaders, Dorion and Grimaldi, had fallen at the first discharge. Then, to add to their men's demoralization, there followed a series of explosions at intervals along the English line, sending balls of iron and stone among the Genoese ranks. Whether or not they caused any casualties the moral effect of this – the first use of artillery in an open battlefield – seems to have been decisive. The Genoese fell back.

There was no love lost, it seems, between the French knights and their hired hands. Suspecting treachery among their Genoese allies, the first French division, led by the king's brother the comte d'Alençon, immediately rode forward, cutting them down as they did so. Some of the Genoese fired back and a short, bloody struggle ensued. 'The English,' says Froissart, 'continued to shoot into the thickest part of the crowd, wasting none of their arrows. They impaled or wounded horses and riders, who fell to the ground in great distress.'

The lethal longbow takes its toll

Brushing aside the Genoese, the fiery D'Alençon now led his men up the gentle slope towards the Black Prince's position. Meanwhile, the following division, led by the comte de Flandre, wheeled into line to the right of D'Alençon's division and attacked Northampton's division on the English left. In the centre, Jacques de Bourbon followed close behind D'Alençon's division, while on the right, Jean de Hainault advanced on Wadicourt. Behind them, other divisions, led by John, the blind king of Bohemia, and the comte de Blois, descended into the valley. Behind *them* came the mass of French infantry. D'Alençon's advance had begun in disorder and, as the French mass began struggling up the slope towards the English line, the confusion increased. The English awaited the approach of the French cavalry with a confidence born of experience. When the French were at very close range, they unleashed a storm of arrows. The chronicler Jean le Bel tells us, 'The archers fired so skilfully that some of those on horses, feeling the barbed arrows, did not wish to advance, while others charged forward as planned; some resisted them tirelessly. While others turned their backs on the enemy.' It seems clear that the archery took its main toll upon horses, whose flesh was more exposed than that of their riders.

Harrowed by this deadly fire, the French closed in, attempting to avoid the archers and approach the men-at-arms. It was here, fighting men of their own calibre and social standing, that glory was to be won, rather than in cutting down mere infantry. And since that infantry was lethally armed, there was all the more reason to avoid them. By the time D'Alençon's first wave hit the English line, it had lost all impetus, as well as all order. Momentum – 'shock action' – was the essence of medieval cavalry's effectiveness on the field of battle. Without it the French cavalry had little hope of breaking through a strong line of well-armed, well-ordered infantry. 'When fighting with the English men-at-arms,' says the chronicler Geoffrey le Baker, 'the French were beaten down by axes, lances and swords. And in the middle of the army, many French soldiers were crushed to death by the weight of numbers.' In a disordered army, numbers can actually be a disadvantage. Crowding into the centre of the prince's line, large numbers of heavily armoured knights seem to have died in the crush.

Here and there, small groups of men, including one led by D'Alençon himself, managed to penetrate the English line, but were soon cut down. In a matter of minutes it was all over, and the French first wave had been utterly defeated. The comtes d'Alençon and de Flandre were both killed, while Louis de Male, De Flandre's son, and Jacques de Bourbon were badly wounded.

A prince wins his spurs

The French were not finished yet, and within minutes a fresh wave of horsemen, led by the duc de Lorraine and Jean de Hainault, rolled up the slope towards the English line. This wave met the fate of the first – and by now the ground in front of Edward's army was littered with dead and wounded men and kicking horses – but as it receded, a third wave appeared on the scene, led by King John of Bohemia. King John was blind, but hearing that the battle had commenced, he turned to his attendants and said 'My lords, you are my men, my friends and my companions in arms. Today I have a special request to make of you. Take me far enough forward for me to strike a blow with my sword.' Tying their bridles together and setting the king in front, his knights rode up the slope towards the English. Followed by the king's German and Luxembourg knights, they charged straight at the Black Prince's division. The flanking archers, preoccupied by the threats to their front, had hardly had time to land an arrow among the blind king's men before they crashed into the prince's line.

> ' let the boy win his spurs, for if God has so ordained it, I wish the day to be his '
>
> EDWARD III

OPPOSITE: *In an image from an illuminated manuscript, Edward III is shown granting his son Edward the Principality of Aquitaine. Known to history as 'the Black Prince', the young Edward 'won his spurs' at the Battle of Crécy.*

As the French knights fell back, however, the archers turned inwards and began firing on the rear of the German column. King John was beaten from his horse and killed, as were all those who had followed him into the prince's ranks, but as his men fell back, some of them to quit the field for good, another division under the comtes de Blois and St Pol charged in.

Made in the half-light of evening, this attack was the crisis of the battle. Despite taking terrible casualties from the English archery, at least six divisions of French knights managed to come to blows with the Black Prince's men-at-arms. At one point, fearing his line would break, the prince's advisors, Oxford, Warwick and Harcourt, sent Sir Thomas of Norwich to his father to plead for reinforcements. 'Is my son dead or stunned' asked Edward, 'or so seriously wounded that he cannot go on fighting?'

'No, thank God, 'replied Sir Thomas,'but he is very hard pressed and needs your help badly.'

'Sir Thomas,' the king replied,'go back to him and to those who have sent you and tell them not to send for me again today, as long as my son is alive. Give them my command to let the boy win his spurs, for if God has so ordained it, I wish the day to be his and the honour to go to him and to those in whose charge I have placed him.'

Heartened by the king's message, the prince's advisors fought on. The king did relent, however, sending a token force of 30 knights to shore up his son's line and ordering Northampton to advance his line to relieve the pressure on the prince.

Slaughter of the nobles

This was the nearest the French came to victory, but soon their knights were falling back, picking their way among their own dead and dying men and horses. Yet the French continued their assaults – as many as a dozen more attempts were made, only to meet the same fate. Not until darkness fell, after six hours of fighting, could the English relax their vigilance. In the meantime a great slaughter went on among the wounded. 'Among the English,' says Froissart, 'there were pillagers and irregulars, Welsh and Cornishmen armed with long knives, who went out after the French ... and when they found any in difficulty, whether they were counts, barons, knights or squires, they killed them without mercy. Because of this, many were slaughtered that evening, regardless of their rank. It was a great misfortune and the king of England was afterwards very angry that none had been taken for ransom, for the number of dead lords was very great.'

King Philippe had fought bravely – he had had two horses killed under him – but as had happened to the English king's father at Bannockburn, he was dissuaded from throwing himself into the fight, and hustled from the battlefield by his advisors. Jean de Hainault seized the king's bridle and led him away from the fighting. Philippe eventually found safety at the castle of La Broye, where he announced himself to its captain as 'the unfortunate King of France.'

The English army slept under arms on the ground they had defended and it was only when the morning's fog had cleared that the extent of their victory was revealed to them. Edward sent his clerks and heralds down into the valley (hence its name, the Vallée des Clercs) to identify and number the French dead. Among the dead of note were King John of Bohemia – mourned by Edward as 'the crown of chivalry'. The Black Prince took John's distinguishing crest, the three ostrich feathers, as his personal emblem – to the present day it remains the emblem of the Prince of Wales. Also numbered among the slain were the duc de Lorraine, 12 counts, 80 knights banneret (knights who fought under their own banner), 1,200 knights and uncounted (and unrecorded) thousands of foot. It was the worst defeat the French had suffered up to that time. English losses amounted to no more than 100 men-at-arms and archers.

The Hundred Years War begins

Following a similar victory by the Black Prince at Poitiers in 1356, the Treaty of Brétigny of 1360 gave Edward Aquitaine in sole right of ownership. The ending of the English king's vassalage to the French did not, however, put an end to hostilities, which continued on and off for another 93 years. It is perhaps ironic that the English should have introduced the use of artillery in this war, for it was the French who would eventually prove the master gunners, using these weapons to blast the English out of their French fortresses and, ultimately, out of France.

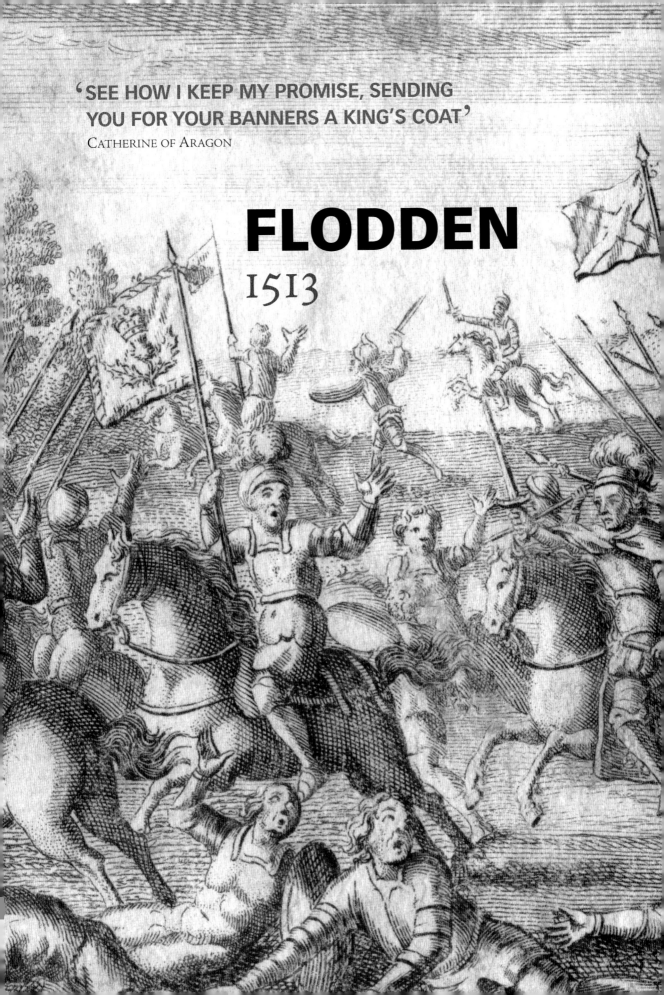

'SEE HOW I KEEP MY PROMISE, SENDING
YOU FOR YOUR BANNERS A KING'S COAT'
CATHERINE OF ARAGON

FLODDEN

1513

Henry VIII came to the throne determined to emulate

his most famous predecessor, Henry V, and win military glory in France. To this end, joining other nations in Pope Julius II's Holy League against France, Henry took a mighty army across the English Channel in the spring of 1513. The French king, to distract Henry, resorted to a traditional French strategy, urging James IV of Scotland to invade England.

James had in the previous years equipped himself with a powerful train of heavy artillery and, more recently, had been importing long pikes from the Low Countries. With the aid of a military mission of 40 French officers, he had persuaded his army to abandon their traditional weapons and train with pikes – the use of which by massed columns had won great success for Swiss and German armies. James's army, the largest Scotland ever put in the field, was state-of-the-art, even if his men were less well trained than their Continental counterparts and uneasy about their new weapons and tactics.

Defence of the realm

With Henry in France, the defence of England fell to the regent, his first wife Catherine of Aragon, and so in practical terms to Thomas, Earl of Surrey, head of the mighty Howard family who held (and still hold) the position of earl marshal of England. Surrey's army was composed of men from the north of England, hastily assembled and mostly armed with their traditional weapons of the bill (an English version of the halberd, a combined spear and battleaxe) and the longbow. Surrey also had a complement of guns, but of much smaller calibre than the Scottish guns.

Traditionally, medieval armies were organized in three divisions – 'vaward', 'main' and 'rearward'. Surrey adapted this slightly, forming his army into two main divisions – the vaward under his son Thomas Howard, the admiral of England, and the main under his own command. Each division had two flanking 'wings', one of which, flanking the admiral's vaward, would be commanded by Surrey's younger son, Edmund Howard. Both armies rode to battle, but would fight mainly on foot.

James encamps on Flodden Hill

James crossed the Tweed on 22nd August, marched south and laid siege to the bishop of Durham's castle of Norham. The bishop of Durham was a major power in the north; his own troops, known as Saint Cuthbert's host, were among the best in Surrey's army. He was confident that Norham could hold out indefinitely, but James's heavy guns battered the medieval fortress into submission in just five days. There followed a delay, which legend, and some chroniclers, put down to James's infatuation with the castle's chatelaine, Lady Heron – the chronicler Robert Lindsay of Pitscottie accuses James of committing 'stinking adultery and fornication' with her. In fact James was merely proceeding

PREVIOUS PAGE: *The defeat of James IV's Scottish army by the earl of Surrey's English troops at Flodden. Unfamiliar with their new weapons and tactics, the Scots fell prey to an opponent fighting in their traditional manner.*

cautiously while he and his commanders scouted out a good position for the Scottish forces on which to confront Surrey and his English army.

By 7th September they had found it – and James and his army were encamped on Flodden Hill facing south. It was a strong position. On a saddle-backed ridge 500 ft (150 metres) above sea level, the Scots were shielded on their right flank by a marsh and on their left by the River Till. In front, almost at the foot of the hill, James had entrenched all his heavy artillery. The river and the marsh would serve to 'channel' any approaching army, whose only option would be a frontal assault in the teeth of James's guns. Assuming the English were bold enough to make such an attempt, and lucky enough to succeed, they would then have to push on uphill and arrive – disordered, breathless, and already having suffered heavy casualties – to face the massed pikes of James's infantry, which would then steamroller them back down the hill. If it was in accordance with the most modern Continental military practice to employ an entrenched camp, it was also in accordance with Scottish military tradition – remember Bannockburn – to use the ground to deny the English the chance to deploy their strongest assets.

Surrey's right hook

Surrey's army was by now desperately short of supplies. He had two choices – he could march his army away in ignominy or he could engage the Scots in battle. He chose the latter. At 5 a.m. on 12th September, Surrey began marching his army from Wooler Haugh to Barmoor Wood, two miles (3.2 km) to the east of the Scots position, separated from it by the River Till and a line of low hills.

Surrey's plan was basically a huge right hook – the vaward under his son Thomas Howard would march north and cross the Till by Twizel Bridge, close to the river's junction with the River Tweed. His son would have to take the artillery along with him, as Twizel Bridge was the only feasible crossing point for the guns. Surrey himself, leading the main body, intended to cross the Till by a much nearer crossing point, the Millford (or Sandy Ford). The two English forces would then line up in a position behind and to the north of the Scots – placing them between Scotland and its army – and attack the Scots from the rear.

'he could march his army away in ignominy or he could engage the Scots in battle'

On the east end of Flodden Edge, at the far left of his position, King James and his advisors watched for most of the morning as Surrey's army abandoned its position and marched away past their left, on its way ... where? What was Surrey doing?

There seemed two possible explanations:

1)   Surrey was marching on Scotland. His intention was to bypass the Scots army, cross the Tweed and ravage the Merse, the area north of the Tweed, in what would now be called a 'counter-stroke'. Thus he would draw the Scots army back to defend their own territory, clearing them out of England without the risk of a battle.

2)   Surrey was marching on Berwick to revictual and replenish his army.

It was not until James's scouts, shadowing the English array from the western side of the Till, brought news that the admiral and his division had wheeled left and crossed the Twizel Bridge, that a new set of possibilities were considered. Either Surrey intended to park his army across James's lines of communications with Scotland and thus manoeuvre him out of position, or he intended to bring on a battle.

The Scots turn about

Thus, James decided – urged on, it is said, by English renegade Giles Musgrave – to turn his army about and march it onto Branxton Hill, keeping the advantage of the high ground. This was a huge undertaking. The whole army had to be inverted – the left would now become the right, an unsettling development with implications for morale – and its heavy guns would have to be dragged out of the emplacements that had been so painstakingly prepared and redeployed at the forward edge of Branxton Hill, pointing north.

While this was happening, the admiral's English division, along with all the artillery, was crossing the Twizel Bridge. Once across the River Till, the admiral formed the vaward in traditional fashion with the main body in the centre and two vaward wings, plus the artillery, and began advancing south towards Branxton Hill. The English vaward was about half the size of the Scots army now forming up ahead on top of Branxton Hill. As he advanced, the admiral would have been casting anxious eyes away to his left, hoping to see his father and the English main body.

On the hill towards which the admiral was advancing, the Scots army was forming up. In the course of breaking up their camp, the king's servants had set fire to the camp's rubbish. The smoke from these fires now blew from behind the Scots, over them and down towards the English, inconveniencing both armies. Smoke or no smoke, the admiral knew that he was not only outnumbered but outflanked – the Scots army's left (formerly their left) extended far beyond his own right. He sent a rider off to the left to find his father and the rest of the army, ripping off his 'Agnus Dei' badge and handing it to the messenger to stress the urgency of the situation.

Surrey proved close at hand. As the vaward reached the foot of the hill, Surrey's division came hurrying up to form on their left – the English army was complete, and only just in time!

The English gunners best the Scots

As soon as the English army arrived within range, the Scots guns opened fire. Despite their advantage in weight of shot, the ensuing artillery duel did not go as James had hoped. The Scots guns were siege artillery, designed for precision fire. Emphasis was on slow, careful loading and aiming – and having a powerful recoil, the guns took some time to be manhandled back to their firing positions. The English guns were lighter field artillery, designed for rapid loading and firing at a constantly moving target – with a lighter recoil, they could be brought back into action more quickly. Thus, although both rates of fire would seem painfully slow by modern standards, the English fire was faster and more effective. The Scots guns were firing downhill – a difficult business due to the mysteries of trajectory – and may even have had problems depressing (lowering) their barrels sufficiently for effective fire. Many of their balls seem to have passed harmlessly over the heads of the English, and those that found a target simply buried themselves in the earth rather than bouncing repeatedly – the desired 'grazing' effect that caused maximum casualties. Firing up the slope, the English balls 'grazed' nicely off the summit giving the English gunners a distinct advantage. The chronicles tell us that Robert Borthwick, the Scots master gunner, was killed, though records reveal that he was alive years later. It may be, however, that a senior Scots gunner was killed, damaging the gunners' morale, for soon the English gunners had the best of it, driving the Scots from their weapons.

'English balls ploughed into the ranks, taking off arms and heads'

Their dominance established, the English gunners now turned their attention to James's densely packed columns. English balls ploughed into the ranks of his infantry, killing men in the front ranks and taking off arms and heads from the men massed behind. This was still a new experience in warfare, and James could not expect his men to stand such punishment for long. He had two options: withdraw his columns out of range of Surrey's guns and await his attack further back – or attack himself. The first option was risky – any withdrawal under fire has the potential to degenerate into a rout, and having seen their gunners bested, Scots morale may have been shaky. Far better, and more kingly, to attack.

As the English, at least on their right, had by now started to ascend the hill, the Scots would still have the advantage of the ground.

The armies line up

If we had taken up a viewpoint behind the advancing Scots we would have seen the following: beyond the Scots army, at the foot of the hill, the English army (divided into two bodies) was coming up the hill. To the left, the admiral's vaward was flanked by two smaller vaward wings – the one to the left of it (on the English extreme right) was commanded by Edmund Howard, and the one to the right by Sir Marmaduke Constable. To the right of Constable's wings we would have seen the English artillery, deployed in the centre of their army and linking the admiral's force with that of his father, Surrey. To the right of the artillery was a wing commanded by Lord Dacre (this was one of the two wings of Surrey's array). Then came Surrey's main division and finally, on the far right (the English far left), a wing commanded by Lord Stanley. The English formations seem to have been more 'linear' than the Scots – that is to say, the frontage of these blocks of men was longer than their depth.

In front of us we would have seen the Scots army advancing downhill to meet them in several great pike columns, each divided into two brigades, one behind the other. From left to right these were: The Scots Borderers under the chamberlain, Lord Home, who commanded the front brigade. Behind him were massed the Highlanders under Alexander Huntly. To their right marched the men of Fife, Angus and Perthshire under

¶ Hereafter ensue the trewe encountre or
Bataple latelp don betwene .Englāde and:
Scotlande. In whiche bataple the .Scottſ=
he .Kpnge was Clapne.

¶ The maner of thaduaūceſynge of my loro of
Surrep treſourier and .Marſhall of .Englande
and leuetenūte generall of the north pties of th
e ſame with .rrvi .M.men to wardes the kyn=
ge of .Scottſ and his .Armve vewed and noin/
bred to an/hundred thouſande men at/theleeſt.

Lord Errol, and their supporting brigade under the earl of Montrose. Each of these
columns numbered between 3–5,000 men. Next came the Scots main body, led by King
James himself and consisting of his personal retinue, backed by the Western Borderers.
This was the largest column, of between 8–9,000 men. To their right was a smaller
column of the men of Lothian under the earl of Bothwell, and finally, on the Scots'

ABOVE: *The earl of Surrey receives news of the Scottish King James IV's death, and his crown, at the English camp, in
this page from a contemporary pamphlet.*

extreme right, a column of Western and Northern Highlanders under the earls of Lennox (commanding the forward brigade) and Argyll (commanding the supporting brigade). These columns were described as being either 'quadrant' – that is square, or 'pike shaped' – with a frontage narrower than the column's depth. They advanced 'in the Almayne's (German) fashion', silently and in good order, and in 'echelon' formation, so that the left-hand column (Home's) was slightly in advance of the others; the next column (Errol's), to its right, was a little further back; the king's column further behind Errol's, and so on. So, by the time Home collided with the English right, Argyll's column – on the Scots right – was still at the top of the hill. The idea, employed so successfully by the Swiss with their pike columns, was to deliver a succession of fatal body blows to the enemy line.

An impenetrable hedge of pike points

The first clash was on the Scots left against the English right. Here for the Scots under Home everything went according to plan. The ground on the Scots left was perfect for a pike column, and the Cheshire and Lancashire men of Edmund Howard's wing found themselves confronted by a moving wall of armoured infantry, preceded by an impenetrable hedge of pike points. With their close-quarter weapons, the English could not even close with the Scots front rank – those who tried were either spitted on pikes or bowled over by the sheer momentum of Home's column. Behind them (or possibly mixed in among the pikes) – also in 'Almayne' style – were Huntly's Highlanders with double-handed claymores and axes. In short order, Edmund Howard's wing was overrun. 'They proched us with spears,' said one English account, 'and put many over, that the blood burst out at their broken harness. Edmund Howard himself was trampled underfoot three times, and his standard bearer 'hewed in pieces'. As Edmund's men scattered and fled, and it looked as if Surrey's younger son himself would be captured by Home's Scottish Borderers, help arrived in the form of an English Borderer – Lord Dacre.

Dacre's light horse charge

Dacre commanded a force of English Border cavalry, which formed the right wing of Surrey's main body, almost at the centre of the English array. Whether he was sent by Surrey or acted on his own initiative is unclear, but his arrival – light horsemen charging into the triumphant but scattered Scots ranks – restored the situation on the English right. Howard himself was rescued by a renowned Border ruffian, John, the Bastard Heron – in those days bastardy was no disgrace in an eminent family such as Heron's. After a bloody fight the two sides drew apart, and at this point the fighting on the English right ended. Home's hitherto victorious column allowed itself to be held by Dacre's smaller force – some said because, both sides being Borderers, they were all related. Some accounts even talk of news and family gossip being shouted across the bloody, corpse-strewn no-man's-land. Whatever the reason, Home's action – or lack of it – proved crucial. If he had regrouped and attacked again he might have brushed aside Dacre's force and turned in against the right of the admiral's main body, which was even now engaged frontally by the earl of Errol's column. Attacked, therefore, in both the front and in the flank, the admiral's body would have melted away, too, and the whole English line could have been rolled up from right to left.

Although victory was at hand for the Scots, Home seemed content that he had done everything that duty required. 'He does well that does for himself', Home is quoted as saying, 'we have fought our vanguard already and won the same therefore let the rest do their part as well as we.'

Errol's stumble

The second Scots column, Errol's, attacking the admiral in the centre of the battlefield, and King James's main column attacking Surrey's main body, did not have Home's good fortune. The ground over which they advanced was not as smooth as on the English right – it was broken by a small stream known as the Pallinsburn, probably invisible from the top of the hill. The whole English line was massed on a small rise just a few yards beyond. Here, the Scots' supposed advantage of ground was reversed. The burn was small enough to hop across, but the effect of the crossing was to disrupt Errol's ranks. Order was everything to a pike phalanx. As the Macedonians had discovered when fighting the Romans, once gaps appear in the pike wall, men with shorter weapons can work their way through the pike points and wreak havoc. A 5.5-metre (18-ft) pike is a poor close-quarter weapon compared to a bill or sword, and the English billmen now had the advantage.

'Isolated, abandoned and soon surrounded, the earls died where they stood'

Disappointed with the new weapon that had been expected to bring them victory, the Scots seem in this moment of crisis to have abandoned their pikes and turned to their old, familiar weapons – swords and axes. However, against a man armed with a 2.4-metre (8-ft) bill, a swordsman is at a disadvantage – the English found themselves fighting with the advantage of ground and 'reach'. With their broader frontage the English infantry was able to lap round the sides of the Scots columns and attack their flanks. What had been supposed, for the Scots, to be a triumphant downhill march to victory now turned into a traditional, and bloody, slugging match.

The Scottish nobles bear the brunt

For the Scots nobles, this was the kind of fighting they were born and bred for, especially against their ancient foe. As the social as well as political and military leaders of their men, they insisted on leading from the front – taking their places in the front few ranks of each phalanx. This, too, accorded with German and Swiss practice, but it had its disadvantages. The well-armoured noblemen of Scotland bore the brunt of the fighting and took the heaviest casualties. In the fierce hand-to-hand fighting at the front of the columns, as the English billmen of the admiral's vaward began to scythe into the Scots ranks, Scots nobles began to fall in sheaves.

For the men further back in the columns, lacking the leadership of their feudal lords, massed and dying in the front ranks, the strain began to tell. When a unit falls apart, the rot usually starts in the rear ranks – and so it was in Errol's column. Their advance stalled, galled by longbow arrows – more effective against their lighter armour – aware of the slaughter at the head of the column, unable to fight themselves and with the English lapping round their flanks, it is perhaps little wonder that men of the rear ranks of Errol's column began to melt away.

Isolated, abandoned and soon surrounded, the earl of Errol – together with 87 of his family – and the earls of Crawford and Montrose died where they stood. The second Scots column had ceased to exist as a unit.

Defensive positions and flank marches

James's position at Flodden is a good example of a defensive position that is too good. A good defensive position should give the defender the advantage of ground, but seem to offer an attacker a reasonable chance of success. Ideally, the defender's advantage should not become obvious until it is too late and the attacker has committed himself. Bruce's position at Bannockburn, and Edward's at Crécy, both fulfilled these criteria – the advantages of James's position on Flodden Hill were all too obvious. No sane commander would consider assaulting it – and Surrey proved no fool. Surrey's march to come round behind the Scots army illustrates the dangers of making a flank march when the enemy's front is not 'pinned' by an attacking force. Had James brought his army down to attack Surrey as he bypassed the Flodden position, he could have caught the English army when it was divided in two by the River Till. Surrey took a calculated risk – and got away with it.

The 'auld enemy'

The main clash, however, and the longest and bloodiest fight, took place 200 yards (180 metres) to the Scots right (or English left) between James's column and Surrey's main body. Seeing Errol's column halted by the admiral's men, King James had hurried his phalanx forward. This, the most powerful of the Scots columns, composed of the king's personal retinue and the leading nobles, all professional fighting men, crashed into Surrey's lines driving them back 200 yards (180 metres) or more. But the English line held. The Pallinsburn had disrupted the king's column, too, robbing them of the momentum that might have shattered the English line. The forces here were of roughly equal numbers and were made up of the toughest and most experienced troops on either side. The Scots were fighting the 'auld enemy' the English, who were

'James was slain, hit in the jaw by an arrow and slashed across the throat by a bill'

mostly northerners in this instance. They were men with generations of bad blood between them. King James fought bravely at the head of his men – it is said he killed five men with his spear before it broke, and he drew his sword – but the fight developed in the same way as that between Errol and the admiral. Even when reinforced from the rear by troops from Bothwell's smaller column, the king's phalanx could not make the crucial breakthrough. Worse, having destroyed Errol's column, the admiral now brought his men to bear on the king's left flank.

Increasingly desperate, the king and his immediate following slugged their way towards Surrey's banner, hoping to salvage victory by killing the English commander. They reached within 'a spear's length' of Surrey's banners before the English billmen surrounded them. James was slain, hit in the jaw by an arrow and slashed across the throat by a bill. With him died the bishop of St Andrews (who was his bastard son) and the earls of Bothwell, Cassilis and Morton, among many others.

The action on the Scots right is quickly told. While Home, Errol and the king battled with the main English array, Lennox and Argyll's Highlanders remained massed on top of the hill. There they provided flank protection to the king's main column, and guarded the Scots camp and artillery. Realizing that their king was losing the battle below, Lennox and Argyll prepared to march their column to his aid. However, before they could do so, the last force to arrive on the English left, under Lord Stanley, reached the battlefield. Exhausted as they were by their long march, Stanley led his men – scrambling on all fours in places – up the hill to attack the Highlanders. Stanley's Cheshire and Lancashire archers found a perfect target among the largely un-armoured Scots force. As Stanley's billmen followed up the arrow storm with a charge, the Highlanders fled, leaving Argyll and Lennox dead behind them.

A generation's leaders slaughtered

By seven in the evening the slaughter was over. Approximately 10,000 Scots had died in the fighting and pursuit, but it was the status and rank of the casualties that was telling. As well as King James there fell two bishops, two abbots, 12 earls, 13 lords, the eldest sons of five peers and 300 of the flower of Scotland's nobility – an entire generation of political and social leaders. English losses were estimated at 1,500, with no peers among them. For Scotland this was a catastrophe made worse by its nobles' insistence on leading from the front. James may have been conforming with Continental practice – and medieval notions of honour – by wielding a pike in the front rank, but by doing so he risked, and brought about, the political decapitation of his kingdom. The appropriate location for a commander has been much debated over the centuries, but one thing is certain – he should not become personally involved in combat. He may on occasion need to come up to the point of maximum danger, but it is not his proper place on the battlefield.

Queen Catherine sent trophies of the battle – including James's surcoat – to her husband in France, writing exultantly 'See how I keep my promise, sending you for your banners a king's coat'. The military glory that had eluded Henry had been won – in proxy – by his wife at home. Such outcomes do not make for happy marriages.

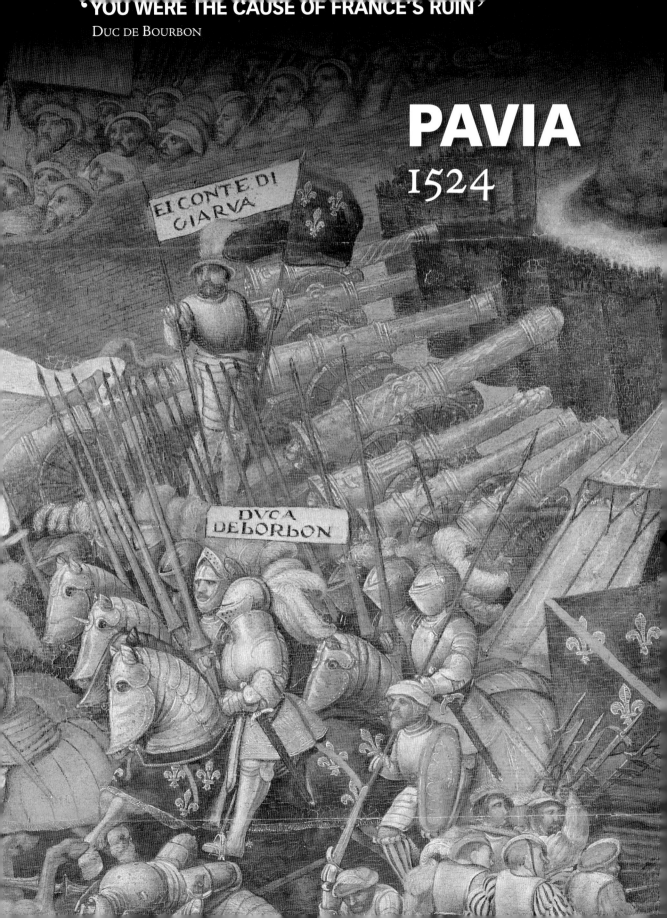

'YOU WERE THE CAUSE OF FRANCE'S RUIN'
Duc de Bourbon

PAVIA
1524

Coming to the throne of France in 1515, Francis I

immediately took up the claims of his Valois predecessors in Italy – not least to the dukedom of Milan. He was opposed by the various states of the 'Italian League', including Venice and the Papal States – and also, crucially, by the Habsburg emperor, Charles V. In 1524, in response to an Imperial siege of Marseilles, commanded by French renegade the duc de Bourbon, Francis launched a counter-stroke: an invasion of northern Italy. This was by no means the Valois' first venture into Italy, though previous attempts had proved more or less disastrous.

This time, however, it seemed likely to be more successful. In October 1524 a plague-ravaged Milan surrendered to Francis. Disdaining to enter the stricken city, Francis turned south to besiege the city of Pavia, a key fortress in northern Italy.

Imperial forces in northern Italy were commanded by Charles de Lannoy, Imperial Viceroy of Naples, assisted by the Neapolitan marquis de Pescara and the French duc de Bourbon, who marched back from Marseilles to join him. Bourbon was a prominent noble in France – too prominent for the liking of Francis. When Francis had met Henry VIII of England, Henry had commented that if he had such a noble in his court he would have his head off. Henry proved as good as his word, executing the duke of Buckingham, largely for being too prominent. Fearing similar treatment from the French king, and angered at being supplanted in the king's counsels by Admiral Bonnivet, Bourbon had taken up service with the emperor.

Mercenary loyalties

Shocking as Bourbon's 'treason' seems to modern eyes, it should be remembered that the armies of this time were largely mercenary – a term that did not have the unfavourable connotations it now carries. Renegades and exiles, commanding bands of mercenaries, abounded in this period. Among Francis's officers were John, duke of Albany, a former regent of Scotland, and Richard de la Pole, 'the White Rose of York' – the last Yorkist claimant to the English throne. Of the mercenaries that made up the bulk of these armies, the Swiss were considered the best, followed by the German *Landsknechts*. These were dressed in similar extravagant fashion and variously armed with pikes, halberds, two-handed swords and an early form of musket, the arquebus. They fought for pay or plunder and would often change sides, though generally when their contract had run out, at the end of a campaigning season. The Swiss at this time nearly always fought for the French – Italian and German mercenaries could be found on both sides. Both sides also had their national contingents: Francis had his French infantry, organized into 'legions', and on the Imperial side, Spanish infantry proved formidable. Light cavalry was often

PREVIOUS PAGE: *Francis I's most dangerous enemy. French renegade the duc de Bourbon (and constable of France) leads Imperial troops against his own king and countrymen at Pavia.*

mercenary, but for heavy cavalry both sides still employed noblemen, equipped in elaborately decorated plate armour, no different from the heavy horse of previous centuries. It was a time of transition, with armoured knights, artillery and muskets all present on the battlefield.

Pavia comes under attack

On 28th October the French army halted in front of Pavia and, after a short bombardment, attempted to take it by storm. The town's western walls were damaged by Francis's heavy guns, but the city's governor, Antonio de Leyva, barricaded the breach and, catching the storming parties in a crossfire, drove them back. Francis's advisors now urged him to continue in pursuit of De Lannoy, who was withdrawing in the direction of Venice, but Francis was determined to capture the town first.

A formal siege was a long, drawn-out process – some of his advisors pointed out the severe conditions his men would have to endure digging and manning trenches through the winter months. They favoured a withdrawal to winter quarters followed by a resumption of operations in the spring. Francis, however, was supremely confident, not least because he had recently received a communication from the pope, Clement VIII, indicating that he was ready to desert the emperor and the 'Italian League'. Clement even claimed he could bring Florence and Venice with him.

Buoyed by this news and his judgement affected, no doubt, by the apparent ease of his conquests so far, Francis now decided to embark on a spectacular coup – an expedition against Naples, 300 miles (480 km) to the south. The pope, when he heard about it, begged Francis to wait until the spring when such a campaign would be more practicable, but the lure of Naples was too great. No sooner had Francis been reinforced – by 8,000 Swiss mercenaries and the 'Black Bands' of Giovanni de Medici (who, having quarrelled with De Lannoy, had decided to switch sides) – than he despatched nearly a third of his army on this fool's errand. John Stuart, duke of Albany, marched off with 600 lances, 10,000 foot, 300 light horse and 12 guns. In the event, Albany's force never progressed further than Rome, where they were delayed by winter conditions – Francis had dangerously weakened his army for no gain.

> 'Francis had dangerously weakened his army for no gain'

The French army digs in

On 31st October the French army began to encircle Pavia according to traditional methods. These involved digging a series of parallels, trench lines parallel to the enemy's walls, then pushing forward zigzag communication trenches until a second parallel could be dug, closer to the walls. Once a parallel was established close enough for the attacking troops to cross the open ground to the enemy's walls fairly quickly, an assault would be mounted on a breach opened up by the guns. While this was in progress, Francis was distracted by another scheme – to divert the course of the River Ticino, which flowed past the south side of the city where there were no proper defensive walls. Here, the river itself formed the city's defence. If it could be dammed, Francis and his men could practically walk into Pavia. Almost the whole of November was spent on this scheme. A dam was built upriver, but just before it could be finished, heavy winter rains swelled the Ticino and swept the dam away.

Work on the trenches resumed. As predicted, it was hard work in appalling conditions. Francis and his nobles lodged in abbeys and country houses, but in the trenches his already depleted ranks were further thinned by desertion and sickness. Even so, Francis remained confident. Among mercenary armies, defections were frequent, and Francis's informants from within Pavia told him that De Leyva's garrison were discontented almost to the point of mutiny. It was true that De Leyva's Spaniards and German *Landsknechts* were suffering from hunger, but they were at least living in town houses – unlike Francis's men strung out in tents and dugouts all round the city's perimeter.

Conditions in Pavia worsen

Still, the prevailing opinion was that Pavia would fall – a wit in Rome offered a reward for anyone who could find an Imperial city 'lost in the Alps'. Charles de Lannoy, however, had not been idle – and nor had Francis's inveterate enemy, the duc de Bourbon. De Lannoy had scraped together what troops he could in northern Italy, and Bourbon had gone to Germany with Imperial cash and returned with 500 Netherlandish horse and 6,000 *Landsknechts* under an old campaigner, Georg von Frundsberg. Altogether the Imperialist generals had mustered an army of 1,000 mounted men-at-arms and 17,000 foot. It seemed unlikely that such a force could take Francis on in a pitched battle, but it might be possible to raise the siege of Pavia in one of two ways: either by placing themselves across his lines of communication with Milan, or by engaging Francis and then retreating – drawing him after them in pursuit. Marching from Lodi, the Imperial army arrived in the vicinity of Pavia on 2nd February. Approaching cautiously from the north, De Lannoy hoped to draw Francis away from the city, but Francis would not be drawn. The following morning he expressed his reasoning in a letter to his mother: 'According to the view I have always held, I think the last thing our enemies will do is fight, because, to be frank, our strength is too much for them… Pavia will be lost to them unless they find some means of reinforcing it, as they have now tried everything in attempting to hold it to the last gasp, which I think is not far away, because for more than a month those inside have not drunk wine or eaten meat or cheese.'

Conditions in the city were desperate, it is true – though rumours that De Leyva had had to execute one of his *Landsknecht* captains seem to have been false. He had, however, been reduced to melting down church vessels and even the gold chain he wore about his neck to pay his men.

Stalemate

Francis reacted to the arrival of De Lannoy by moving the bulk of his army into a defensive position to the east of the city along the line of the Vernacula Brook, a tributary of the Ticino. It was a good position – the Vernacula was only narrow but deep-sided.

Francis fortified the 2-mile (3.2-km) line with earthworks and studded it with guns.
It was a line of 'contravallation' (see page 21) – in accordance with classic practice, which
was much studied at the time. His right flank rested on the River Ticino itself, his left on
the wall of the park of Mirabello, a hunting palace 3 miles (4.8 km) north of the city.
Most of the French army was now manning this east-facing position, with only 2,000
Swiss and De Medici's Black Bands facing west.

Unable to draw Francis away from the siege,
De Lannoy began entrenching his own army
directly opposite the French. Before long, the armies
were staring at each other across the brook from two
lines of entrenchments that were in places only 50 yards (46 metres) apart. Attack was
impractical in either direction and, apart from occasional exchanges of artillery fire,
no action was taken for three weeks.

> 'Both sides were playing the waiting game'

Both sides were playing the waiting game. Francis was waiting for Pavia to fall
through starvation; De Lannoy for desertion and sickness so to deplete the French ranks
as to make the siege unviable. De Lannoy had his own problems, though – both armies
were dependent on the good will of their mercenaries, and his *Landsknechts'* pay was long
overdue. Cold weather, rain and mud had taken their toll on morale, and they were
demanding payment or, failing that, a battle – the plunder from which they would accept
in lieu of pay. De Leyva was sending De Lannoy messages warning him that he would
soon be compelled to surrender, and De Lannoy's subordinates, the fiery Bourbon and
even the cautious Neapolitan Pescara, were urging him to fight.

De Lannoy finally makes a move

It was events in the French camp that finally made De Lannoy's mind up for him.
Repelling a sortie from Pavia on 17th February, Giovanni de Medici was badly wounded
in the foot and withdrew to Piacenza – over the next few days, two-thirds of his Black
Bands dispersed and went home. At the same time, news arrived from the north that a
band of Milanese mercenaries had captured a key fortress in the Valtelline – the main
route between Italy and Switzerland. Those of his Swiss mercenaries who came from the
threatened region – some 6,000 men – marched out of Francis's camp on the 20th, despite
the king's entreaties. In three days the French army had lost nearly 8,000 men. Francis's
army was reduced to 1,300 men-at-arms, 4,000 German *Landsknechts*, 5,000 Swiss and
9,000 French and Italian infantry. Now he scarcely outnumbered the Imperial relief force,
except in heavy cavalry.

Two of Francis's most senior captains, La Palice and La Tremouille, backed by most
of the generals, urged Francis to cut his losses and withdraw, but Admiral Bonnivet, who
spoke last, told them they were too old and had lost their nerve. 'We Frenchmen,' he said,
'never refuse battle, are not used to waging war by little stratagems, but instead show forth
our banners proudly, especially when we have for general a brave King, who can make
even cowards fight … Sire, give battle!' When dealing with kings, flattery rarely fails –
Francis decided to stay put.

A stealthy march under cover of night

De Lannoy, too, had decided on battle. On the night of 24–25th February, while Imperial artillery bombarded the French all along the Vernacula line, De Lannoy took virtually his entire force on a huge flank-march, comparable with Surrey's at Flodden. From its position facing the French along the trench line east of Pavia, the Imperial army in effect made a huge right turn and marched off north. They marched at night in five divisions of infantry, flanked by cavalry, with an advanced guard of pioneers. Like Surrey's flank-march it was a risky venture, although in this case the enemy's front was 'pinned' by the Imperial artillery and the skeleton force manning the entrenchments. Better still, in this case, far from watching the flank-march, the enemy were blithely unaware of it – or at least were as blithe as they could be, huddled in their entrenchments on a wet, windy night. Francis was short of light cavalry, the arm he needed for patrolling and scouting, and to ask the nobles of his heavy cavalry, his *gendarmerie*, to perform such menial tasks was unthinkable, so the Imperial move went unnoticed. As Demosthenes learned at Syracuse, any attack at night risks causing confusion among the attackers as much as the defenders. To guard against this, the Imperial troops wore white shirts over their normal clothes so that the men could distinguish each other in the darkness. By the time the last man of the last Imperial column was clear of the Imperial trench line, the pioneers at the head of the army were at work making breaches in the wall of the hunting park. The Mirabello park, it will be remembered, was the left anchor of Francis's defence line. With its high walls it seemed so secure that it was only lightly defended. If the Imperialists could break into the park without arousing the French, they could sweep down through it and roll up the French army from left to right.

> 'When dealing with kings, flattery rarely fails. Francis decided to stay put'

At length, three breaches were made in the brickwork of the wall and the Imperial columns poured through. A small force of Genoese mercenaries, caught napping, were swiftly dispersed. Behind a screen of light cavalry, Italian mercenery commander Del Vasto's leading column overran the camp around the Mirabello hunting lodge, scooping up numerous civilians, camp-followers and a papal legate. A 'snatch squad' of *arquebusiers* (soldiers armed with an early type of musket) burst into the lodge, no doubt hoping to catch Francis asleep there, but he had elected to spend the night among his troops.

Francis launches a 'spoiling attack'

The unfortunate king was roused from sleep – it was dawn on 24th February, the Feast of St Matthew – to learn that the enemy had marched round him in the night and was now descending on his left rear. The enemy were forming up in battle order. His army was in disarray. The troops closest to him were the nobles of his *gendarmerie*. Placing himself at their head, Francis rode north to confront the enemy, leaving orders for the Swiss under Diesbach to come up on his left, and the German *Landsknechts* under Francis of Lorraine and Richard de la Pole on his right. The bulk of his Italian and French infantry he left,

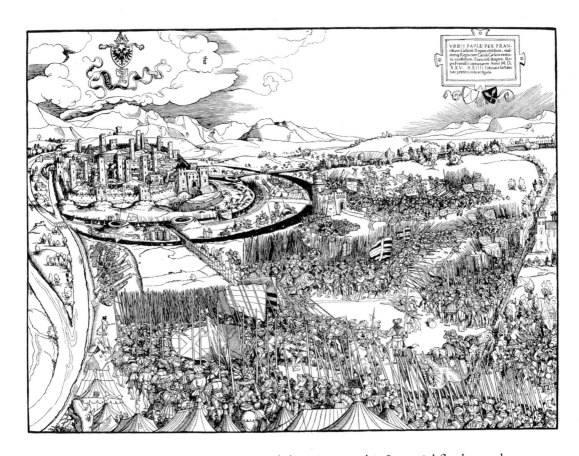

under Bussy D'Amboise, to man the trench line, in case this Imperial flank attack was merely a distraction.

Other troops of Francis's army, the remains of De Medici's corps and Italian troops watching the west walls of Pavia, were distracted by a sortie from within the city. De Lannoy had succeeded in getting a message through to De Leyva the previous day asking him to co-operate with his attack in any way possible. This was the sort of diversionary attack from within that Edward II had been hoping for from the besieged troops in Stirling Castle – only a legal technicality had prevented it. Here, De Leyva's attack prevented Francis's troops in that sector from joining the main battle.

The Mirabello park was typical of royal – or, in this case, ducal – hunting lodges, with open parkland, rides and copses. On reaching it, Francis saw ahead of him, in the light of dawn, the Imperial army still forming up. He had with him only his heavy cavalry and a scratch force of artillery, scraped together by his senior gunner, Galliot. A bold attack now – a 'spoiling attack' – might just stall the Imperialist advance long enough for his own troops to form up on his flanks. Francis was nothing if not bold – after a brief artillery fire, he charged a Spanish-Italian column in the Imperial left-centre, sweeping it away in confusion and with heavy casualties. Then he turned left and attacked the cavalry in their centre. In doing this he 'masked his guns' – artillery at this time was not capable of 'overhead fire', and if friendly troops passed in front of the guns, they fell

'thousands ran to the river, only to be drowned or slaughtered on its banks'

ABOVE: *A contemporary woodcut depicting an overview of the Battle of Pavia. The besieged city can be seen top left; to the right, Imperial troops storm through the park of Mirabello, after their overnight flank-march.*

An opening fusillade

Commentators at the time agreed that Pavia showed the increasing importance of gunpowder on the battlefield. Compared to later firearms the *arquebus* was crude and unreliable. Its powder, ignited by a slow match, proved vulnerable to wet weather, and it took several minutes to load. But if fired in volleys by men protected by trees, hedges or a 'sleeve' of pikemen, its fire could be devastating. Pavia also marked the beginning of a process that would see, in the 19th century, the rifle become the 'queen of the battlefield'.

silent. Even so, Francis and his knights crashed into the Netherlandish and Austrian horse, scattering them and killing their commander. So far things had gone well. Turning to one of his entourage, Thomas de Lescun, Francis cried, 'Now I really can call myself Duke of Milan!' For his part, De Lannoy was dismayed by the speed and ferocity of the French response, crossing himself and declaring 'There is no hope but in God!'

The infantry that might have followed up Francis' initial success, however, had yet to arrive on the battlefield. The horses of his *gendarmerie* were blown now, and further attacks failed to break into the Imperial infantry columns. At last Francis's Swiss and German infantry arrived on the field of battle. On the French left the Swiss, under Diesbach, attacked Del Vasto's corps, which had been the first Imperial troops into the park. Del Vasto's men – and Pescara's, who joined the fight – were mostly *arquebusiers*, and the Swiss pike columns were shattered by their massed fire before they could close. The Swiss fled the field, making for the Milan road. Francis rode over to try to rally them, but to no avail. On the French right the German *Landsknechts* did better, wading into a corps of their countrymen led by De Lannoy himself. The fighting here was severe, only ending when Georg von Frundsberg brought in more Germans on the Imperialist side. Francis's Germans died where they stood. Both their commanders, Lorraine and De la Pole (the Yorkist claimant to the English throne), died with them.

The French are overwhelmed

In the centre, Francis and his noblemen charged time and again into the Imperialist ranks and the fighting here was a portent of the future – armoured knights against musketeers. The Imperialist *arquebusiers* took shelter behind hedges and in copses from where, out of the reach of the lances and swords of the cavalry, they shot down their high-born opponents point-blank. Last on the scene were Francis's French infantry led by D'Amboise, who had finally realized that the attack through the park was the main Imperialist effort. Too late to affect the course of the battle, they were overwhelmed by the same Germans who had slaughtered the *Landsknechts*.

Up to this point the comte d'Alençon, commanding the French 'rear', had made little impression on the battle. Described by one chronicler as 'a man of shallow understanding', he had found himself without orders and had confined himself to watching Del Vasto's men overrun the grounds of the Mirabello lodge and the subsequent fighting there. D'Alençon had sufficient understanding, though, to see that the day was lost and he retreated south, crossing by the bridges over the River Ticino and destroying them behind him. By so doing he condemned to death thousands more French, Germans, Italians and Swiss who, in the general collapse of the French army, ran to the river, only to be drowned or slaughtered on its banks by the exultant Imperialists.

Francis fights on, on foot

Now Francis and his immediate entourage fought on alone – desperate men on tired horses. Nearly 70, the aged veteran La Tremouille was slain, as was his old comrade-in-arms La Palice. Bonnivet went looking for death. Crying 'I cannot survive such disaster, such destruction for anything in the world. I must die', he opened his visor and charged into the enemy ranks. His arch-rival Bourbon found his body after the battle, declaring, 'Wretch! You were the cause of France's ruin – and mine!'

Francis fought on alone until his horse was shot under him, then continued fighting on foot. Wounded in the face, arm and right hand, he was struck to the ground by Spanish *arquebusiers*, who, not knowing who he was, began to strip off his surcoat and armour. The Spanish were not taking prisoners and it was only the arrival on the scene of the Sieur de Pomperant, a supporter of Bourbon's, that saved his life. De Pomperant begged the king to surrender to his master, Bourbon, but the king refused to yield to a traitor. In the nick of time, De Lannoy and his

> ' In less than three hours the army in Italy had ceased to exist '

bodyguard forced themselves through the press. De Lannoy dismounted, knelt, kissed the king's hand and received the king's sword, amidst the cheers of the Spaniards: '*Vittoria! Vittoria! Viva Espana!*'

The consequences of a king's ambition

In less than three hours – it was now 10 am – the French army in Italy had ceased to exist, losing 8,000 men to the Imperialists' toll of 700. As at Crécy, the casualty list looked like a roll-call of French nobility. Francis was taken to a nearby monastery where he wrote to his mother: 'Madame. To let you know the extent of my misfortune, nothing remains to me but my honour and my life which are safe.' The Emperor Charles's terms for the release of Francis were severe – so severe that Francis, once returned to France, felt able to renege on them with a clear conscience, not that his conscience ever seemed to trouble him much. The war continued, but Pavia effectively marked the end of the Valois cause in Italy. The duchy of Milan became a vital part of the Habsburg empire in Europe – a source of both men and cash, and a strategic link between Habsburg lands in Germany and the Netherlands, Spain and Naples.

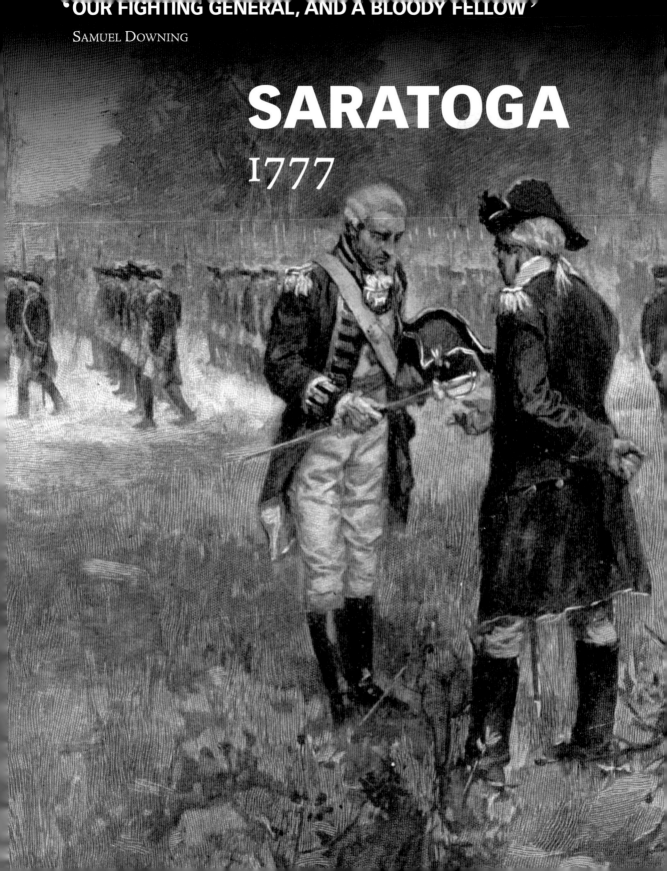

'OUR FIGHTING GENERAL, AND A BLOODY FELLOW'

SAMUEL DOWNING

SARATOGA
1777

For the British government to pick a fight with its own colonists in America was an act of purest folly. In the French and Indian War, these colonists had proved capable, to a great extent, of defending themselves, though it had taken British regulars to complete the expulsion of the French from Canada. When political dissension turned, in 1775, to open rebellion by the colonists, the British government relied on British regulars to regain control. The regulars were reinforced by German mercenaries – another act of political folly.

By December 1776 it seemed that the government was on the road to victory – General Howe had seized New York and driven Washington and his 'Continental Army' out of New Jersey, and a rebel invasion of Canada had proved a catastrophe.

It was at this point that a British general, John 'Gentleman Johnny' Burgoyne, approached London with a plan to isolate and subdue New England with a three-pronged attack. Burgoyne would advance south from Canada; a smaller force under Colonel St Leger would advance east along the Mohawk River from Oswego; and General Howe would march north from New York. New York State and Mohawk Valley loyalists would flock to the king's colours and the back of the rebellion would be broken – the war would be over in a year. It was a plan that looked good on paper, but in execution it relied too heavily on loyalist support in the areas to be invaded, underestimated the problems of logistics, and called for a great deal of co-ordination between widely scattered forces with no means of communicating with each other. Nevertheless the Secretary of State for the Colonies, Lord George Germaine – who had been cashiered from the army as 'unfit to serve his Majesty in any military capacity whasoever' at the Battle of Minden some years earlier – gave the plan the go-ahead.

'The Gibraltar of America'
On 21st June 1777, at the head of Lake Champlain in Canada, Burgoyne embarked his force of 9,500 British regulars, German mercenaries from Brunswick and Hesse-Hanau, Canadian irregulars and Indians. His flotilla, consisting of 200 boats, 20 gunboats and three frigates, sailed south down Lake Champlain. Burgoyne expected the toughest resistance of the entire campaign to be at Ticonderoga, at the southern end of the lake – a wood-and-earth fort considered 'the Gibraltar of America'. Its works were designed to be defended by a force of 10,000, but its commander, General St Clair, had just 2,546 American regulars (Continentals) and 900 militia. Arriving in front of the fort, Burgoyne discovered that the rebels had failed to defend 'Sugar Loaf Hill' – the 'vital ground' that dominated the fort. Burgoyne's gunner-general needed only to have two heavy guns dragged up to the top of the hill to render the fort untenable. St Clair, recognizing his error, declined to sacrifice his men needlessly and, on the night of 6th June, broke out.

OPPOSITE: *'Gentleman Johnny' Burgoyne surrenders his sword to American general Gates after suffering defeat at Saratoga. A former British officer, Gates granted generous terms which Congress refused to honour.*

Pursued by Brigadier-General Simon Fraser, Burgoyne's commander of light troops, St Clair lost 400 men in a clash at Hubbardton, but succeeded in extracting the remainder of his force. Ticonderoga had been expected to hold out for several weeks, yet had fallen within days. The campaign could hardly have got off to a better start – in 20 days Burgoyne had travelled over 100 miles (160 km) and, for the loss of only 200 men, had captured the rebels' chief fortress with its 128 guns. By 10th June Burgoyne was just 60 miles (96 km) from Albany – all seemed set fair for a triumphal progress to his link-up with St Leger and Howe.

'The campaign could hardly have got off to a better start'

A crucial error

It was at this point that Burgoyne made what we can see with hindsight to have been a crucial error. Rather than marching his force back to Ticonderoga, re-embarking them and continuing down Champlain by boat, he decided to advance overland. It must have seemed that he was on the verge of a career-making victory – this was no time for retrograde movement. Leaving 900 men to garrison Ticonderoga, he plunged his force into the thick woods, streams, marshes and the broken ground of Wood Creek leading to Fort Edward on the Upper Hudson River. Burgoyne placed great reliance – in the event of any future clash with the rebels – on the firepower of his artillery. So, struggling along behind his men, as they hacked and stumbled their way through the dense forest, was a train of 52 guns – imposing frequent delays on the column, which was forced to halt repeatedly while they caught up. Progress was further hindered by a corps of American woodsmen ordered up by General Philip Schuyler, American commander of the Northern Department. The woodsmen felled trees across the British line-of-march. As a result of Schuyler's initiative it took Burgoyne 24 days to march the 23 miles (37 km) to Fort St Edward.

With Americans clearing the country ahead of him of provisions, Burgoyne's communications with Canada became his only lifeline, and the need to detach troops to guard them was a constant drain on his force. Progress continued to be slow – by 16th September he had advanced only another 7 miles (11 km) to Fort Miller, an abandoned trading post.

The Fate of St Leger and Howe

Meanwhile the other two 'prongs' of Burgoyne's offensive had come to grief. St Leger's advance – with 1,500 British Regulars, American Loyalists (called Tories by American Patriots) and Indians – had, on 6th August, been met by a force of American militia at Oriskany. St Leger won through, but at a high cost and a few days later, while he was besieging Fort Stanwix, rumours reached him of an approaching American relief force under Benedict Arnold. His Indian allies melted away and soon his whole force was in disorderly retreat back up the Mohawk.

St. Leger's defeat was damaging to Burgoyne's strategy, but not fatal. There was still Howe marching up from New York – surely at any time now the sound of Howe's drums would be echoing up the Hudson Valley. In fact Howe was not marching anywhere – he was at sea. In April, while Burgoyne was still en route to America, Howe had decided on a venture of his own – to embark his force and take them up the Delaware to seize Philadelphia. Almost incredibly, this plan had gained the approval of Lord Germaine in London who, ever the politician, added a vague proviso that it should be done in time to co-operate with the force advancing from Canada. By August, having spent four months assembling a fleet and having changed his mind on en route to Delaware, Howe was now at anchor in the Chesapeake. The only troops left in New York were Sir Henry Clinton's 8,000 men, and before Clinton could attempt to advance up the Hudson he would have to wait for reinforcements from England.

In the meantime, Burgoyne had suffered a further reverse. A column of 800 Hessians, Loyalists and Indians, under the Brunswicker Colonel Baum, had been sent into the Green Mountain country to forage for supplies. Here the column was cut to pieces by some 2,000 American troops at Bennington. With 200 killed and 700 captured, Burgoyne had lost ten per cent of his army – the news reached him on the same day as that of St Leger's defeat. Undeterred, Burgoyne was determined to press on with his plan.

Benedict Arnold joins the fray

The Americans, meanwhile, had not been idle. By this time, 7,000 Americans under a former British officer, General Horatio Gates, had entrenched themselves on Bemis Heights. These were soon reinforced by Benedict Arnold's men, fresh from their repulse of St Leger's advance down the Mohawk, and thousands of American militiamen, drawn by tales of Indian and Tory atrocities. The recruitment of Indians to fight against colonists had always been controversial, even in England. In a speech in the House of Lords, Lord Chatham had painted a picture of 'the cannibal savage torturing, murdering, roasting, and eating the mangled victims of his barbarous battles.'

In fact both sides employed Indians – Burgoyne's order book for 30th September refers to seven deserters who were 'scalped by the Enemy's Indians'– and in the merciless civil war between Rebel and Loyalist, both sides committed atrocities. The murder and scalping of Miss Jane MacCrea, a clergyman's daughter, by one of Burgoyne's Indians, however, proved a gift to American propagandists and brought a flood of recruits – not to the king's colours, but to Gates's camp on Bemis Heights.

Gates was confident that the wooded terrain around Bemis Heights would enable his men to stand up to Burgoyne's regulars, whose training would have placed them at an advantage on an open, European-style battlefield. His position was strong one – on high ground, facing the plain of the Hudson Valley on one side and the forests on the other. The Polish patriot Thaddeus Kosciuszko had fortified the line with breastworks (temporary defences) and batteries. Gates's force had been augmented by 330 riflemen under Dan Morgan, who had been sent north on the orders of George Washington, and

‘a bloody fellow he was, he didn't care for nothing; he'd ride right in ’
SAMUEL DOWNING

200 light infantrymen under Major Henry Dearborn. Perhaps the Americans' greatest asset on Bemis Heights – though Gates would have disagreed – was the newly arrived Benedict Arnold. Like many American officers, Arnold had served with the British in the French and Indian Wars. In the Revolutionary War he had taken part, in 1775, in a disastrous American attempt to capture Quebec. Samuel Downing, who served with him, described him thus: 'He was our fighting general, and a bloody fellow he was, he didn't care for nothing; he'd ride right in. It was "Come on boys!" – it wasn't "Go boys." He was as brave a man as ever lived.'

Burgoyne plans his assault

Burgoyne identified an undefended height to the west of Gates's position from which he believed his heavy guns could force the rebels out of their position. On 15th September Burgoyne advanced in three columns. The left column, commanded by Simon Fraser, consisted of the elite 'flank' companies of the regular regiments, Grenadiers and light infantry, as well as Canadian and Tory regulars and the few remaining Indians. The centre, under Brigadier-General Hamilton, accompanied by Burgoyne, was made up of the bulk of the British regulars. The left, under the experienced campaigner Baron von Riedsel, consisted of all the German troops and six British companies. The total British force was 3,500 men and 35 guns. To oppose them, Gates had five brigades of Continental infantry: those commanded by Brigadier-Generals Poor and Learned, which he placed on his left and centre, and a further three, those of Nixon, Patterson and Glover, which he kept under his own hand on the right. Together with Morgan's and Dearborn's men and the volunteers, he had 7,000 men. He was adequately supplied with artillery – 22 guns, though outnumbered by Burgoyne's 35.

Burgoyne's plan was to seize the high ground and bombard Gates out of position. He ordered Von Riedsel to hold his column back until signal guns told him that Fraser and the centre column were in place. Then all three columns would advance together against the American line. The plan was sound enough in itself, but the three-column advance required a degree of co-ordination – between detached columns in a thick fog – that would be difficult to achieve in an age before radio communications.

Hollow victory at Freeman's Farm

Gates was kept well informed of the British advance but, reluctant to engage in an open battle, remained behind his defences, despite the urgings of his more aggressive commanders, headed by Arnold. At length he compromised, allowing Morgan's and Dearborn's men to probe forward. Morgan's men made contact with Burgoyne's centre column at 12.30 at a clearing at Freeman's Farm – after which the ensuing battle was named. Having driven into the British pickets, they were then driven back by Burgoyne's superior firepower. Morgan himself then rallied his troops, supported by two regiments of Continentals from Poor's brigade, sent up by Arnold. After a lull in the fighting, Burgoyne continued his advance across the clearing. Morgan's sharpshooters drove them back with heavy casualties, especially among the officers. Then Morgan's men charged,

and were themselves driven back. The fight raged back and forth across the clearing for
three hours, the American line being gradually thickened by Arnold. He was determined
to prove that his Continentals were more than mere snipers and defenders of barricades
and continually fed fresh regiments into the struggle.

Obsessed with an imagined threat to his right, Gates kept 4,000 Continentals under
his own hand, men who might have swung the battle in the centre. As it was, Burgoyne's
men were close to being overwhelmed when – acting on his own initiative – Von Riedsel
brought a part of his column into the fight. Together with the arrival of Simon Fraser
from the right, Von Riedsel's arrival swung the balance in favour of the British, and as
dusk fell the Americans withdrew.

Raging at Gates's 'cowardice', Arnold returned to the American lines, leaving Burgoyne
in possession of the field – but it was a hollow victory. Burgoyne's advance had stalled, he
had lost a further 600 men and the Americans were still in position. Now Burgoyne
established his own fortified line. On his right, and detached from his main trench line,
he placed – under Lieutenant-Colonel Breymann – a German battalion that had suffered
badly trying to relieve Baum. Next in line, at Freeman's Farm, he erected a redoubt named
after its commander Lord Balcarres, which was linked by fortifications to Burgoyne's
headquarters. Burgoyne's left was guarded by a 'Great redoubt' overlooking the Hudson.

Burgoyne's dilemma

Burgoyne now had two options: a retreat overland to Canada, which promised to be as
painful and bloody as the advance had been, or a second attempt to break through and
link up with Sir Henry Clinton. Reinforced at last, Clinton had pushed upriver with
2,000 men – although the defence of New York remained his priority. Burgoyne decided
to attack. The three weeks since the Battle of Freeman's Farm had been miserable ones
for his army. Demoralized, down to half rations and under constant sniper fire, his army
was dwindling day by day. Gates's force, by contrast, was steadily increasing and on 7th
October – the very day Burgoyne selected for his next attempt – he was reinforced
by a further 4,000 militia.

Wooded terrain favours the Americans

Burgoyne decided to push forward a reconnaissance force of 1,500 men under Major-
General Phillips, accompanied by Simon Fraser and Von Riedsel (both of whom had
urged Burgoyne to retreat to Canada while there was still half a chance). This force was
to probe the American left and open up the way for a full-scale attack by the rest of the
army if that proved feasible. Phillips' column marched out of the British lines at noon
on 7th October.

Sulking in his tent, having been dismissed from his command by Gates after a series
of arguments following the Battle of Freeman's Farm, Benedict Arnold was roused by the
sound of gunfire when the first clash occurred. He rode at once to the scene of action and
took command. Morgan and his men were already engaged with Phillips's column, which
was deployed at the edge of a wheat field. Fraser was on the British right with his light

'**The fight raged back and forth across the clearing for three hours**' infantry and a battalion of British regulars; Von Riedsel and his Germans held the centre; and Major Acland was on the left with a battalion of British Grenadiers. Both flanks were anchored on thick forest. This was European practice, woodland being well-nigh impossible for regulars to advance through, but for American infantry it merely offered cover from which to fire and, when the moment was right, charge. Soon, Acland's grenadiers were suffering heavy casualties from Poor's brigade, firing out of the woods to their left. On the other flank, Fraser's light infantry suffered a similar fate at the hands of Morgan's riflemen. Fraser, attempting to rally his men, was shot and mortally wounded –

ABOVE: '*As brave a man who ever lived*' – American general Benedict Arnold is wounded in the leg storming the Hessian redoubt. Frustrated at lack of recognition, Arnold was later to defect to the British.

his light infantry fell back. Now Arnold led Learned's brigade against Von Riedsel's Germans in the centre. After repulsing Arnold's first effort, the Germans also found themselves exposed on both flanks, and fell back.

Arnold's tenacity wins the day

The arrival of 2,000 New York militia decided the battle and the British retreated to their breastworks at Balcarres Redoubt and Freeman's Farm. They had fought well – outnumbered three to one, they had held their ground for three hours – but now the entire army was faced with annihilation. Burgoyne's 'reconnaissance' had cost him 400 men killed or captured and the loss of eight guns – and Arnold was not finished yet. Keen to capitalize on his success, he threw his men against the Balcarres Redoubt. There they were repulsed by the British artillery – but still Arnold would not give up. Having led Learned's brigade against Burgoyne's centre and again been repulsed, he cried: 'Well then, let us attack the Hessian lines.' With that he rode to the extreme right of the British position to attack the isolated Breymann Redoubt. The Canadian skirmishers in front of the redoubt having fled, Breymann's already shaken troops were exposed to the full fury of Arnold's fresh onslaught. After a brief resistance, during which Arnold received a severe wound in the leg, Breymann's men fled. Breymann himself was killed.

Although Arnold, to his extreme frustration, had to be carried from the field, he had successfully turned Burgoyne's right flank and rendered Burgoyne's entire position untenable. British losses were 176 killed, 250 wounded and 200 prisoners, as well as tents, baggage and guns. The Americans lost 50 killed and 150 wounded.

The second Battle of Saratoga turned into a mirror-image of the defeat Burgoyne had tried to inflict on Gates during the first clash at Freeman's Farm. By the following day, American artillery was in place on the newly won ground, shooting into the great redoubt. Meanwhile, as he had requested with his dying breath, Simon Fraser was buried in the lines where he had been stationed. Informed that the gathering they saw was a funeral procession, the gunners ceased their fire. Fraser's burial was almost the last act before Burgoyne's withdrawal from his lines.

Rebels *v.* Regulars

At Saratoga we see an example of a phenomenon that occurs throughout military history, and that might be termed 'Rebels versus Regulars'. This kind of warfare is characterized by a strong, well-trained regular army fighting in hostile territory against an irregular opponent for whom the terrain is familiar. Whether it is Varus's legions in the Teutoburger Wald, Burgoyne's redcoats or the French at Dien Bien Phu, the regular forces are placed at a disadvantage. Their strengths – superior training, discipline and firepower – designed to bring victory on a very different kind of battlefield, are nullified in thick forest or jungle against a determined and elusive enemy with the high morale that comes with fighting on, and for, 'home turf'. Irregular warfare alone, however, is rarely enough to ensure victory. All three 'rebel' armies in the examples above contained 'regular' elements willing and able to take on the professionals at their own game.

Burgoyne surrenders

The withdrawal took place by night, in pouring rain. By the morning of 9th October Burgoyne's army was in a new position on the heights of Saratoga. During the previous three weeks, he had lost approximately 1,000 men – the Americans had lost half that number and within days their numbers had swelled to 14,000. Surrounded and now subjected to a ceaseless bombardment, Burgoyne recognized at last that the game was up, raised a flag of truce and sent to ask for terms. Gates, seemingly surprised at a victory to which he had contributed little enough, and wishing to be free to turn on Clinton, offered Burgoyne generous terms. Burgoyne's men were to be allowed to march out of their camp with full honours of war, and – on parole not to serve in America again – to be conveyed to Great Britain. The Convention of Saratoga was signed on 16th October, but Congress had other ideas. Realizing that Burgoyne's 'parolled' troops could be used to relieve troops at home who could serve in America, they sensibly – though perhaps not very honourably – repudiated the convention. Most of Burgoyne's men never saw their homes again.

The beginning of the end for the British in America

It is an irony that what was surely the most significant American victory of the Revolution should have been won by an officer who held no official command in the army – for beyond all doubt this was Arnold's victory. Without him it is possible that Burgoyne might have reached Albany. Instead, by the end of the year, all the British had achieved was the capture of Philadelphia – a city of only symbolic significance.

Burgoyne's strategy had foundered for a number of reasons, not least Howe's decision to embark on a campaign of his own. Given that, Burgoyne's decision to try and go it alone was optimistic to say the least. He failed to appreciate the problems of supply and the difficulties of the terrain, and his decision not to march back to Ticonderoga and re-embark his force was a major error. More critical still – and Burgoyne was not alone in this – was an underestimation of the enemy. The belief that the Continental army could not face British and German regulars in a 'stand-up fight' was a fatal delusion. Burgoyne's army found itself fighting an irregular foe in difficult and unfamiliar terrain where the superior firepower of their artillery was not enough to win the day – a situation familiar to Western armies in our own times.

By 7th December, Benjamin Franklin in Paris heard the news of Burgoyne's surrender. Two days later, King Louis XVI gave his approval to an alliance with the United States, bringing into the conflict a naval power that could challenge British control of the American seaboard – Spain and Holland would soon join the alliance. It was the beginning of the end for the British in America.

'WINTER WILL FIGHT ON OUR SIDE'
Tsar Alexander I

MOSCOW
1812

Having defeated Austria and Prussia in 1805 and 1806, and fought the Russians to a standstill at Friedland, Napoleon concluded a peace with Tsar Alexander at Tilsit, on Russia's Baltic coast, in 1807. However, it proved uneasy for a number of reasons: the tsar was vulnerable to a 'war party' from among his own aristocracy; Russian participation in the 'Continental System' (Napoleon's ban on British imports to Europe) was damaging the Russian economy; and Alexander was growing increasingly suspicious of the Grand Duchy of Warsaw, established by Napoleon, which he saw as a nascent Polish state on Russia's border. Despite the efforts of Armand de Caulaincourt, the French ambassador to Russia, relations worsened to such a point that, by the autumn of 1811, Napoleon had determined on war.

The invasion

Napoleon's blueprint for war was always the same: a swift advance into enemy territory and a decisive battle in which the enemy's main army was destroyed, after which an unfavourable peace was dictated to a prostrate enemy. This strategy had served him well so far, and was dictated as much by political as military considerations – as a military dictator, Napoleon could not afford to be away from his capital for too long. In so far as they had a plan, the Russians intended to draw Napoleon into the Russian interior and wear his forces down. As the tsar said to Caulaincourt, 'Your Frenchman is brave, but long privations and a bad climate wear him down and discourage him. Our climate, our winter, will fight on our side.'

By late June 1812, Napoleon had massed 450,000 men on the western bank of the River Nieman, on the southwest Russian border. His army consisted of Frenchmen, Poles, Italians, Bavarians, Saxons, Westphalians, Württemburgers, Croats, Spaniards and Portuguese – drawn from across the Napoleon's empire. They were organized into three 'army groups', commanded by Napoleon, his son-in-law Prince Eugene and his brother Jerome. On the night of 24–25th June, the Grande Armée crossed the Niemen and advanced broadly in the direction of Moscow. Napoleon took Kovno, at the confluence of the Rivers Viliya and Nieman, without opposition.

The Russians had two main armies, commanded by General Barclay de Tolly in the north (sometimes accompanied by the tsar), and by General Peter Bagration in the south. Napoleon learned from captured despatches that the tsar and Barclay's army were at Vilno, the intended meeting point of the two Russian armies. Napoleon arrived at Vilno, however, to find that the Russians had burned the bridge over the Vilnia, along with their

OPPOSITE: *Moscow in flames, the result of fires started deliberately on the orders of city governor Rostopchin. Enough of the city survived to tempt Napoleon to remain there until it was too late.*

supplies, and withdrawn. Vilno was taken, therefore, without a shot being fired, but amidst scenes of indiscipline and looting. The Russians' 'scorched earth' policy thus ensured that Napoleon's army was already hungry and its cavalry desperately short of forage for its horses.

Bagration slips the net

Napoleon decided to split his forces. He sent Joachim Murat, king of Naples, with five cavalry divisions (supported by Marshals Oudinot and Ney) to keep up the pressure on Barclay, while he turned his attention to Bagration. On 1st July, hearing that Bagration, the Georgian 'hero of Austerlitz', was moving northeast to link with Barclay, Napoleon ordered Marshal Davout and his brother Jerome, to trap Bagration between their two forces. However, Jerome moved too slowly and, crucially, failed to keep Napoleon informed. Bagration, a wily campaigner, slipped the net. Napoleon was furious with his brother 'Tell him,' he raged, 'that it would be impossible to manoeuvre in worse fashion ... tell him that he has robbed me of the fruit of my manoeuvres and of the best opportunity ever presented – and all on account of his singular failure to appreciate the first notions about warfare.' Out of his depth, Jerome left the army and went home. Still hoping to trap Bagration, Napoleon ordered Davout to drive him into the vast Pripet Marshes. Once again, the Georgian proved elusive, doubling back towards Bobruisk.

His first plan having failed, Napoleon now turned his attention to Barclay. Rather than attack him frontally, Napoleon tried to manoeuvre round Barclay's rear, crossing the River Dvina and threatening his communications with St Petersburg, while Murat 'pinned' him frontally. On 19th July, Napoleon was informed by Murat that Barclay had moved out, and on the 24th that he had taken up position at Vitebsk (in modern-day Belarus), which the Russians had now settled on as the meeting point for their armies. Bagration was marching towards it when he was blocked by Davout at Mogilev. Napoleon decided against attacking Barclay immediately, preferring to wait until he could bring up more troops, but hearing of Bagration's check at Mogilev, Barclay withdrew once more, in the direction of the next rendezvous – Smolensk, around 225 miles (360 km) west of Mosow.

Napoleon enters Smolensk

Yet again, Napoleon had failed to force a decisive battle on a divided enemy. His troops were hungry and exhausted – 100,000 men had dropped out through sickness and fatigue, and many horses had been lost. He was forced to call a halt for eight days – during which time Davout marched up to join him – before advancing on Smolensk. Bagration and Barclay finally linked up at Smolensk on 4th August. Now was Napoleon's chance to force a decisive battle, and once more he attempted a massive right-flanking manoeuvre, crossing the Dnieper River on the night of 13–14th August. By dawn, 175,000 men were across the river and marching northeast towards Smolensk. At 3 p.m. – at Krasnoe, southwest of Smolensk – Murat's advance guard encountered General Neverovski with 8,000 infantry and 1,500 cavalry. Without waiting for the infantry of Ney's III Corps, which was following on behind, Murat threw in his cavalry, only to see them shot down by Russian infantry. Ney's corps was unable to deploy before Neverovski made his escape towards Smolensk – but for him the French would have been in the city that afternoon. When he finally reached it, Napoleon ordered a halt for 24 hours – the following day was his 43rd birthday, which he intended to celebrate with a grand review of the army. Thus the surprise achieved by crossing the Dnieper was lost – now aware of the presence of Napoleon south of Smolensk, Bagration ordered Nikolay Raevsky's VIII Corps into the city.

Although of little strategic value, Smolensk was home to the icon of the 'Black Madonna', to which many miracles had been attributed and which was therefore of huge spiritual significance to the Russians. Napoleon could have bypassed the city, crossing the river east of it and placing his forces across the line of the Russian army's communications. Instead, he decided to assault the city, convinced that the Russians would come out to defend it. However, Barclay and Bagration simply watched from the banks of the Dnieper, north of Smolensk, as Napoelon's army attacked its ancient walls. An initial assault on 16th August having failed, Napoleon attacked the following afternoon with 200 guns and the three corps of Davout, Ney and Poniatowski's. Now defended by 30,000 Russians, the fighting for the city was fierce. The French lacked siege guns or even ladders to scale its ancient walls as they battled though the city's suburbs. From the heights opposite, Auguste Thirion, a heavy cavalryman, watched Marshal Poniatowski's Poles attack the eastern walls of what had once been a Polish stronghold. 'These brave men tried to scale them by climbing on each others' shoulders. But the nature of the terrain would not permit of success, and it was a curious spectacle to see that ant-like mass of men crawling over the rocks in such a picturesque manner while above their heads the cannon which were the object of their efforts thundered against their brothers in arms.' By nightfall the Russians were evacuating the blazing city. Napoleon lost approximately 7,000 men, and, while he was able to inflict 11,000 casualties on the Russians in return, they were better able to absorb those losses.

> 'before a month is out we shall be in Moscow'
> NAPOLEON

Napoleon's reward was a burned-out city. Military historian Carl von Clausewitz considered the decision to assault Smolensk the biggest mistake of the entire campaign.

The Russian retreat continues

Failing once more – this time at Valutino – to trap the retreating Russians, Napoleon's army plodded wearily on in their wake. The army was still 280 miles (448 km) from Moscow and had already exhausted its supplies. Marauding Cossacks were everywhere, burning, harassing and swooping on any troops foraging for food – inflicting damage out of all proportion to their numbers. The marching and fighting of the last two weeks had cost the Grande Armée another 25,000 men. Briefly, Napoleon appeared to listen to his chief-of-staff Berthier and his aide Caulaincourt's call for a winter halt at Smolensk, but he soon changed his mind. 'Before a month is out,' he said, 'we shall be in Moscow; in six months we shall have peace.'

On the Russian side there were recriminations about the loss of Smolensk. Much blame was attached to Barclay, who, as a German-speaking Livonian (Livonia – present-day Latvia and Estonia) of Scots ancestry, was automatically regarded with suspicion by the Russian aristocracy. They urged the tsar to appoint Mikhail Ilarionovitch Kutuzov as commander of the combined armies. Immortalized by Tolstoy in *War and Peace* as the embodiment of the earthy wisdom of old Russia, Kutuzov was in fact an experienced campaigner and courtier. He was described by the British liaison officer Sir Robert Wilson as 'polished, courteous, shrewd as a Greek, naturally intelligent as an Asiatic, and well instructed as a European'. A former comrade of Russia's national hero, Alexander Suvarov, morale soared when Kutuzov joined the army on 29th August.

Attack and counter-attack

Kutuzov was determined to fight for Moscow. He selected a site at Borodino, 60 miles (96 km) from the capital. As Napoleon approached with 133,000 men, Kutuzov set about improving the position with earthworks, behind which he arrayed his force of 120,000. A bloody battle at an outlying earthwork, the Shevardino Redoubt, on 5th September gave Napoleon a foretaste of the fighting that would follow when he assaulted the main position. Rejecting Davout's plan for a wide flanking movement by his own and Poniatowski's Polish Corps, Napoleon opted instead for a frontal assault that, he believed, would break the will of the Russian army.

'Marauding Cossacks were everywhere, burning, harassing and swooping'

The battle began with massive and lengthy bombardments from both sides, with 650 Russian against 597 French guns. The French army then launched a succession of frontal assaults on the Russian positions, which lasted most of the day. It was bloody, attritional warfare

made up of attack and counter-attack, and was the type of fighting at which the Russians excelled. Borodino, however, did not show Napoleon at his best – he seemed to have sunk into lethargy and depression, sitting in the early morning with his head in his hands declaring 'What is war? A trade of barbarians, the whole art of which consists in being the strongest at a given point.' At the critical moment, when the Russians appeared to be forming a new line in the rear of their main position, Napoleon, uncertain of the situation on his extended flanks and disturbed by rumours of a huge Cossack host to his north, refused to commit his Guard.

'What is war? A trade of barbarians'
NAPOLEON

ABOVE: *In Russia, handling armies greater than had ever been seen before, Napoleon showed only flashes of his former genius. At times he seemed lethargic, and even war-weary.*

A priceless opportunity was accordingly lost. By the time darkness fell, 30,000 of Napoleon's army had been killed or wounded (including 43 generals), yet just one mile of ground had been gained. The Russians had lost 44,000, including their hero Bagration, while their line, though pushed back a little, had held. The Russian army was in no condition to fight again the following day, but remained in being (intact). As Napoleon sat in his headquarters composing a bulletin that would 'spin' Borodino as a triumph under the walls of Moscow, he could hear the Russians in their new positions shouting 'Victory!' Then, overnight, the Russians withdrew.

Moscow in flames

At a council of war on 13th September, Kutuzov decided to abandon Moscow to the enemy in order that his army might rest and regroup. The following day an advance party from the French army arrived on the heights west of Moscow. Sergeant Bourgogne of the Imperial Guard later wrote: 'All the sufferings, the dangers, the hardships, the privations, everything was forgotten and swept from our minds by thoughts of the pleasure of entering Moscow, of taking up comfortable winter quarters in it and of making conquests of another kind.' He was to be disappointed. As Murat's vanguard was entering the city, the bulk of the population – some 180,000 out of a total of 200,000 – was leaving it via the eastern gates at the instigation of the governor Rostopchin. Napoleon entered that evening and took up quarters in the Kremlin, only to be roused from his bed a few days later to find Moscow in flames. The fires had been started deliberately on the orders of Rostopchin. Looters – both French and Russian – and a stiff wind caused the flames to spread, and over the next few days three-quarters of the city was destroyed. The part that remained, which included the Kremlin, was saved by a change of wind. Ironically, had the whole city been destroyed, Napoleon would have been forced to withdraw immediately, sparing the Grande Armée what followed.

> 'The Grande Armée returned north … and its fate was sealed'

Confident that the tsar must now negotiate, Napoleon sent a message suggesting that a peace might now be agreed, but received no reply, nor to a subsequent message. Meanwhile, at their fortified camp at Tarutino, some 50 miles (80 km) southwest of the capital, the Russians were rearming and reinforcing – by late October their numbers had risen from 85,000 to over 120,000.

On 17th September, realizing that the tsar had no intention of negotiating, Napoleon ordered the evacuation of Moscow. He planned to march southwest and return to Smolensk by a southerly route, through land that had not been devastated by either the advancing French or the retreating Russians. The tsar's plan was to catch Napoleon in a giant pincer movement. Kutuzov would pursue the retreating French army while General Ludwig Wittgenstein descended from the north and Admiral Pavel Chichagov advanced from the south.

At Maloyaroslavets, south of Moscow, on 24th October, Napoleon's advance guard was halted by a force under the Russian general Dokhturov. In the fighting that followed – in which Prince Eugene's Italian troops distinguished themselves – the all-important crossing of the River Lusha changed hands several times. As night fell it was in Eugene's hands, but after an unsettling encounter with marauding Cossacks, Napoleon concluded that his army was too weak to fight its way through to the southerly route. The Grande Armée returned north – along the route by which it had previously advanced – and its fate was sealed.

A pitiful retreat

From now on Kutuzov contented himself with marching parallel to the French, denying them the fertile lands to the south, while hordes of Cossacks – joined now by bands of partisans composed of peasants and stragglers from the Russian armies – harassed them at every turn. However, on 1st November at Viazma, General Miloradovitch saw an opportunity to cut off the French rearguard, formed by I Corps, commanded by Davout. After a hard day's fighting, with the help of divisions sent back by Eugene and Ney, Davout managed to extricate what was left of his corps, but it had almost ceased to exist as a fighting force. Marshal Ney's III Corps then took over as rearguard.

The first snow fell on 5th November, by which time Napoleon's army was already falling apart. Some regiments – many pitifully reduced in numbers – still maintained discipline under their officers, but much of the army was by now a mob of fugitives stumbling towards the supposed safety of Smolensk. In fact, Wittgenstein's army, the northern arm of the Russian pincer, had captured Polotsk (about 150 miles [240 km] northwest of Smolensk). Realizing his line of retreat was now at risk, Napoleon knew it would not be possible to winter in the city and that he would have to continue. Having driven his army on through blizzards, on 9th November the emperor reached the burned-out city to find that the provisions stored there had nearly all been consumed by the garrison. What little had remained had then been looted by the advance guard.

The retreat continued in intense cold and thickening snow, which, together with starvation, took a terrible toll. Count Langeron – a French émigré commanding a Russian division – described some of the horrors he witnessed as his column followed the French. Passing through a forest, he wrote: 'the Pavlograd Hussars, who formed the advance-guard and moved on foot, were obliged to lift bodies and throw them aside to clear a path for the column … I saw a woman who had just given birth to a child and had then died beside her dead baby. One cannot imagine the number of women the French army dragged along … I saw a dead man, his teeth in the haunch of a horse which was still quivering. I saw a dead man inside a horse which he had disembowelled and emptied in order to crawl inside and get warm. I saw another man tearing with his teeth at the entrails of a dead horse. I did not see the wretched French eating one another, but I did see corpses from the thighs of which strips of flesh had been cut for eating.'

On 16th November, at Krasnoe, Miloradovitch struck again, allowing Napoleon and his Imperial Guard to pass and then inserting a force across the road behind them, cutting off the rest of the army. Eugene and his 4,000 Italians managed to fight their way through, but Davout and Ney remained isolated. So often afflicted by lethargy during this campaign, Napoleon now showed flashes of his old energy and genius. Sending his

'I saw a dead man inside a horse which he had disembowelled and emptied in order to crawl inside and get warm'

COUNT LANGERON

Guard to the aid of Davout, he succeeded in extricating what remained of Davout's corps. This left Ney's 6,000 still cut off from the main French force. Ney arrived on the scene to find Miloradovitch's force arrayed across the road, blocking his way west. The French commander launched a series of desperate attacks, but after a day of hard fighting he failed to break through.

Furious that Napoleon had continued retreating towards Orsha, southwest of Smolensk – 'The bastard has abandoned us!' – Ney led his men on a night march north of the road through forests knee-deep in snow and across the frozen Dnieper. Aware of the appalling conditions – 'Those who get through this will show they have their balls hung by steel wire!' – Ney lived up to his own words, bringing his remaining 2,000 men safely through to link up with pickets (infantry outposts) of Eugene's corps near Orsha. Although he was later criticized for his conduct at Waterloo, Ney received high praise during this retreat, earning Napoleon's soubriquet 'the bravest of the brave'.

Marching on Moscow

One of British Field Marshal Montgomery's two famous rules of war was 'Never march on Moscow'. Russia is not just big, its vast distances seem never-ending. Marching on Moscow can be likened to entering a funnel from the wrong end. When Napoleon's armies crossed the Nieman, they were operating on a front that was 250 miles (400 km) long. By the time they reached Smolensk it had grown to 500 miles (800 km). Nor are the problems caused by the Russian climate confined to the freezing winter. The baking heat and dust of the Russian summer were equally damaging to an army confined to moving at the speed of the slowest hungry horse. Even discounting Borodino, Napoleon lost more men on the advance to Moscow than during the retreat.

Massacre at the Berezina

Ahead of the French, running southeast to northwest across the road from Smolensk, lay the River Berezina. The only crossing, the bridge at Borisov, had been captured on 22nd November by Admiral Chichagov's forces – advancing from the southeast. Arriving with the French advance guard, Marshal Oudinot immediately attacked and regained the town, but the Russians succeeded in burning the bridge. The Grande Armée was due a change in luck, however, and it arrived in the discovery of a ford, 12 miles (19 km) to the north at Studianka, by a detached unit of lancers. By the afternoon of 26th November, working up to their necks in the icy water, General Eblé's engineers had succeeded in constructing two new bridges across the river. On the 27th, the part of the army that was still combatant crossed the Berezina, while the mass of fugitives and stragglers that trailed behind them, threatening to swamp the bridges, were held back by force. With the bridge at Borisov rebuilt, Chichagov's force on the west bank and Wittgenstein's on the east launched a concerted attack on the French bridges. Held off by Marshals Oudinot and Victor, the Russians contented themselves with bombarding them. By 6 p.m., Victor's rearguard had crossed the river, forcing a way through a throng of desperate refugees. Then, having enabled as many as possible of the refugees to cross, at 8.30 on the morning of the 29th Eblé destroyed the bridges, still leaving many thousands at the mercy of the Russians. The Count de Rochechouart, an eyewitness, described the carnage on the east bank that morning. 'Nothing in the world more saddening, more distressing! One saw heaped bodies of men, women, and even children; soldiers of all arms, all nations, choked by the fugitives or hit by Russian grapeshot; horses, guns, ammunition wagons, abandoned carts. One cannot imagine a more terrifying sight than the appearance of the two broken bridges, and the river frozen right to the bottom.' Napoleon may have escaped the pincers of the Russian forces, but his army had been destroyed. He lost between 20,000 and 30,000 men at the Berezina, as well as countless non-combatants.

> 'Those who get through this will show they have their balls hung by steel wire!'
>
> MARSHAL NEY

A terrible price

Napoleon's fears about Paris were justified. On 5th December, learning of an attempted coup led by General Malet, he left the army to return to the capital. Joachim Murat took over command of the Grande Armée. His attitude at the time was summed up by the answer he gave to an artillery officer who had been sent to reinforce the rearguard. Struggling to get his guns up the icy road to the top of a nearby hill, the artillery officer asked the king of Naples for advice. 'Major we're —ed,' said Murat, 'get on your horse and run.' Of the original force of 450,000, barely 20,000 emaciated men staggered back across the Niemen at Kovno on 11–12th December. Five days later, at Gumbinnen in East Prussia, the French army's intendant-general, comte Dumas, was confronted by a red-eyed, ragged, bearded man in a brown coat. 'What General Dumas,' the man cried, 'do you not recognize me? I am the rearguard of the Grande Armée. I am Marshal Ney.'

The cost of the 1812 campaign to Napoleon's empire was terrible – approximately 300,000 men had been killed and 200,000 captured, along with 1,000 guns and 200,000 horses. Russian casualties amounted to 150,000 killed and countless thousands wounded. By the end of 1812, it must have seemed that Napoleon was finished, but by the spring of 1813 he was preparing to fight in Germany with a newly raised army.

'HE IS A—WHO WILL HAVE US ALL KILLED'
NAPOLEON'S STAFF OFFICERS

LEIPZIG
1813

The destruction of Napoleon's army in Russia marked the beginning of the end for his empire. A Sixth Coalition was formed against him in June 1812, consisting of Great Britain, Russia, Spain and Portugal, and other nations soon joined in. Prussia, only ever a reluctant ally of Napoleon, joined in February 1813. Under Napoleon's father-in-law, the emperor Francis, Austria held aloof from the fighting at first, but was sympathetic to the coalition. This combination, and the after-effects of the Russian debacle, might have finished a lesser man, but amazingly, Napoleon returned to Germany in spring 1813 with a new army.

Napoleon's comeback

It was an army he had scraped together from wherever he could, scouring depots and garrisons and calling up young conscripts, national guards and customs officers, as well as bringing sailors ashore to man artillery, and redeploying the forces that he had in Spain. On paper its 200,000 men looked impressive, but in practice it was woefully under-trained. A particular weakness was the cavalry, which was under-strength in trained men and horses.

Still, in the initial campaigning, Napoleon showed some of the old genius that had deserted him in Russia, defeating the Russian general Wittgenstein at Lützen on 2nd May and at Bautzen on 20th and 21st. However on each occasion lack of cavalry prevented him from fully exploiting his victories.

There followed an armistice in June and July, which allowed Napoleon time to train his young recruits, but during which his enemies also grew in strength. In August, Austria declared war on Napoleon, and Sweden, under Napoleon's old colleague and rival Marshal Bernadotte, joined the Sixth Coalition against him. Despite bearing a tattoo declaring 'Death to Tyrants', Bernadotte had swallowed his republican principles and accepted the offer of Sweden's vacant throne.

French manoeuvres against the coalition

When the campaign resumed, Napoleon faced three armies: the Army of Bohemia, under the Austrian general Karl Schwarzenberg; the Army of Silesia, under Wittgenstein's replacement, the Prussian Gebhard Leberecht von Blücher; and the Army of the North, under Bernadotte. The Allies adopted a policy of refusing battle with Napoleon, in favour of engaging his marshals individually. Bernadotte defeated Oudinot at Grossbeeren and Blücher bested Macdonald at the Battle of Katzbach, but Napoleon defeated Schwarzenberg's Army of Bohemia at Dresden on 26th and 27th August. Even this success, though, failed to raise morale among his war-weary army. Captain Coignet, then serving as the emperor's baggage-master, recalls in his memoirs a conversation he heard

OPPOSITE: *Prussian and French cavalry clash at Möckern on the northwest edge of Leipzig. Prussian successes here drew Napoleon away from a potential victory in the south. The following day Napoleon gave orders for a retreat.*

among a group of staff officers after Dresden. 'This was a memorable victory but our generals had had enough of it... They cursed the Emperor; "He is a—," they said, "who will have us all killed." I was dumb with astonishment. I said to myself, "We are lost".

Napoleon failed to follow up his success at Dresden and when General Vandamme attempted to exploit it, in pursuit of the retreating Coalition forces, he was captured, along with 13,000 men, at Kulm on 29 –30th August. Only days later, on 6th September, Marshal Ney was defeated by Bernadotte's Swedes at Dennewitz, while trying to capture the Prussian capital Berlin.

Napoleon now decided to gather his forces west of the River Elbe, and at 3 a.m. on 14th October he gave orders to concentrate the troops at Leipzig. By now, Blücher and Bernadotte were advancing on Leipzig from the north, and Schwarzenberg from the south. 'The three armies,' Blücher had written on the 13th, 'are now so close together that a simultaneous attack against where the enemy has concentrated his forces might be undertaken.' Napoleon was of the same opinion, writing to Macdonald: 'There can be no doubt that tomorrow – the 15th – we shall be attacked by the Army of Bohemia and the Army of Silesia.' Neither side was in any doubt that a battle was approaching that would determine the future, not just of Germany, but the whole of Europe.

> 'a battle was approaching that would determine the future, not just of Germany, but the whole of Europe'

As Napoleon entered Leipzig he could hear the sound of fighting to the south of the city at Liebertwolkwitz, where Murat had, against orders, engaged in a huge and indecisive cavalry battle. By nightfall, Napoleon had concentrated 177,000 men in Leipzig – a further 18,000 would arrive from the north over the next 48 hours. Against him, the Allies were assembling a vast force – Schwarzenberg's Army of Bohemia was arriving from the south with 203,000 men, Blücher's Army of Silesia arriving from the northwest numbered 54,000, and Bernadotte's Swedish army from the north, 85,000.

Napoleon's plan of defence

At Leipzig, Napoleon had the advantage of fighting on interior lines, with a city at his back. Communication between the Allies, arrayed around the city's perimeter, was hampered by the distances involved and the fact that French engineers had destroyed all the bridges. What the engineers had not done was build extra bridges over the River Elster to provide Napoleon with an escape route west, via Lindenau – all traffic had to pass along a single causeway (over the marshes between the Rivers Pleisse and Elster – at the end was the crucial bridge over the Elster). Every good general fights – as Wellington said – 'with one eye on the back door'. Napoleon was no exception, but, based on a misreading of the Allied positions, his planned line of retreat was northwards, not westwards. Surveying the massed camp fires to the south of the city on the night he arrived, Napoleon came to the conclusion that, after arriving from the north, Blücher and Bernadotte had passed round the city and massed their armies to the south of it, alongside Schwarzenberg's Austrians. In fact they were in the north, positioned right across his projected line of retreat – if Napoleon was forced out of Leipzig, his entire army would have to pass over the narrow causeway to Lindenau.

Napoleon was not, in any case, planning a passive defence – his plan was to attack the Allied armies and defeat them in detail (separately), before they could combine effectively against him. He intended to launch a big attack southwards against Schwarzenberg's army with three corps – 37,000 men under Marshals Poniatowski, Victor and Lauriston, supported by cavalry. This main attack would pin the Austro-Russian forces frontally, while a further 23,000 men, consisting of XI Corps and Marshal Sebastiani's cavalry, enveloped their right. Then, at the crucial moment, another 62,000 men – the Imperial Guard, Marshal Augereau's corps and two more cavalry formations – would deliver the coup de grâce. This final attack would be supported by another corps, either that of Marshal Marmont or Count Bertrand, brought down from the north of the city. Ney would hold this northern sector with four corps plus the Leipzig garrison. This plan had one major flaw: it was based on the assumption that all of the enemies' forces were in the south, and that those to the north were just token, covering forces that could easily be contained by Ney.

An attack planned like clockwork

The Allied plan was to attack from all around the city. It is easiest to imagine Leipzig at the centre of a vast clock. If Napoleon and his army were at the centre, Blücher was advancing roughly between the 10 and the 12, Austrian general Gyulai between the 9 and the 10, Bernadotte and his Swedes between the 1 and the 2, and Schwarzenberg between the 4 and the 8. Blücher's, Gyulai's and Bernadotte's attacks would be subsidiary ones – the main effort would be in the south.

Here, the Russian general Barclay de Tolly would commit 77,500 men under Kleist, Eugen, Gortchakov and Kenau, supported by Count Pahlen's cavalry and the Russian reserve cavalry, against the three villages to the south of the city, centred on Liebertwolkwitz, the focus of the previous day's fighting. Wittgenstein, who was to command the attack, decided to attempt to outflank the French left, as well as sending General Merveldt through the marshes of the River Pleisse against their right. As a result, he spread his men over six miles (9.6 km), which both weakened the blow and, crucially, meant that the attacking columns couldn't see each other. The essence of Napoleonic warfare was concentration of force at what Prussian military historian Carl von Clausewitz would later call the 'critical point'. For this battle in the south, Napoleon had concentrated two-thirds of his force, the Allies only one-third.

A critical error

Napoleon had by now become aware that Blücher and Bernadotte were not south of the city, but deciding they were to the west, he still anticipated that the crucial battle would take place in the south. In fact it was their subsidiary attacks from the north that would destabilize Napoleon's plan. Still under the illusion that the only real threat came from the south, at 7 a.m. on the morning of the 16th Napoleon ordered Marmont to abandon

Lindenthal to the northwest of the city. Marmont was to take up a position in the southern outskirts of Leipzig, to support his main attack. Marmont had been observing Blücher's camp fires overnight from the church tower of Lindenthal, but despite his doubts he started marching south. He had not been on the march long when Blücher attacked, forcing Marmont to execute a quick about-turn and dash back to the village of Möckern. Realizing that, in the absence of Marmont, Napoleon's southern attack needed support, Ney ordered Bertrand to take his corps south, but as Bertrand did so, Gyulai attacked Leipzig from the west. Bertrand too was forced to abandon his southward march, and turned west to meet the new threat. The only troops that remained at Ney's disposal to send south were the remains of Count Souham's corps, but this under-strength formation spent the day receiving orders and counter-orders, and marching fruitlessly back and forth between the front lines.

The attack from the south

The Allied attack in the south was slow in getting started. It was not until 9 a.m. that the four dense columns of men – 120,000 Russians, Austrians and Prussians – moved off in the cold, mist and wet. The attack was disorderly and piecemeal, hitting the French line between 9 and 9.30 a.m., with the distances between the columns making it difficult to co-ordinate the attacks. In particular there was a large gap between the columns of Prince Eugen of Württemberg and the Russian Prince Gortchakov. Here was the perfect time and situation for a French counter-attack, but the troops who might have made it – Macdonald's corps and Sebastiani's cavalry – had, like their enemy, been delayed by the mist. Instead, Napoleon had to content himself with fighting a direct, frontal battle for two hours until approximately 11 a.m.

'Here was the perfect time and situation for a French counter-attack, but the troops who might have made it had been delayed by the mist'

On the extreme Allied left, Austrians under General Merveldt captured the château of Dölitz, but were held there by part of Poniatowski's Polish Corps. Also on the left, the Prussian Kleist captured the village of Markleeburg, but was then held up by massed French artillery fire. In the centre, Prince Eugen took Wachau but was ejected by a counter-attack, and on the right, at Liebertwolkwitz, Prince Gortchakov fell into a trap set by Lauriston and suffered heavy casualties from well-sited guns.

Now Napoleon decided to thicken up his line, calling up Augereau's and Oudinot's corps and two divisions of his Young Guard to support Poniatowski and Victor, while Marshal Mortier took the remainder of the Young Guard to aid Lauriston. Napoleon brought up all available guns, Murat's cavalry and the Old Guard to support his centre; some noted that it was unusual for the Guard to be committed to battle that early.

By 11 a.m. it was evident that Schwarzenberg's attack was falling away, but the Allied leaders were already preparing for a fresh effort. The tsar himself called the Prussian and Russian Guards to take up positions behind Prince Eugen and Gortchakov, and messages were sent to hurry up the dilatory Klenau, as well as to Generals Bennigsen and Colleredo, who were en route from Dresden with 70,000 men.

Klenau arrived on the Allied extreme right and took Kolmberg Heights, preparatory to attacking Lauriston at Liebertwolkwitz from the east, but any further forward movement by Klenau was stalled by the arrival of Macdonald. Meanwhile, to the north-west of the city, Blücher had been probing the village of Möckern – he was aware of the presence of more French troops to his north, marching towards the concentration of Napoleon's forces at Leipzig. In the west Bertrand had halted Gyulai's advance and restored the situation. Things had gone well for the French on both these fronts, although the fighting had tied down the two corps of Marmont and Bertrand, which Napoleon had earmarked for his effort in the south. Nevertheless, once it was clear that the Allied effort on that front had exhausted itself, Napoleon resolved to counter-attack.

France counter-attacks

The plan was a classic example of the tactics employed by Napoleon towards the end of his career – Drouot was to mass 150 guns between Victor and Lauriston's corps and blast a hole in the Allied centre. This would be followed by a general advance along the whole front, with Macdonald (supported by Souham) hooking in round the Allied right to threaten their rear and centre. At the crucial moment, Murat would lead the massed cavalry forward, supported by Drouot's guns, and carve a way through for the infantry, hopefully driving the Allied centre and right off in confusion. By 2 p.m., despite the fact that neither Marmont (engaged at Möckern) nor Souham (marching back and forth through Leipzig) were present on the southern front, and Macdonald's outflanking move had not materialized, Napoleon decided to attack. As Drouot's guns fired into Kleist's and Eugen's formations, French columns advanced all along the line, and 12,000 cavalry, led by Murat, moved into place to deliver the coup de grâce. Once again, Liebertwolkwitz was the scene of heavy fighting. Murat's cavalry rolled forward, driving back Kleist's column, smashing an Austrian cavalry brigade, overrunning a 30-gun Austrian battery and riding down two battalions of the Russian Kremenchuk Regiment. Russian Guard light cavalry counter-attacked, but were driven off.

> 'Drouot was to mass 150 guns between Victor and Lauriston's corps and blast a hole in the Allied centre'

> 'Thus, at the crucial moment – when he might have won the day in the south – Napoleon was riding north'

Things were going well for the French: Murat's cavalry had created confusion in the Allied ranks which Napoleon could now exploit decisively – but Napoleon wasn't there. Even as Murat's cavalry had advanced, the sound of gunfire was heard in the north – it was coming from Möckern, where Blücher's Prussians were now pressing Marmont hard. Napoleon turned his horse about and rode back towards the city.

Thus, at the crucial moment – when, by throwing his infantry reserves in behind Murat, he might have won the day in the south – Napoleon was riding north. Murat had attacked where the Allied reserves were strongest. Now he decided to press home his attack over ground that Count Pajol, one of his light cavalry generals, had warned him was swampy. Some of his units got to within 300 yards (274 m) of the hill where the tsar and the king of Prussia stood, before getting into difficulty in the unsuitable ground. It was the tsar himself who ordered up two batteries of horse artillery and his Guard Cossacks, supported by two Prussian cavalry regiments. With grapeshot, lance and sabre they drove the French cavalry in confusion right back to Drouot's grand battery. The French infantry continued to advance until fresh Austrian reserves under General Bianchi halted them and pushed them back. At length, one division of the Old Guard and, at last, the leading elements of Souham's corps, who had countermarched through the city once more, stabilized the French front and Bianchi was driven back. On the Allied extreme left, Merveldt's Austrians were driven back across the River Pleisse, and Merveldt himself was captured.

A bloody stalemate

The day's fighting in the south had cost the Allies 37,000 men. The French lost 27,000, killed or wounded, including 12 generals, losses they were far less able to bear. The battle had ended in a bloody stalemate, chiefly through Schwarzenberg's skilful use of his reserves, feeding them in at the right time and place, and Blücher's attacks in the north-west, which had drawn in Napoleon's reserves and, ultimately, Napoleon himself.

At Möckern, in some of the most intense fighting of the whole war, the Prussians had slowly, bloodily pushed Marmont back. A French officer described the fighting thus: 'Besides the enemy's artillery, which was killing us at point-blank range, an imposing force of cavalry waited a mere twenty yards away for us to be put to flight when they would spring on us like a tiger.' By the end of the day, Blücher's Prussians had captured Möckern at loss of 5,600, but had taken 2,000 prisoners, one Napoleonic Eagle, two colours (regimental flags) and 40 guns – half of Marmont's artillery. Marmont estimated his losses at 6–7,000.

> ‘an imposing force of cavalry waited for us to be put to flight when they would spring on us like a tiger ’
>
> FRENCH OFFICER

On the following day, 17th October, there was a lull in the fighting, as both sides considered their options. Having failed to win another victory like Dresden, now was the time for Napoleon to withdraw, but that would mean abandoning his garrisons on the Rivers Vistula and Oder and losing control of Germany. Napoleon decided to fight on. His situation, however, was deteriorating by the hour. During the course of the 17th, as Napoleon organized his defences around the perimeter of the city, Bernadotte's Swedish army was approaching from the northeast, and Bennigsen's Russians were reinforcing the Allies in the east and south. Apart from his new line of retreat to the west, Napoleon was now surrounded. Worse still, he was desperately short of ammunition. As he later wrote to his son-in-law Prince Eugene, 'If on the eve of the 18th I could have had 30,000 cannon balls, I would be master of the world today.' It was an act of desperation to fight on in such a situation, with the city – and the River Elster – at his back.

Saxon silence

At 7 a.m. on the morning of 18th October, the Allies launched a concentric attack on the city, with 300,000 men and 1,500 guns. The biggest battle of the Napoleonic wars, this has rightly been named the Battle of the Nations. Even the British were represented by a rocket battery attached to Bernadotte's army.

In the south, the Army of Bohemia began a general advance over the same ground that had been so bitterly contested two days earlier, but after some initial success, their

> 'The response from the Saxon ranks, however, had been a sullen – and ominous – silence'

offensive ground to a halt. In the northwest, Blücher's Army of Silesia was fought to a bloody standstill, but on all other fronts the French were being slowly driven back. At about 2 p.m., advancing from the northeast Bernadotte's Swedes formed up on the right of Bennigsen's Russians. Together they advanced and took the village of Paunsdorf. Napoleon retook it with the Imperial Guard but, finding it untenable, was forced to abandon the village once more. Ney, to his right, withdrew too.

As the French withdrew, however, their Saxon allies were advancing towards the enemy – or so it seemed. Recently their loyalty had been tested to the limit. On 9th October Napoleon had made an inspiring speech to the Saxon VIII Corps, at the conclusion of which the French officers present had cried out '*Vive l'Empereur!*' The response from the Saxon ranks, however, had been a sullen – and ominous – silence. Now, seeing Saxon infantry and guns dashing towards the enemy, the French cavalry cheered them on, only to see their hopes dashed as the Saxons surrendered en masse to the advancing Allies.

With this defection, Napoleon lost at a stroke a division of infantry and 19 guns. As the fighting drew to a close at the end of the day, both sides were completely exhausted. The French line to the south of the city still held, but they had been driven in everywhere else. The ammunition situation was also desperate, and casualties were still mounting. Finally on the evening of 18th October Napoleon decided to give the order for a general retreat to the west.

The nation in arms

'These animals have learned something!' Watching the Russians advance at Bautzen, Napoleon was referring to the fact that, by 1813, the Allied forces had learned a good deal from the French about how to handle troops on the battlefield. It is the fate of armies who start a war with a technical or systemic advantage, to be their enemies' tutors. The Allies, however, had also learned something else. It had been the French who first mobilized the 'nation under arms' against the professional armies of the European ancien régime. First in Spain, later in Russia, and now in Germany in the 'War of Liberation', it was – by a supreme irony – those same monarchies who would mobilize their nations against the French.

The evacuation

At 2 a.m. the following morning, the bulk of the army began moving out west, towards Lindenau – the Imperial Guard leading, followed by three infantry and two cavalry corps. The remainder of the army, which was covering the retreat, began to thin out soon after, while still holding the line. The Allied pickets (infantry outposts) heard some noise, but did little to investigate. Not until 7 a.m. did they begin to take an interest, by which time the French had been retreating for five hours. Fighting did not recommence until 10 a.m. An hour later, Napoleon rode out of the city through crowded streets, crossed the last remaining bridge over the River Elster, rode into Lindenau, dismounted, dictated some orders and fell asleep. If the battle had only been drawn, at least – it seemed – he was about to lead his army out of the threatened encirclement.

Traffic on the causeway and on the bridge over the Elster was heavy and confused. One eyewitness described it as follows: 'Ammunition wagons, vivandiers, gendarmes, cannon, cows and sheep, women, grenadiers, post-chaises, soldiers – unharmed, wounded and dying – pell-mell struggled together in so great a confusion that it was all but impossible to continue on the march, and much less to defend oneself.'

Blown too soon

A whole army retreating over one bridge is a recipe for disaster – especially when that bridge has been prepared for demolition. Bridge demolitions are a difficult operation of war. If the bridge is blown too late, it is captured intact by the enemy; if too soon, a portion of the retreating army is stranded on the enemy bank. At 1 p.m. the colonel in command at the bridge rode back into the city to ascertain which corps would be the last to cross. Shortly afterwards, Napoleon, who had slept despite the gunfire, was aroused by

a terrific explosion. The corporal left in charge of the bridge while the colonel rode into the city had panicked and blown it, leaving 37,000 men and all their artillery, 20,000 walking wounded, 30 generals and two Marshals on the wrong side of the river with no means of escape. In an instant a drawn battle had turned into a French catastrophe.

Many, among them the two marshals, tried to swim across the Elster. Macdonald got safely across with the cries of his men – 'Monsieur le Maréchal, save your men, save your children!' – ringing in his ears. Only recently created marshal, Poniatowski was already

ABOVE: *After the premature destruction of the one remaining bridge, the newly created Marshal Poniatowski plunges into the River Elster. Like hundreds of others, he was swept to his death. Thousands more were stranded and captured.*

'Monsieur le Maréchal,
save your men,
save your children!'

FRENCH TROOPS

wounded and, like many others, was swept away by the river. Generals Lauriston and Reynier, two of Napoleon's best, were taken captive. Many of lower rank were slaughtered by vengeful Allied troops.

The biggest battle of the Napoleonic Wars, Leipzig cost Napoleon 38,000 men, killed or wounded. Another 50,000 were captured and a further 5,000 defected. Allied losses were approximately 55,000. The battle marked the end of Napoleon's German empire – Bavaria had already switched sides and Saxony and Württemberg would soon be forced to abandon the emperor. Napoleon had lost two-thirds of his army excluding the forces that remained in Spain, along with his reputation for invincibility. The French retreat was now headed towards France's border on the Rhine. Crossing the bridge at Mainz, one French officer looking back to the pursuing Allies remarked: 'We have done well to go all the way to Moscow, and bring the Russians back with us!'

'I AM NOT COMPETENT TO COMMAND
SUCH A LARGE ARMY'
GENERAL AMBROSE BURNSIDE

FREDERICKSBURG
1862

By the end of the second year of the American Civil War, both sides had realized that there was little hope of a negotiated peace. The Battle of Antietam in September 1862 had given Abraham Lincoln his first major victory, though at a terrible price. With the Confederate Army of Northern Virginia finally driven away from the banks of the Potomac, Lincoln felt that now was the time to deliver a second blow to Robert E. Lee's already disorganized army. He planned a drive against Fredericksburg, Virginia – an old colonial town on the Rappahannock River – and on to Richmond, 50 miles (80 km) beyond. Lee would have no choice but to fight the more numerous Union Army, or abandon the Confederate capital.

Getting the army of the Potomac's commander, General George B. McClellan, to move, though, was another matter. If 'Little Mac' was the soldiers' favourite, he was less popular with Lincoln, who thought him slow-moving and over-cautious. To do McClellan justice, it was thanks to him that the Union now had a well-trained army. Lincoln, however, had had enough. In the first week of November 1862 he sacked McClellan and replaced him with the commander of the army's IX Corps, General Ambrose E. Burnside. Burnside initially refused the appointment, saying 'I do not want the command. I am not competent to command such a large army.' But Lincoln was insistent and Burnside gave way.

A well-defended position
With 113,000 men to Lee's 80,000, the odds were promising. At first Burnside moved swiftly, concentrating his army opposite Fredericksburg by 17th November. The two wings of Lee's army were 60 miles (96 km) apart – the one commanded by Major-General James Longstreet was at Culpepper Court House while Brigadier-General Thomas 'Stonewall' Jackson's wing was in the Shenandoah Valley. Lee was confident that he could concentrate his army at Fredericksburg if, though he could scarcely believe it, the town proved to be Burnside's main axis of advance.

Lee's doubts were based on the fact that, from the Confederate side of the river, Fredericksburg was eminently defensible. An assaulting force would first of all have to cross the 400-foot (122-m) wide Rappahannock River, fight its way through the town and then form up and advance across broken but open ground to seize the ridge of hills beyond the town. Of these, Marye's Heights was the closest and would have to be captured if the town was to be held and a way forced through to Richmond. The ridgeline was topped with roads and stone fences, but the greatest boon to a defender was the Sunken Road, which ran virtually along the foot of Marye's Heights. Twenty-five feet

(7.6 m) wide and fronted on the side facing the town by a strong stone wall, the Sunken Road formed a natural entrenchment in which several regiments could take shelter. What was more, thanks to the earth piled up against the wall, it was practically invisible from an attacker's point of view. Viewed from the edge of town or from across the river, the ground appeared to slope gently and uninterruptedly up to the top of Marye's Heights.

Burnside drags his heels

Even before he arrived at Fredericksburg, Burnside had ordered up the pontoon bridges he would need to force a crossing. A combination of poor weather and appalling staff work, however, delayed the arrival of the bridges by three weeks. 'If the pontoons had been there,' commented one Union General, 'we might have crossed at once. Yet we lay there nearly a month, while they were fortifying before our eyes.'

Two days after Burnside's advance guard had seized Stafford Heights, a position that overlooked the town and river from the Union side, Confederate Major-General James Longstreet, a master of defensive warfare, was on Marye's Heights on the opposite bank, fortifying his positions and extending the defences on the Sunken Road by a series of rifle pits at each end. Longstreet had a new artillery commander, Lieutenant Edward Porter Alexander, who observed the way the obstacles on the ground below Marye's Heights would channel an attacker towards the Sunken Road. With his 300 guns recently augmented by two 30-pounder Parrott guns from Richmond's defences, Porter Alexander felt able to boast to Longstreet that 'a

> 'a chicken could not live on that field below when we open up on it'

chicken could not live on that field below when we open up on it.' Questioned by an anxious Lee, Longstreet reassured him: 'General, if you put every man now on the other side of the Potomac on that field to approach me over the same line, and give me plenty of ammunition, I will kill them all before they reach my line.'

Even when the bridging equipment did arrive, Burnside still dragged his heels, and it was not until 11th December that he was ready to force a crossing of the Rappahannock. His plan was to launch simultaneous attacks against both wings of Lee's army – Longstreet's and Jackson's – to force a way onto one or other of the two roads leading to Richmond. Having watched the Confederates fortifying over the previous weeks, those ordered to make the assault viewed it with foreboding. 'There were not two opinions among the subordinate officers as to the rashness of this plan,' wrote one staff officer. Many men among the assaulting divisions wrote their names and those of their next of kin on their handkerchiefs and sewed them onto the backs of their tunics, in order that their bodies might be more easily identified.

Bridging the Rappahannock

In the early dawn of 11th December, regular and volunteer Union engineers went down to the riverbank and pushed the first two pontoons out into the Rappahannock. No sooner had they started than Brigadier William Barksdale's Mississippian sharpshooters, hidden in buildings on the town's waterfront, opened up. They took a heavy toll – according to a Confederate observer, 'Nine distinct and desperate attempts were made to complete the bridges ... but every one was attended by such heavy loss that the efforts were abandoned.' Burnside now unleashed his artillery on the town. Several hours and 8,000 shells later, the town was ablaze, but Barksdale's Mississippians were still stubbornly emplaced. At length, a body of volunteers – men from Michigan, Massachusetts and New York – using the pontoons as assault craft, crossed the Rappahannock and gained a foothold on the far bank. Fighting street by street, they succeeded in driving the rebel sharpshooters from the town.

Lee watched all this, still unconvinced that this could be Burnside's main effort. Throughout the night of the 11th and 12th and the following day, Union troops marched across the now-completed pontoons.

During the night of the 11th and 12th, Union Major-General William B. Franklin marched 45,000 men and 116 guns across the southernmost pontoon bridge. This force deployed along the railway leading to Richmond, which ran through the river valley.

> 'A cavalryman sat down at a fine rosewood piano ... drove his saber through the polished keys'
>
> FEDERAL CHAPLAIN

Meanwhile, Major-General Edwin Sumner marched 31,000 men, via the northernmost bridge, into Fredericksburg itself. By dawn of the following day, Lee, from his position on what is now know as Lee's Hill, could see both forces preparing to assault his positions. Of the two Confederate wings, the right, based on Sudley Heights, was the weaker. Aware of this, Lee ordered Jackson to summon the divisions of D.P. Hill and Jubal Early, which were covering other crossings of the Rappahannock. On receipt of Jackson's order, Hill's division began an 18-mile (29-km) forced march to join him.

Burnside made no effort against Lee's positions on 12th December. As Fredericksburg was 'secesh', 'Secessionist' and thus rebel territory, his men felt free to loot the town. While this behaviour might be understandable on the part of an army only intermittently supplied in the depths of winter and desperate to survive, much of the destruction was utterly wanton. One eyewitness , a federal chaplain, wrote 'I saw men break down the doors to rooms of fine houses, enter, shatter the looking glasses with the blow of the axe, knock the vases and lamps off the mantelpiece with a careless swing ... A cavalryman sat down at a fine rosewood piano ... drove his saber through the polished keys, then knocked off the top and tore out the strings.'

The start of the offensive

By the morning of the 13th, Burnside was ready to launch his offensive. Lee's right wing seemed to Burnside the weaker of the two, and it was his plan to turn it with Franklin's force. Jackson's command, though, was not as weak as it appeared – by dawn D.H. Hill's division had arrived and formed on Jackson's right, and Jubal Early's division arrived to be placed in reserve behind A.P. Hill's. The bulk of Jackson's command was concealed

by thick woods. Even so, Lee was concerned enough to ride over and join Jackson, as the vanguard of Franklin's 'Grand Division', General George Meade's 5,000 men, began driving into Jackson's skirmishers. Soon Meade came under a raking fire from batteries on Jackson's extreme right, which stalled his advance until Union batteries could suppress their fire. By midday, Meade was able to continue his advance, but he once again came under fire – this time from Jackson's main artillery, which inflicted heavy casualties on the left of his division. Before they could even come to within rifle range of Jackson's positions, Meade's division was forced to withdraw.

ABOVE: *Burnside's Union troops push pontoons out into the broad Rappahannock River, preparing to cross it to reach the old colonial town of Fredericksburg. The looting of the town by Union soldiers brought a new bitterness to the conflict.*

The death trap of the Sunken Road

Lee now rode over to assess the situation on his left. Here, at 11 a.m., Sumner had launched his attack out of Fredericksburg. General Nathan Kimball, commanding the leading brigade of William H. French, led his men out of the now-blazing town and into the open country between Fredericksburg and Marye's Heights, 400 yards (366 m) away. Picket fences and a drainage canal slowed his men's progress, the latter forcing them to 'bunch' dangerously as they queued to cross by plank bridges. By now, Alexander's Confederate artillery had opened up, catching Kimball's brigade in a deadly crossfire as they attempted to deploy from columns of march into columns of attack. 'It was,' Kimball wrote, 'a most murderous fire ... several shells bursting in the ranks and destroying a company at a time. Yet all the regiments, without an exception, moved steadily forward without confusion, those in the rear quickly closing up the gaps left by their fallen comrades.'

Watching from Marye's Heights, Adjutant Owen of the (Confederate) Washington Artillery was equally impressed. 'How beautifully they came on! Their bright bayonets glistening in the sunlight made the line look like a huge serpent of blue and steel.' Among Brigadier-General Thomas Cobb's Georgians manning the Sunken Road was Sergeant Montgomery of the Georgian Philips Legion. 'It would have made your blood run cold,' Montgomery wrote, 'to have seen their great numbers coming over to oppose our little handful.' Kimball's men had been taking casualties from the rebel artillery, who had been firing on them from three different directions from the moment they left the edge of Fredericksburg. By the time they finally began to ascend Marye's Heights they were already exausted from a fast-paced advance over muddy, broken ground.

> '**It would have made your blood run cold to have seen their great numbers coming over to oppose our little handful**'
>
> SERGEANT MONTGOMERY

Leaning into the gradient, they pushed on up the hill, still, it seems, unaware of the presence of the stone wall or of Cobb's Georgians hunkered down behind it. The first they knew was when a line of heads and shoulders appeared as if out of the ground in front of them at a distance of about 200 yards (183 m). On the heights above, among the Confederate guns, Adjutant Owen watched what followed as 'the Georgians in the road below us rose up, and glancing along their rifle barrels, let loose a storm of lead into the faces of the advance brigade.'

The opening volley shredded the front ranks of Kimball's brigade. As they reeled, the Georgians ducked down behind the wall and then, after furiously reloading, rose up again to deliver a second shattering volley. 'We poured volley after volley into their ranks' wrote Sergeant Montgomery, 'which told a most deadening effect.' Most of the Confederate infantry behind the stone wall were firing cartridges containing a ball and three rounds of buckshot – not as effective at long range as the Minie bullets of the Union rifles, but devastating at close range. Raked by volleys of 'ball and buck', Kimball's line wavered and the men scattered, fell back or went to ground where they could. Since crossing their 'start line' at the edge of Fredericksburg, Kimball's brigade had suffered 520 casualties; Kimball himself (hit in the groin) and three regimental commanders had fallen wounded. 'They soon began to waver,' wrote Montgomery, 'and at last broke for the rear.' The Georgians cheered, but even as they did so they were aware of another Union brigade commanded by Colonel John W. Andrews, coming up to replace Kimball's.

A repeating pattern

This was the beginning of a pattern that would be repeated throughout the afternoon as brigade after brigade was thrown by Burnside onto Longstreet's killing ground. In the Sunken Road, Brigadier-General Cobb did not have long to enjoy his triumph. Not all of Kimball's men fell back when the first attack was stopped in its tracks – some had taken cover in the railroad cutting that ran up the hill to their left, others in the buildings at the edge of town. Experienced troops with good rifles, these men now commenced firing 'at will' at any target that presented itself. Sheltered against the wall and exposing themselves only briefly to fire before ducking down again, the riflemen in the Sunken Road made a difficult target; not so any troops sent to thicken up Cobb's firing line. Brigadier-General John R. Cooke and his two regiments of North Carolinians had to make their own way over open ground before they could drop into the relative safety of the Sunken Road. Those huddled up against the wall were well protected against Union cannon fire and rifle bullets, but the field officers, at the rear of their regiments, were more exposed in the middle of the road. Two captains and one regimental commander had already been struck down, and now, as the two brigadier-generals greeted each other, Cooke was hit in the head and Cobb in the thigh. Cooke's wound, although it took him out of the fight, was not fatal, but Cobb's wound severed the femoral artery and within minutes he was dead. For the men in the Sunken Road this was the crisis point of the battle – they were running low on ammunition, their two commanders had been struck down and fresh Union troops – of General Hancock's division – were advancing up the slopes towards them. Into the breach stepped Colonel Robert McMillan, commander of the 24th Georgia Regiment and one of the few unwounded officers left in Cobb's brigade. McMillan walked up and down the line between assaults, calming and encouraging the men.

Hancock's division attacks

Hancock's men came on in three lines, with Colonel S.K. Zook's brigade leading. The riflemen behind the stone wall waited until they were at close range, then greeted them with a 'rebel yell', the spine-chilling, high-pitched hunting holler that was the hallmark of the Confederate soldier, followed by a succession of volleys. Zook's brigade suffered the same fate as Kimball's. Unable to advance, they tried to hold their ground under withering fire, before falling back.

Next came Brigadier–General Caldwell's brigade who, suffering the same treatment, also retreated. Confederate riflemen had never had it so easy – able to steady their rifles on the stone wall and engage the enemy with 'ball and buck' at perfect range, they carpeted the ground before the embankment with blue-coated bodies. Nonetheless, many of

Caldwell's brigade went to ground, joining those of Zook's and Kimball's troops who had refused to retreat, adding to the growing fusillade against the rebel positions.

The next of Hancock's brigades was Colonel Thomas F. Meagher's 'Irish Brigade'. Now they, too, came under fire from McMillan's Georgians and Carolinians – many of whom, including Colonel McMillan, were themselves of Irish origin. Colonel St. Clair Mulholland, commanding the 116th Pennsylvania Volunteers, on the left of Meagher's line, described what followed: 'The Irish Brigade had reached a point within thirty yards of the stone wall and began firing. All the field and staff officers of the Regiment were wounded. The colour sergeant, William H. Tyrell, was down on one knee (his other being shattered) but still waving the flag... Five balls struck him in succession; a dozen pierced the colours; another broke the flagstaff, and the colours and the colour sergeant fell together. The orders were to retire passed down the line and the command began falling back.'

Reinforcements for the Sunken Road

From his position on Marye's Heights, Brigadier-General Joseph Kershaw had become aware of the desperate situation of the Georgian and North Carolinian regiments in the Sunken Road. Galloping his horse down the slope, he led two fresh South Carolinian regiments, taking heavy casualties as they crossed the open ground into the Sunken Road.

'That's our boys cheering the Yankees!'
CONFEDERATE TROOPER

'Just in the nick of time,' wrote Sergeant Montgomery, 'here came the old 2nd S.C. Vols. Like so many wild Indians. I tell you I felt good for we had shot away 70 rounds of cartridges and the Yankees were still coming.' The South Carolinians lined up behind their comrades from Georgia and North Carolina. According to Kershaw, 'my troops could only get into position by doubling on them. The troops accordingly doubled up and the formation along most of the line was consequently four deep.' Further reinforcements thickened the Confederate firing line until it was six deep, creating some confusion and even some 'friendly-fire' casualties. However, with McMillan and Kershaw controlling their fire, the rebel riflemen could now fire one 1,000-rifle volley every 15 seconds.

The South Carolinians arrived just in time because at 1 p.m. a new Union division commanded by General Oliver O. Howard advanced to the attack. Though previously the Union armies had not shown much fight, Antietam had shown the Confederates what they had not believed before – that Union soldiers could and would fight. If anything good emerged from the carnage below the stone wall, it was a new respect on the part of the rebels for their Union counterparts. At one point a Confederate officer on Marye's Heights, enquiring about the commotion below on the Sunken Road, was told 'That's our boys cheering the Yankees!'

Burnside's despair

By the time Howard's division fell back, they had added another 700 to the dead and wounded in front of the stone wall – Sumner's corps had done all it could. From his viewpoint, Burnside could see the failure of his attacks on Lee's left – now he ordered

'It is well war is so terrible or we should grow too fond of it'

ROBERT E. LEE

Franklin to make a fresh assault against his right. Supported by 51 guns, Meade's and Gibbon's divisions went forward. Union scouts had found a weakness in Jackson's line – a tongue of woodland protruding from the main position. Because of its boggy ground the woodland had been considered impassable and was therefore only lightly defended. Plunging into it, Meade turned Jackson's left, driving off the first of A.P. Hill's two lines, but a timely counter-attack by Jackson's reserves, Early's and General William Taliaferro's brigades, drove Meade's now-disorganized bluecoats back down to the river.

While this was going on, from his vantage point on the ridge line, Lee watched the fourth Union attempt, by Major Samuel D. Sturgis's division of IX Corps, falter and fail in front of the stone wall. With the two extra regiments Lee had personally sent down, there were now nine Confederate regiments in the Sunken Road, and another seven supporting them from above on the heights along with fresh artillery – Alexander's batteries had replaced the Washington artillery, which was almost out of ammunition.

Burnside was growing frantic. He ordered Franklin to make yet another assault on Jackson's positions – orders which Franklin flatly refused to obey. The battle on the Confederate right (Union left) ground to a halt. By now, General General Andrew Humphreys' Pennsylvanians were attacking the stone wall with no more success than their predecessors. It was dusk, and Humphreys' men could only see the rebels' positions by the flashes from their muskets. Against the advice of General Joseph 'Fighting Joe' Hooker, Burnside then decided to throw V Corps into the cauldron. Hooker obeyed the order as far as was necessary – using General George Sykes' corps to extricate Humphreys and sending two brigades on a failed attempt to turn the rebel right. Then '... finding I had lost as many men as my orders required me to lose, I suspended the attack.'

A distraught Burnside announced that he would place himself at the head of his

Open or close order

The tactic of attacking in close-order columns in the face of massed rifle fire, as employed by mid-to-late-19th-century armies, may appear suicidally stupid, but the problem faced by attacking troops was one of command and control. Troops attacking spaced out rather than shoulder to shoulder may suffer fewer casualties, but are much more difficult to command when an officer or NCO can only see one or two men to his left or right. After the Seven Week War of 1866 in which they suffered severe losses at the hands of troops armed with Austrian Lorenz rifles, the Prussians carried out a study. They concluded that the ability to control and manoeuvre attacking formations was all-important and that the close-order column delivered troops onto the enemy's position more quickly and in better order than the alternatives. The tacticians of most other armies invariably came to the same conclusion.

old corps, the IXth, and personally lead them up Marye's Heights. Perhaps, like many another commander in this situation, he was seeking redemption in death. Dissuaded from this, however, he broke down and wept. 'Those poor men,' he sobbed, 'Those poor men.' Surveying the carnage from the opposing heights, Lee had remarked earlier in the day, 'It is well war is so terrible or we should grow too fond of it.'

A hollow victory

In the fighting that took place on 13th December, the Army of the Potomac lost 12,600 men, two-thirds of whom fell before the stone wall below Marye's Heights. During a total of 14 assaults, not a single Union soldier succeeded in setting foot on the Heights. Confederate losses amounted to 5,300. It was a timely victory for the Confederacy, but ultimately a hollow one. Union losses were soon made up – but, lacking the manpower of the north, the men that Lee had lost would be harder to replace. One immediate outcome in the aftermath of Fredericksburg was that Burnside was dismissed and replaced by 'Fighting Joe' Hooker.

The Army of the Potomac would have its revenge. In July 1863, under George Meade, who had headed the assault on Jackson's wing at Fredericksburg, it would halt Lee's invasion of Maryland at Gettysburg. On the second day, as they mowed down General George Pickett's Confederates charging up Cemetery Ridge, the Union riflemen taunted their opponents with cries of 'Fredericksburg!' 'Fredericksburg!'

'NOUS SOMMES DANS UN POT DE CHAMBRE'

GENERAL AUGUSTE-ALEXANDRE DUCROT

SEDAN

1870

The Franco-German war of 1870–1 was caused by the rivalry between Napoleon III's France and the emerging power of Prussia. The Prussian Minister-President, Otto von Bismarck, was determined to unite all of Germany under Prussian leadership. For most of the previous 200 years, France had been the paramount power in Europe, and was determined to remain so, fearing a united Germany would threaten her dominant status. Burdened as we are with more modern stereotypes, it is now hard to imagine that in the first half of the 19th century it was France that was considered the aggressive, militaristic nation and the Germans a nation of poets, philosophers and dreamers.

If Franco-Prussian rivalry was the underlying cause of the war, the *pretext* was the succession to the Spanish throne. When this fell vacant in 1870, the Prussians put forward a candidate from the Prussian ruling house, the Hohenzollerns. This caused outrage in France, who felt herself about to be encircled. French protests proved effective and the Hohenzollern candidature was withdrawn. This was not enough, though, for Napoleon III, nephew of the first Napoleon, who had already shown a taste for military adventure.

A secret weapon

Although there was always more than a hint of comic opera about the 'Second Empire', the French army had established a reputation second to none in Italy, the Crimea, China, North Africa and Mexico. It was, though, as one of its generals described it, 'a nice little African army' ideal for colonial 'bushwhacking' expeditions against native forces in France's North African empire, but in no way prepared for a major continental war. The armies of the Prussians and their German allies, on the other hand, were organized with just such a war in mind, employing the first modern-style professional general staff, universal conscription and a railway network designed to rush men swiftly to the frontier. If the French *chassepot* rifle was superior to the Prussian Dreyse, the Germans – with their steel, breech-loading Krupp artillery – enjoyed a distinct advantage over the French bronze muzzle loaders. That the French were not overly worried about this was due to their secret weapon, the *mitrailleuse*, a 25-barrel machine gun that could fire 125 rounds a minute. So secret was it that it was only issued to the army a few days before the outbreak of war.

War breaks out

Eager for *la gloire*, confident in the power of his army to inflict a crushing defeat on the Germans, and in need of the distraction of a foreign war to shore up his shaky and

PREVIOUS PAGE: *Bloody, hand-to-hand street fighting in Bazeilles, near Sedan, between French and Bavarian troops. French civilians found under arms were executed.*

unpopular regime, Napoleon decided to overplay a weak hand. The withdrawal of the Hohenzollern candidature had handed him a diplomatic coup on a plate. Now Napoleon demanded a public apology from Prussia – an apology that the Prussian king, William I, could not make without massive loss of face. No apology being forthcoming, France declared war on 19th July. France's mobilization was chaotic, with units marching all over the country in different directions to their concentration areas. At length, two armies coalesced – one under Marshal Patrice de MacMahon at Strasbourg, the other under Marshal François Bazaine at Metz – a total of 250,000 men. When Napoleon took personal command of the 'Army of the Rhine' at Metz, there was still no strategic plan, other than a vaguely conceived push to the north to drive the Prussians and their German allies off the west bank of the Rhine.

Again, the contrast with the Prussian army could not have been more striking. Under their commander Field Marshal Helmuth von Moltke, they used their railway network to assemble three armies, totalling 400,000 men, along the Franco-German frontier. The French having obligingly divided their armies, Moltke was able to contain MacMahon's army with one of his, while the other two swept round to the south and west of Bazaine's army at Metz, cutting him off from Paris and MacMahon. It was as well for Napoleon, already desperately ill from a bladder stone, that he had earlier left the Metz army to join MacMahon. Bazaine attempted to break out westwards, but after a bloody battle at Gravelotte-St. Privat he was forced back into Metz.

MacMahon leaves Paris wide open

With Bazaine trapped in Metz, MacMahon had no choice but to retreat to where, at Châlons-sur-Marne, he could protect Paris. His best strategy at this point would have been to stay put and concentrate on the defence of the capital, but political pressures intervened. Frantic messages from the empress and the Council of Regency made it clear that a merely defensive posture would imperil the regime – what was needed was some spectacular, Napoleonic coup. Napoleon found himself agreeing to a scheme whereby, it was hoped, MacMahon's army might link up with Bazaine's. It involved a flank march to the northwest, towards the Belgian frontier at Montmédy, leaving Paris unprotected. There, it was hoped, the whole army would be able to slip past the right flank of the advancing Prussian armies and march around them to join Bazaine's army. The united French armies could then fall on the Prussians' rear and attack their lines of communication.

'Cries of *'Vive l'Empereur'* were met with *'Un! Deux! Trois! Merde!'*'

It was another of those plans that look good on paper – and the hastily-improvised Army of Châlons – 130,000 men with 423 guns – looked good on paper, too. In fact, the regular element was exhausted and demoralized, the new recruits scarcely able to handle their weapons, and the 18 battalions of the Paris Garde Mobile openly seditious. Cries of *'Vive l'Empereur'* were met with *'Un! Deux! Trois! Merde!'* Nevertheless, by 20th August, the Army of Châlons, with the emperor little more than an ailing passenger now, was on the march northwards through the wild forests of the Argonne.

By the 25th, Moltke – who had been expecting to march westwards to a decisive battle in front of Paris – learned to his amazement that MacMahon had left Paris wide open and was marching across the front of the Prussian armies, heading towards the Belgian frontier. Moltke did not stand amazed for long, ordering two of his armies – the Third Army and the Army of the Meuse – to swing northwards too, staying between MacMahon and Metz, and blocking any move MacMahon might make to link up with Bazaine. Shadowing MacMahon's march, Moltke was ready to meet him when he tried to turn south. At Beaumont-sur-Meuse, on 30th August, Moltke barred his way, inflicting 5,000 casualties and capturing 40 guns. Confounded, and with his flank march over, MacMahon had no choice but to withdraw to the northwest *away* from Metz – towards the frontier city of Sedan.

The French make a stand

Sedan was a 17th-century fortress, chiefly famous for the chair that bore its name and for being the birthplace of the great French marshal, Turenne. The marshy Meuse Valley protected the city from the south and west, and to the northeast a triangle of ground rose up into the hills beyond. With Sedan at the centre of the triangle's base, the villages of Floing and Bazeilles formed its western and eastern corners respectively. The two sides of the triangle were formed by the valleys of the River Givonne to the east and the River Floing to the west. The apex of the triangle ended at the heights the 'Calvaire d'Illy'. The interior of this huge defensive triangle, which sloped down from its apex to the city at its base, was filled with a vast forest, the Bois de la Garenne. At first, MacMahon only intended to regroup at Sedan and consider his next move, but he appears to have finally decided to make a stand, despite the fact that his army was low on ammunition. As his army reached Sedan on 31st August, it took up positions along the sides of the triangle, with a reserve in the centre.

> 'what was needed was some spectacular, Napoleonic coup'

When one corps commander, General Douay, mentioned the need to entrench his positions, MacMahon commented that he would not be fighting a defensive battle but intended 'to manoeuvre in front of the enemy'. 'M. le Maréchal,' replied Douay, 'tomorrow the enemy will not give you time.'

Moltke manoevures into position

Douay was right. Even as MacMahon was making his dispositions Moltke, a keen student of Hannibal, was positioning his forces to envelop the French army, crowd it in upon Sedan and destroy it. His plan was to use his two armies as a giant pair of pincers. The Army of the Meuse, under Crown Prince Albert of Saxony, would be the right pincer, attacking MacMahon in front, and turning his left. Albert was to advance up the Givonne Valley to the high ground beyond. Once there, Albert would detach a force to link up with troops of the left pincer. The Third Army, led by the Prussian Crown Prince

ABOVE: *Prussian infantry in attack formation in the fighting around Sedan. Like Burnside's infantry, the Prussians generally attacked in close columns and suffered heavily from French rifle and mitrailleuse fire.*

> **'Now we've got them in a mousetrap!'**
> FIELD MARSHAL HELMUTH VON MOLTKE

Frederick William, was to be the left pincer, attacking MacMahon's centre at the villages of Bazeilles and Balan, but then overwhelming the French right. When the two pincers met on the high ground near the Calvaire d'Illy, the French would be completely surrounded, and the greatly superior German Krupp guns, deployed on the heights, would do their terrible work and pound them into submission.

Approaching Sedan from the south on the afternoon of 31st August, the Saxons, part of the right pincer, crossed the Meuse below Sedan, while the Prussian Guards pushed out beyond *their* right towards the Belgian border. If the French regarded the Belgian border as a protection, Moltke saw it as a wall against which he could pin MacMahon's army. Meanwhile, commanding the left pincer, Crown Prince Frederick William brought his troops up to the line of the Meuse and began shelling the railway line that ran through the city. Now MacMahon had only one avenue of retreat left: north of the city, the Meuse makes a huge hairpin bend before turning west, through Donchery, in the direction of Mézières. There – 15 miles (24 km) away – was General Vinoy with his newly formed XIII Corps. However, by the evening of the 31st, any chance MacMahon had of falling back and joining him was lost. Even as the Prussian crown prince's guns were shelling the railway line, troops of General Blumenthal's corps, the tip of the left pincer, were pushing on to cross the bridge at Donchery and seal off the Meuse Valley. By the evening, Bavarian troops of the Prussian Third Army had thrown two pontoons across the river to the south of the city. 'Now we've got them in a mousetrap!' remarked Moltke to King William as he looked at the maps at Third Army headquarters. On the French side, General Auguste-Alexandre Ducrot had come to a similar conclusion expressing it in words that might have been the epitaph of the Army of Châlons. '*Nous sommes dans un pot de chambre,*' he said, '*et nous y serons emmerdés* ('We are in a chamber pot and are going to be shit on'.)

The trap snaps shut

The following morning, under a thick fog, the German attack began, and by 6 a.m. French and German artillery were engaged along the whole line. In the French centre the Bavarians attacked Bazeilles once more, supported by crossfire from their gun batteries. Well aware of the importance of this village, the French marines, the best troops in MacMahon's army, disputed the ground inch-by-inch, assisted by *franc tireurs* – armed French civilians. The fighting was bitter and bloody, and the Bavarians executed any French civilians found under arms. Neither side knew it yet, but this sort of warfare and this sort of atrocity were to become regular features of the later stages of the war as the Germans found themselves confronted by a nation under arms.

On the French left, Crown Prince Alberts' Saxon forces pushed up the Givonne Valley – the right-hand side of the French triangle. While one Saxon column linked with the Bavarians to their left, another attacked the village of Daigny. Here they were held for nearly

> **'the encirclement of the Army of Châlons was complete'**

three hours by Ducrot's Zouaves, North African-style light infantry. However, the gradual build-up of Saxon infantry and gun batteries eventually proved too much for these elite troops, who withdrew up the slopes of the valley. By 10 a.m. the Saxons were pushing on up to the apex of the triangle, near the village of Givonne itself – the German right pincer was almost in place. Here MacMahon had placed the troops in which he had least confidence, and at the approach of the Germans they panicked and gave way. Thus the French left was turned.

> 'Within two hours from now we will have driven the enemy into the Meuse'
> GENERAL DE WIMPFFEN

The Prussian crown prince, Frederick William – son of the Prussian king and father of 'Kaiser Bill' (William II, the last German Emperor) – was commanding the German left pincer. At 7.30 a.m. King William and his staff rode to a hill near the village of Frénois to watch his son's Third Army complete the encirclement of the French. By the time they reached the hill, the crown prince's troops were astride the Sedan-Mézières road and were marching east towards the city. By 9 a.m. they were setting up gun batteries opposite the left-hand side of the French defensive triangle, and Frederick William's left-hand V Corps was pushing up towards its apex. Still, the advancing Germans did not have it all their way – the massed fire of the French infantry took its toll on their columns. One of the Prussian king's 'celebrity' guests – the American general Phil Sheridan, reporting on the war for the United States – listening to the rolling fire of the French *chassepot* rifles and the deep bark of the deadly *mitrailleuses*, commented that he had never heard such well-sustained small arms fire. However, as in the Givonne Valley, weight of numbers and Krupp artillery carried the day for the Prussians. Shortly before midday, the left-hand corps of the Third Army met the advance guard of the Prussian Guard cavalry coming from the other direction on the high ground near the farm at Olly. The pincers had closed – the encirclement of the Army of Châlons was complete.

Misplaced confidence

The fighting at Bazeilles claimed an early and significant casualty. As soon as the fighting started, MacMahon rode into the village and was soon hit in the leg by a shell splinter. Carried into Sedan, he appointed Ducrot commander-in-chief in his place. Ducrot immediately ordered a general retreat to the west. Told that the emperor should first be informed, Ducrot replied '*Que l'Empereur aille se faire foutre où il voudra*' (the Emperor can go **** himself). Ducrot was unaware that the Germans were already in Donchery, astride his intended escape route. He was also unaware, as was MacMahon, that another corps commander, General de Wimpffen, had a letter in his pocket from the war minister appointing *him* commander-in-chief should MacMahon be incapacitated. Now the Army of Châlons had its third commander-in-chief in as many hours. De Wimpffen countermanded Ducrot's orders for a retreat,

> 'Que l'Empereur aille se faire foutre où il voudra'
> GENERAL DUCROT

confidently assuring the emperor: 'Your Majesty need have no fears. Within two hours from now we will have driven the enemy into the Meuse.'

Military fashion

Throughout history, military fashion has provided a good indication of which nation's army is the most highly regarded. In the first half of the 19th century it was the French. Both armies in the American Civil War, for example, chose to adopt French-style uniforms – including the kepi, and even the exotic, North African-style 'Zouave' dress – as an indication that their volunteer armies would aspire to the highest military standards. Although French soldiers did not disgrace themselves in the battles of the Franco-Prussian War, the nation's military reputation was to suffer for a generation, and military fashion changed once again to ape the victors. By the end of the century, most armies, including the American and the British, were wearing spiked helmets.

The bitter truth

Once in command, De Wimpffen soon learned the true state of affairs – bombarded from all sides by massed batteries of Krupp guns, his front was collapsing and troops were now pouring into the illusory shelter of Sedan.

The superiority of the German guns is illustrated by the account of a staff officer with Napoleon III. The emperor was in Bazeilles encouraging the defenders when he became aware of a French brigade coming under enemy shell fire. 'The men fell like wheat battered by a storm', he wrote. 'The emperor was incredulous; he could not believe in their murderous effects at such a remote range. He, however, immediately ordered cannon to play upon the newly discovered battery, but to no purpose. The balls chiefly fell in the River Meuse at a distance of only 1,500 metres!'

The emperor then rode back into the city. 'He had scarcely entered Sedan,' the staff officer wrote, 'when he found soldiers flying in various directions, utterly panic-stricken. They rapidly filled the town. At the same time, a terrific cannonade resounded from the very heights which Marshal MacMahon ... had ordered to be occupied by the French troops, but which were now in the possession of the Crown Prince... This advantage was fatal. Then and there the day was lost.' One of the shells burst under the emperor's horse, killing the horse of a general behind him. 'He himself was untouched,' an eyewitness wrote, 'and he turned around smiling, though my friend thought he saw tears in his eyes, which he wiped away with his glove.'

At 2.30 p.m., at the other end of the battlefield, on the heights overlooking the village of Floing, King William of Prussia was looking through binoculars at the spectacular chessboard view his position afforded. Nearby was *The Times* correspondent William Howard Russell. 'That awful Prussian artillery,' he wrote, 'circled the whole of the French in a continuous smoke belt.'

'Ah! Les braves gens'
KING WILLIAM I OF PRUSSIA

'So long as there's one of us left!'

Observing a mass of French cavalry moving in the direction of Floing, King William commented to bystanders: 'That, I think, must be an attempt to break through.' He was right. On his own initiative General Ducrot was determined to make one last attempt to break out of the Sedan 'chamber pot'. His plan had the simplicity of desperation. He ordered General Marguerite's cavalry division to attack in two lines, acting as a battering ram to hammer a way through the German encirclement. Ducrot himself and his infantry corps would follow, before marching west to Mézières. Marguerite rode forward to reconnoitre the ground, only to return moments later fatally wounded in the face – he pointed towards the enemy before falling from his saddle. With cries of 'Vengez-le!' the mass of horsemen moved off at a walk, trot, canter and finally at a gallop towards the German infantry and guns in Floing. It was a charge worthy of the high traditions of French chivalry – but against modern artillery and breech-loading guns it was utterly, heroically futile. Led by General Gallifet, the first line of troops, heavy-armoured *cuirassiers*, drove back the German skirmishers, but before the massed volley fire of the main German infantry, they divided right and left and fell back, leaving the ground strewn with men and horses.

> 'they swerved … right and left, as water divides upon a rock, pursued by death as they rode'
> WILLIAM HOWARD RUSSELL

Asked by Ducrot if he could attempt another charge, Gallifet replied: 'As often as you like, *mon général*, so long as there's one of us left!' and rode off to lead the second wave. This charge met the same fate. Russell, watching from above, described the attack of a regiment of French chasseurs against Prussian infantry. 'It was not until the front had reached within a couple of hundred yards of the infantry ... that there came out the whiff and roll of a volley, which was kept up like the rattling of a catherine-wheel. The result was almost incredible. The leading squadron was dissolved into a heap of white and grey horses, amidst which men were seen trying to disengage themselves, while others held up their hands as if to avert the charge of the squadrons behind them. The survivors, dropping fast, passed round upon each flank of the infantry and, as the second and third squadrons came in a confused mass over the plain, filled with the carcasses of horses and men, they swerved from rushing upon their fate, and wheeling past the infantry, rode off right and left, as water divides upon a rock, pursued by death as they rode.'

Watching this from the heights, the Prussian king was moved to remark: '*Ah! Les braves gens!*', and as Gallifet led back the pitiful remnants of a third attempt, one German regiment ceased firing and its officers saluted with their swords.

The French collapse

With the failure of Ducrot's break-out, the whole French front from Floing northwards crumbled, the men fleeing into the Bois de la Garenne or pouring into Sedan. 'Within Sedan the situation was indescribable,' wrote Ducrot later, 'streets, open places and entrances were blocked with wagons, carts, cannon and all the impedimenta and debris

of a routed army. Bands of soldiers without rifles or equipment rushed here and there seeking refuge in the houses and churches, while at the gates of the town they crushed each other to death. Athwart this rabble galloped troopers *ventre à terre* (belly to the ground – at speed) and gunners on limbers (gun carriages) lashed their way through the maddened mob. Such as were not completely insane had set to work to pillage, and others shouted: 'We have been betrayed, we have been sold by traitors and cowards!'

At an angry council of war, the emperor finally asserted himself over his discordant generals and insisted on surrender, sending General Reille with a personal note to the Prussian king which read, 'As I have not been able to die in the midst of my troops, it only

ABOVE: *Prussian infantry and horse-artillery parade on the Champs Élysées, January 1871. The Prussian occupation of Paris was to leave lasting bitterness and a desire for revenge, which found its expression in 1914.*

remains for me to put my sword in Your Majesty's hands. I am Your Majesty's good brother.' That night the exhausted victors camped on the heights around the city and from thousands of campfires rose the haunting strains of the old Lutheran hymn, as sung by Frederick the Great's troops on the night of the Battle of Leuthen, *Nun danket alle Gott (Now Thank We All Our God)*.

The following day Napoleon III surrendered himself,104,000 French troops, their guns and baggage to the Prussian king. For a loss of 9,000 of their own men, the Prussians had inflicted 17,000 casualties on the French, as well as taking many prisoners. With Napoleon in captivity in Germany, the Second Empire collapsed, but a new French republic, proclaimed in Paris, fought on. In October 1870 Bazaine surrendered the only remaining imperial army of 179,000 men at Metz. However, Paris fought off a Prussian siege until forced to capitulate in January 1871. Despite Bismarck's urgings, triumphalism prevailed. German troops held a victory parade in Paris and the new German Empire – with King William as its kaiser – was proclaimed in the Hall of Mirrors at Versailles. These humiliations fuelled a French desire for revenge in the years leading up to the Great War, which in turn created a similar desire on the part of Germans following their defeat in that conflict. A mere 70 years after Sedan, in the skies above the place where King William watched the last charge of Napoleon's cavalry, Stukas would be circling.

'I COULD WHIP ALL
THE INDIANS ON THE
CONTINENT WITH
THE 7TH CAVALRY'
GEORGE ARMSTRONG CUSTER

LITTLE BIGHORN
1876

The white man's relentless drive into the American West in the second half of the 19th century inevitably brought conflict with the Plains Indians. The discovery of gold in the Black Hills of Dakota, and the ensuing gold rush, bringing with it ever greater numbers of white prospectors, led hostile Sioux and Cheyenne warriors to form a coalition. In 1876 General Phil Sheridan was tasked with dispersing this coalition. Sheridan planned a three-pronged offensive by columns of troops under General Crook from the north, Colonel Gibbon from the east and General Terry from the west. Included in Terry's command was the 7th Cavalry under one of the most controversial characters in American military history – George Armstrong Custer.

Custer's luck

Custer had been the 'Boy General' of the Civil War, the protégé of General Sheridan himself, and 'Custer's Luck' was proverbial. To some he was the epitome of the *beau sabreur* and a future president; to others he was a reckless showman who had ridden to glory over the corpses of his own men. If it is true that many of his victories had been high-casualty affairs, it is also true that men like Phil Sheridan did not bestow their regard lightly. Under a cloud after having offended President Ulysses S. Grant, Custer's inclusion in the campaign was only due to his personal knowledge of the Black Hills and his experience as an Indian fighter.

Eight years earlier, in November 1868, Custer had commanded the 7th US Cavalry during a punitive expedition against the Cheyenne and Arapaho. He had come upon a large camp on the Washita River. Without reconnaissance and splitting his command into four groups, Custer attacked at dawn while his band played the regimental march 'Garryowen'. From four directions, Custer's troopers galloped into the camp, shooting anything that moved.

'To some he was the epitome of the *beau sabreur*'

In Indian-fighting terms it was a great success, resulting in over 150 American Indians killed or captured, though critics noted that many of these were squaws or young boys. With hindsight, though, there are elements of this victory that boded ill for the future. Custer soon discovered that he had attacked the tail-end of a much larger Indian winter camp, containing Kiowas, Arapahoes, Commanches and Apaches – before long he felt compelled to withdraw in the face of superior numbers. As he did so, a detachment of 18 men under Captain Joel Elliott was overwhelmed and massacred. Some, including one of Custer's own troop commanders, Frederick Benteen, felt that Custer had abandoned Elliott to his fate.

OPPOSITE: *General George Armstrong Custer, a Civil War hero and, by 1876, an experienced fighter of American Indians. Custer's luck was proverbial in the army – but it was to desert him by the Little Bighorn River.*

Custer's confidence

The 1876 campaign went wrong from the start. Gibbon encountered the main Indian encampment in March, but let it escape. In June, General Crook fought a large Indian concentration at the Rosebud River and was forced to withdraw. Later that month, Terry and Gibbon joined forces and considered a new plan. Terry intended to use Custer's cavalry as a hammer to drive the Indians – now under the leadership of the Hunkpapa Sioux Medicine Man, Sitting Bull – against the anvil of Gibbon's infantry. This plan gave Custer the independent command he craved, and Terry's orders were vague enough to allow him plenty of latitude. Convinced that 'I could whip all the Indians on the Continent with the 7th Cavalry', Custer refused Terry's offer of four troops of the 2nd Cavalry and two Gatling guns, and set off with his command up the Rosebud River towards the Little Bighorn Valley. As Custer's regiment marched off, Gibbon, perhaps mindful of Custer's reputation, called out to him: 'Now, Custer, don't be greedy, but wait for us.' Waving his hand, Custer replied, ambiguously, 'No, I will not.'

'Heaps and heaps of Injuns'

During two and a half days' hard marching 60 miles up the Rosebud and west into the Little Bighorn Valley, all the signs – large areas of grass cropped by ponies, burnt-out campfires and lodge-pole trails – indicated that there were 'heaps and heaps of Injuns' ahead. Unknown to Custer, Sitting Bull's village on the Little Bighorn had swelled, with the arrival of reservation Indians, from 400 to 1,000 lodges. There were now roughly 2,000 fighting men – one of the largest-ever concentrations of Plains Indians. Indian numbers, however, were not Custer's main concern. That Indians would disperse rather than stand and fight was well known – and everything in his experience of Indian fighting confirmed it. What Custer did not – could not – know was the mindset of the Sioux and Cheyenne gathered along the Little Bighorn. They were assembled for one last glorious summer of the old life – it was a way of life that in their hearts they knew was dying. They were determined that it would die hard.

At 8 a.m. on the morning of 26th June, Custer's scouts reported that they had seen the main Indian village. Going forward to join them on a mountain top known as the Crow's Nest, Custer could see through the summer morning's haze the southern end of Sitting Bull's encampment, stretched out along the Little Bighorn River, 15 miles (24 km) away. The bluffs to the east of the river, to Custer's right, obscured the rest of the village, leaving him unaware of its full extent. His immediate worry was the other news his scouts gave him. They had seen three parties of Indians, any one of which might already have observed Custer's advance and reported it back to the camp. As far as Custer was concerned, all the information he had received left him only one option – immediate attack.

Custer acts fast

There was not even time for a proper reconnaissance – if the Indians were to be engaged before they could pack up and flee, he must advance at once and improvise an attack off the march. At noon, Custer's command – 600 men and a mule train – arrived at the head of the stream now known as Reno's Creek, a tributary of the Little Bighorn. Here he divided his command into four 'battalions' for the attack. Companies A, G and M (140 men), under Major Marcus Reno, and Companies D, H and K (125 men), under Captain Frederick Benteen, were to act independently. Two other battalions – Companies E and F under Captain George Yates, and Companies C, I and L under Captain Myles Keogh (225 men) – Custer kept under his own hand. Company B and the pack train, under Captain Thomas McDougall, were to follow the main advance at best speed.

Benteen was an experienced Indian fighter who had distinguished himself at the Washita River where he had conceived a lasting hatred for Custer for – in his view – abandoning Captain Elliott. To ensure there were no more Indians in the Upper Little Bighorn Valley, Custer detached Benteen on reconnaissance. He instructed him to make a long left hook to the west, then climb the far ridge line, observe the valley below and ensure that Custer's rear would be safe as he attacked the main village.

Custer pushed ahead with the remainder of the force. McDougall and the mule train followed, but soon began to lose ground. After 3 miles (4.8 km), Custer and Reno came to an abandoned Indian village – the remains of Sitting Bull's earlier camp, now just one teepee containing a dead warrior, wounded in the fight at the Rosebud. From here one of Custer's white scouts, Frank Gerard, reported that he had seen a party of Indians racing their ponies down towards the main camp – if the Indians there were not aware of Custer's presence, they soon would be.

Sitting Bull's vision

If Custer thought he had caught the Indians by surprise, he could not have been more wrong. The Indian leaders, Sitting Bull, Gall of the Hunkpapa and the Oglala Sioux, Crazy Horse, had been receiving messages from outriders all morning. They knew the cavalry were approaching, were expecting an attack and were preparing for a fight – not flight. Earlier that month at a big Sun Dance (ritual tribal ceremony), Sitting Bull had had a vision in which he saw 'soldiers and some Indians on horseback coming down like grasshoppers, with their heads down and their hats falling off. They were falling right into our camp.' The Indians Custer had seen from the Crow's Nest were, in fact, one of a number of decoy parties whose aim was to draw the white soldiers into the valley – to make them 'fall' into the camp as in Sitting Bull's vision. Unknowingly, Custer was doing just what his enemy wanted.

> 'Unknowingly, Custer was doing just what his enemy wanted'

A rout and retreat to Reno Hill

Custer trotted his cavalry forward for another 3 miles (4.8 km) before sending his adjutant William Cooke forward with orders for Reno. Cooke told Reno to advance the 2 miles (3.2 km) to the Indian village and then charge. 'You will be supported by the whole outfit,' Cooke told him. Reno assumed this meant that Custer would be bringing the other two battalions up behind him, but Custer decided instead to support his attack

by a right hook, climbing the high ground to the east of the valley, further upriver, and falling on the Indian camp from above. He expected that the Indians were preparing to run for it – that the fighting men would rush forward to try and hold Reno while the women, the children and the old fled in panic down the river valley. He, with his battalions, would pitch into this mob and carry all before him – it would be a repeat of the Washita River.

'Braves came boiling out of the camp in large numbers, firing as they came'

In two columns of two, Custer led his men off to the right and up onto the high ground, halting just below the crest. Mounting the crest with his Crow scouts and his trumpeter, he looked down into the main valley. For the first time the full extent of the Indian camp was revealed – and below and to his left he could see that Reno was already engaged.

Reno had been ordered to 'charge' into the southern end of the Indian encampment, but his men, exhausted by long marches and almost no sleep, were in no condition to charge. Instead of galloping into the camp, Reno dismounted his men short of it and opened fire. 'When they rode up,' Sitting Bull later said, 'their horses were tired and they were tired. When they got off from their horses, they could not stand firmly on their feet.

ABOVE: *A contemporary photograph of bones collected from Custer's last stand. Custer's defeat and death at the hands of 'savages' sent shock waves through the United States in its centennial year.*

They swayed to and fro – so my young men have told me – like cypresses in a great wind. Some of them staggered under the weight of their guns.' Whoever organized the Indians' response – most evidence points to Gall – it was fast and furious. Braves came boiling out of the camp in large numbers, firing as they came, and driving Reno's men back into the cottonwoods that lined the river. If anyone regretted the absence of those four troops of the 2nd cavalry and the two Gatlings, it must have been Reno now – the missing cavalry might just have bolstered his attack enough to throw the Indians off-balance and start the rout Custer had wanted. Instead it was Reno's men who were being routed, and as he conferred with his Crow scout, Bloody Knife, a Sioux bullet shattered the Indian's head, spattering Reno with his brains. Unnerved and exhausted, Reno ordered a further retreat up onto the high ground of the bluffs. There, on the spot now known as Reno Hill, he and his men started digging in.

'Big village. Be quick.'

On the bluffs, Custer conferred with his officers. It was clear that this was going to be a bigger fight than he had anticipated. It was as the Crow scouts had warned – there were more Indians down there than the 7th had cartridges. His men had 100 carbine rounds per man – ammunition resupply was going to be crucial. Custer sent a sergeant back to find Captain McDougall and hurry him forward with the mule train. 'Come quick,' was the message, 'Big Indian camp.' Despite the large numbers of Sioux he had seen in the valley, Custer was still – outwardly at least – confident. 'We've caught them napping!' he shouted, waving his hat. 'We've got them!' He knew, however, that he needed every man he could muster. He decided to send his trumpeter, John Martin, back to fetch Benteen. Martin was an Italian immigrant, his real name was Giovanni Martini, and it is perhaps for this reason that Custer's adjutant, Captain Cook, added a scrawled note to Custer's verbal message. The note read: 'Benteen. Come on. Big Village. Be quick. Bring Packs. W. W. Cooke. P. Bring packs.' As he rode off, Martin glanced over his shoulder and saw Custer's command galloping off down a broad ravine, now known as the Medicine Tail Coulee, which led to the river. It was the last any white man was to see of them.

Exactly what followed is a matter of conjecture – Indian accounts were not collated until much later and are coloured by a number of factors, including the tendency of old men to forget, and a desire to tell the white men, the eventual victors, what they wanted to hear. From these, and aided by the work of battlefield archaeologists and forensic scientists, it is possible to make a reasonable guess at the fate of Custer's command. While waiting for the arrival of Benteen, Custer seems to have felt the need to take the pressure off Reno's battalion. To this end, he divided his force once more, sending Captain Yates with Companies E and F down the coulee (a deep ravine) to the river in a diversionary attack, which he may have hoped would draw away some of Gall's warriors, who were giving Renos' troops such trouble. Custer ordered Keogh's command to dismount and move onto the high ground between the coulee and another ravine, now known as the Deep Coulee, further along the ridgeline. Keogh's role would have been to form a secure base to cover Benteen's arrival.

Yates and Keogh are forced back

Arriving at the foot of the Medicine Tail Coulee, Yates immediately came under heavy fire from Indians on the opposite bank of the river. At first there may have been as few as 30 warriors there, but the Indian firing line was soon thickened by men riding down from the pony herd and others who had been fighting under Gall, now freed up by Reno's withdrawal. Before long, Gall himself arrived – very few Indians seem to have followed Reno's helter-skelter flight to the high ground – and under him the Indians crossed the river, forcing Yates back. Bodies found after the fight suggest that Yates's command withdrew up the second ravine, the Deep Coulee.

'If Custer was still alive, he was now on his own'

We have Indian accounts of his rearguard firing their carbines dismounted, their reins looped over their arms, while their horses kicked and flung their heads in the air, causing the troopers to fire high.

Gall's men also attacked Keogh's dismounted troopers. They were deployed on the high ground between the two ravines in skirmish order – with horses gathered at the rear by horse-holders – and so were better placed to meet the onslaught. For a time, Keogh's men held the Indians to their front, but those pushing Yates up the Deep Coulee were soon threatening Keogh's right rear. To avoid being cut off, and in order to reunite Custer's command, Keogh ordered his men to mount and withdraw to the north. This was easier said than done. Indian fire seems to have hit a number of horse-holders and caused the horses to stampede, taking much of Keogh's reserve ammunition with them. Keogh's men were now mostly on foot, and many were reduced to using their revolvers, as they fought a rearguard action to their link up with Yates's men on an eminence now named Calhoun Hill, after Custer's brother-in-law James, the commander of Company L. The whole of Custer's command was now spread out across what is today called Battle Ridge and under attack from several directions. One thought must have been on their minds: where was Benteen?

Trumpeter Martin had had no luck urging Benteen to hurry, though in fairness to Benteen, his men and horses must have been as exhausted as Reno's. By the time Benteen arrived on the battlefield, Reno was already established on Reno Hill. Benteen joined Reno

'there were more Indians down there than the 7th had cartridges'

there and came under his command. Shortly afterwards, McDougall and the pack train joined them. If Custer was still alive, he was now on his own, with 7 of his 12 companies out of action.

Retreat to Custer Hill

On Battle Ridge, Custer's men were under increasing pressure, their numbers being steadily whittled down as the Indian numbers increased moment by moment. Again, battlefield archaeology has helped us to recreate the elements of this fight: the Indians took advantage of the rough ground, working their way forward slowly on foot, keeping up a heavy fire with rifles and bows. As individual troopers were disabled by wounds, braves would close in to deliver the coup de grâce with club or tomahawk. Many of the skeletons examined show signs of massive blunt trauma to the head – others seem to have been dispatched with a variety of pistols. At this stage, though, Custer's battle, if it could no longer be won, was far from lost. If he could get his command onto the high ground, there was a good chance he could hold out there until either Benteen or Gibbon, with the main column, could come to his aid. With Gall and his warriors pressing him, Custer led his command up towards the height that is now known as Custer Hill.

Crazy Horse arrives late

Unknown to Custer, the crucial decision that would decide the outcome of the battle had already been taken – down in the valley. According to most accounts, Crazy Horse had arrived late at the Reno fight. One warrior, Short Bull, later claimed that he had taunted Crazy Horse with this, and that Crazy Horse, making a joke of it, had replied: 'Sorry to miss this fight. But there's a good fight coming over the hill. That's where the big fight is going to be. We'll not miss that one.' It seems that Crazy Horse already had a plan – there is a hint of this perhaps in Sitting Bull's 'vision' in which he saw the white soldiers 'falling' into the Indian camp. Over many years of fighting the white man, Crazy Horse had learned to fight the white man's way. Custer had expected that his right-flanking manoeuvre would catch the Indians by surprise while they were fighting Reno to their front. In fact the opposite seems to have happened. It was Reno's attack that took them by surprise – Custer's attack, down from the bluffs, they were ready for. As Custer's flanking move was being rebuffed and his men were being driven back up onto the high ground by Gall's men, Crazy Horse had already embarked on a flanking move of his own.

While Custer's flanking move was held by Gall's men, Crazy Horse intended to race up the Little Bighorn Valley, cross the river, ascend the bluffs himself and fall on Custer's right flank. Custer would thus find himself trapped between Gall to his front and Crazy Horse to his right and rear. It was a plan that required – in a commander of an irregular force – phenomenal powers of leadership.

> 'It is a good day to fight! It is a good day to die!'
> CRAZY HORSE

Splitting forces

Fighting between European-style armies and native warriors was a feature of the colonial campaigns of the 19th century. In his classic *Small Wars* (1896), the British officer Colonel C. E. Callwell discusses the tactic of splitting a regular force in the face of irregular warriors. Whilst commenting that 'irregular warriors above all things fear a situation where their escape ... is jeopardized,' he goes on to point out the dangers involved. Different elements of a split force may fail to co-operate effectively, he says, due to the problems caused by time and distance. At the same time, an enemy commander in a central position may seize his opportunity to defeat the separate detachments in detail. One of the examples he cites is the Battle of Little Bighorn.

That Crazy Horse was at this point able to lead nearly a thousand men, fired-up Oglala, Hunkpapa and Cheyenne warriors, away from the direction of the fighting is a tribute to the power of his name. Shouting 'Ho-ka Hey! It is a good day to fight! It is a good day to die! Strong hearts, brave hearts to the front! Weak hearts and cowards to the rear', he galloped his pony through the Indian camp and led his followers up the valley.

Custer's luck finally runs out

As Custer was leading his men towards the imagined safety of Custer Hill, Crazy Horse was approaching the same height from the opposite direction. Custer's command was strung out, with Custer and his command group in the lead and Calhoun's company in the rear, hard pressed by Gall's pursuing warriors. To Custer, the summit of the hill offered safety – a chance to rally and form an all-round defensive position as Reno and Benteen were doing 4 miles (6.4 km) to the south. However, as his leading elements approached the summit, they suddenly saw Crazy Horse and his thousand warriors sweeping over it and down towards them. Within seconds, the whole slope of the hill became a killing ground, with Custer's men fighting in small groups and the Indians coming and going in all directions – 'like swallows' – as one Oglala recalled. The Cheyenne leader, Two Moons, described the fighting thus: 'the shooting was quick, quick, pop-pop-pop very fast. Some of the soldiers were down on their knees, some standing...

'Custer and 225 men lay slaughtered – stripped and butchered like buffalo'

ABOVE: *An ink drawing on paper of Reno's retreat by Amos Bad Heart Buffalo. The warriors on the right are shown with captured cavalry horses.*

We circled round them – swirling like water round a stone. We shoot, we ride fast, we shoot again. Soldiers drop and horses fall on them.' A Crow scout who heard the shooting said it was so fast it sounded like the tearing of the threads when a blanket is ripped in half. This rapid fire was coming from the Indians – as many as one in five were armed with 1866 Winchester repeaters, which could fire 13 rounds without being reloaded. The troopers' Springfield carbine was a single-shot weapon.

In less than half an hour it was over. Custer and 225 men lay slaughtered – stripped and butchered like buffalo. Custer's own family suffered particularly heavily – killed with him were his brothers Tom and Boston, his nephew 'Autie' Reed, as well as his brother-in-law 'Jimmi' Calhoun. Of Custer's own death – which has been immortalized in numerous paintings and movie reconstructions – there are numerous accounts. Perhaps the most interesting is that of Sitting Bull. Although he was not on the spot – he was in his teepee 'making big medicine' – he talked with many of his own Hunkpapa Sioux minutes after the battle. Interviewed by the *New York Herald* in 1877, he gave the following account:

Sitting Bull: *... the Long Hair stood like a sheaf of corn with all the ears fallen around him.*
Reporter: *Not wounded?*
Sitting Bull: *No.*
Reporter: *How many stood with him?*
Sitting Bull: *A few.*
Reporter: *When did he fall?*
Sitting Bull: *He killed a man when he fell. He laughed.*
Reporter: *You mean he cried out?*
Sitting Bull: *No, he laughed. He had fired his last shot.*

It is not uncommon to read of men laughing hysterically in conditions of extreme stress. It may be that this was one such case. Custer, though, was a man who revelled in the excitement of battle or the hunt – in that respect he had more in common with his enemy than with his own people. Maybe this was his normal demeanour in the thick of a fight, or maybe he was simply laughing – a recognition, perhaps, of the fact that after a lifetime of living on the edge, Custer's luck had finally run out.

Last stand of the Plains Indians

That night, Reno's command endured a siege by the victorious braves until General Terry's column arrived, late the next day. Some have blamed the two officers for failing to support Custer, though neither suffered for it officially. The massacre of Custer's command, which hit the headlines in the week of the country's centennial celebrations, caused shockwaves across the nation, but ultimately merely roused it to greater efforts. Within a very few years the Plains Indian tribes and their way of life had all but disappeared. Little Bighorn was not just Custer's last stand.

'OH, BRITISH TROOPS ARE ALL RIGHT,
WE DO NOT LAAGER'
LORD CHELMSFORD

ISANDHLWANA
1879

Empires expand for a number of reasons – one of them being paranoia. In December 1878, perceiving in the Zulu Kingdom a threat to his proposed confederation of South Africa, the British governor of the Cape Colony, Sir Bartle Frere, sent an ultimatum to the Zulu king, Cetshwayo, calling on him to disband his army. The Zulu *impis*, or regiments, composed of every able-bodied man, had terrorized southern Africa earlier in the century under the great Shaka, the legendary king credited with uniting the Zulu kingdom.

The *impis* were armed with a large shield of hide and a short stabbing spear, or assegai, known as the *iklwa* from the noise it made when pulled out from a man's stomach. The very existence of such an army bordering British territory was deemed unacceptable. Frere's ultimatum, as expected, was refused, and the British prepared to invade Zululand.

The British commander, Lord Chelmsford, planned to invade Zululand with five columns. The main column, which he would accompany, consisted of two battalions of Her Majesty's 24th Foot (2nd Warwickshire) and seven field guns, as well as assorted mounted infantry, mounted volunteers, Natal Mounted Police, the Natal Native Horse (NNH) and the Natal Native Contingent (NNC), the two last being African irregulars. The African horse were of varying quality – some were very good, but the NNC were ill-armed and poorly trained. The Natal Volunteers and Natal Mounted Police were colonial troops with valuable experience of fighting Zulus, but the British imperial battalions, with their disciplined firepower, were the mainstay of the column, producing massed volleys from breech-loading Martini-Henry rifles. Chelmsford was certain they would prove irresistible.

The sphinx-shaped hill

Chelmsford's column crossed the Buffalo River into Zulu territory on 11th January, intending to march on the Royal Kraal (village) at Ulundi with the aim of finding and engaging the main Zulu *impi*. On 20th January he set up camp at Isandhlwana, a prominent sphinx-shaped hill running roughly north–south, to the north of the main track to Ulundi running east–west from Rorke's Drift. From the hill a spur runs 1,500 yards (1,372 m) north to the Nqutu Plateau, which dominates the northern landscape. East of Isandhlwana Hill is a featureless plain broken only by boulders and by two deep stream beds, or 'dongas' – the Narrow Donga and the Big Donga. Beyond the dongas is another high hill known as Conical Kop. The plain is best imagined as a rough square with the Nqutu escarpment forming its northern side and the track to Ulundi forming its southern. At its western side is Isandhlwana Hill and the spur running up to the Nqutu Plateau, and at its eastern side open ground with the Conical Kop at its centre.

The British camp was formed on a north–south line on the eastern side of the hill. The regimental transport was between each unit and the hill, while the heavier wagons

OPPOSITE: *The 24th Foot and a force of Natal Volunteers under Colonel Durnford are overwhelmed and massacred by the Zulu forces at Isandhlwana. The sphinx-shaped Isandhlwana Hill is in the background.*

were placed behind the mounted camp. The column commander, Colonel Richard Glyn, wanted to fortify the camp by drawing the wagons into a 'laager' (wagons used to form a defensive perimeter, protecting the camp within), but Lord Chelmsford believed that manoeuvring the heavy wagons would take too long. Even the rudimentary precautions of creating a thick thorn fence and scattering broken bottles on the ground were neglected. A number of experienced officers of the 24th expressed anxiety about this and some of the men were said to be uneasy about the hill's resemblance to the regiment's sphinx cap badge, seeing this as an ill omen.

Chelmsford's opinion on the fortifying of camps had been noted the previous year by Melton Prior of the *Illustrated London News*. Prior had been present at a conference where various Boers and leaders of mounted volunteers, men with much experience of fighting Zulus, had assured Chelmsford that a force operating in Zulu territory would need to laager at every halt. 'Oh, British troops are all right,' Chelmsford had replied, 'we do not laager – we have a different formation.' On his return to England, Prior had commented to his newspaper's owner, William Ingram: 'You take my word for it, if we do have a war with the Zulus, the first news we shall get will be that of a disaster.'

> ' if we do have a war with the Zulus, the first news we shall get will be that of a disaster '
> MELTON PRIOR

The elusive *impi*

Chelmsford was placing his trust, with some reason, in the firepower of his imperial battalions, but his next decision was to halve the firepower of the Isandhlwana camp. On 21st January, one of his patrols – a mixed force of Natal Mounted Police, Volunteers and NNC under Major Charles Dartnell – encountered between 1,500 and 2,000 Zulus 10 miles (16 km) east of the camp in the direction of Ulundi. On learning this, Chelmsford concluded that the Zulus must have been part of the main *impi*. Accordingly, at first light on 22nd January, Chelmsford marched out to link up with Dartnell with the intention of engaging the Zulus. He took with him the 2nd Battalion/24th Foot minus one company, 84 mounted infantry, and four guns. The camp at Isandhlwana was left under the command of Lieutenant-Colonel Henry Pulleine of the 1st/24th. To guard the camp, Pulleine had five companies of his own battalion, one company of the 2nd Battalion/24th, 115 mounted men (a combination of Natal Mounted Police, mounted infantry and Natal Volunteers) and four companies of the NNC – making a total of 822 Europeans and 431 Africans. To bolster this force, Chelmsford sent a message to Colonel Durnford, commanding Number 2 Column to 'march to this camp at once with all the force you have with you'. Pulleine was told to stay strictly on the defensive, keep his cavalry vedettes (outposts) well out and his infantry well in. If attacked, he was to fight close in to the camp, relying on the volley fire of his 597 regulars.

By 6.30 a.m., Chelmsford had linked up with Dartnell. In the absence of further evidence of the elusive main *impi*, the combined British force – some 2,500 men and four guns – pushed on eastwards in the direction of the Mangeni River. By 9.30, having encountered nothing but a few small parties of Zulus, Chelmsford halted the column for breakfast. Shortly afterwards a messenger galloped up the track from Isandhlwana with a note from Pulleine timed at 8.05 a.m. 'Report just come in that the Zulus are advancing in force from left front of the camp.' Confident that Pulleine's force was strong enough to deal with any attack, Chelmsford saw no cause for alarm. A naval officer equipped with a telescope, sent to a nearby height to observe the camp 12 miles (19 km) away, reported that he thought the oxen had moved but that all appeared normal. Chelmsford marched on.

The *impi* are found

At Isandhlwana, as Pulleine's men were breakfasting, a messenger rode down from the vedettes on the spur to report a large force of Zulus on the Nqutu Plateau. Pulleine quickly wrote out the message that Chelmsford received at his breakfast an hour later, and ordered his force to fall in, forming his infantry up in their defensive positions. A second message from the plateau informed him that the Zulus had dispersed to the north and northeast. A little later, heavy firing was heard in the general direction of Ulundi. This seemed to suggest that Chelmsford had found and was engaging the main Zulu *impi*. Nothing more occurred until 10.30 a.m., when Durnford rode into the camp with his force – five troops of NNH, followed at a distance by Major Russell's Rocket Battery and two companies of NNC. Durnford's arrival confused the issue as to who was in command. Chelmsford had left Pulleine in command of the camp, but Durnford was the older man, three years senior, and an experienced African campaigner. Durnford quickly took command, with Pulleine's agreement.

While the two men were at lunch, they learned that a Zulu force of 500 had been sighted to the northeast, moving eastwards. Durnford decided to follow this force and prevent it from moving in Chelmsford's direction. He would take the two remaining troops of his African horse, plus the Rocket Battery and a company of NNC. He also decided to send mounted patrols onto the plateau to clear it of Zulus. Durnford asked for the support of two regular companies. At first Pulleine reluctantly agreed, but Pulleine's adjutant, one of the officers who had expressed concern about the camp's lack of fortification, objected so strenuously that Durnford finally agreed to do without them. However, when he left the camp at 11.30, he stressed to Pulleine that if he got into difficulty he would expect to be supported. Durnford's command rode east, past the Conical Kop and then swung north, skirting the edge of the Nqutu Plateau. At this point he detached some parties of NNH and NNC (under Lieutenants Charles Raw and J.A.Roberts) up onto the plateau. Shortly afterwards, Raw's patrol saw a group of Zulu boys driving cattle. Giving chase they pulled up sharply at the edge of a deep ravine and gazed in horror and amazement at what they saw below them: 20,000 Zulu warriors sitting silently in massed ranks. Raw had stumbled upon the main *impi*, 11 miles (17.6 km) to the east of Isandhlwana where Lord Chelmsford was now searching for them, but 5 miles (8 km)

'the Zulus rose as one man and began swarming up out of the ravine'

to the north of it. As they watched, the Zulus rose as one man and began swarming up out of the ravine, ready to descend like a tidal wave onto Pulleine's camp.

The water buffalo attacks

The *impi*, under its *induna* (commander) Tshingwayo, had left Ulundi and marched westwards, camping on the night of 20th January at Isipezi Hill. It had then marched up onto the Nqutu Plateau and gone to ground in the Ngwebeni Ravine, intending to attack the camp at Isandhlwana at dawn on the 23rd. Discovered now by Raw's patrol, the whole *impi* came boiling up out of the ravine, deploying as they came. The Zulus traditionally attacked in a formation based on the water buffalo – reputed by hunters of big game to be the most dangerous animal in Africa. Two central divisions – forming the chest and, behind it, the loins of the buffalo – would engage the enemy's main body while two 'horns' would encircle it left and right, and then close in for the kill. The Zulus had not intended to attack that day, but now they swept up out of the ravine, spreading out into a huge, mile-wide arc. In the centre were the umCijo, umHlanga and uThulwane regiments. The right horn was formed by the Nokenke, Nodwengu, umKhulutshane, uDududu and Isanqu regiments, and the left by the uVe, inGobamakosi and umBonambi. As Raw's Sikali Horse fell back before the advancing Zulu 'chest', they joined Robert's troop and together the patrols fell back towards the camp, stopping from time to time to fire their carbines from horseback.

Pulleine sounds the 'alarm'

Neither Durnford, still riding towards the plateau, nor Pulleine, in camp, were yet aware of the impending attack. However, they could hear the fire of Raw's troops, joined now by that of Lieutenant Cavaye's company of the 24th, which Pulleine had earlier sent up onto the spur. Cavaye's men, in skirmish order, were now firing into the Zulu right horn as it passed across their front. At almost the same time, Durnford saw the Zulu *left* horn appearing on the escarpment ahead of him. Immediately he halted his men, fired off a volley and began to retire. He also sent a warning message to Russell's Rocket Battery and its NNC escort. Fired from the ground out of iron 'troughs', rockets had been used by the British army since Wellington's time. Although erratic and inaccurate, they were believed to have an unsettling effect on irregular forces. Russell barely had time to deploy his weapons, close to the Conical Kop, and loose off a salvo before the Zulus were on him. The rockets exploded without apparent effect, the NNC escort fled, Russell and his men were slaughtered, and the Zulu tide rolled on.

> 'his men were slaughtered and the Zulu tide rolled on'

By now, Pulleine had ordered that the 'alarm' be sounded and sent a messenger to inform Chelmsford. He then sent a second company, commanded by William E. Mostyn, to thicken up Cavaye's firing line on the spur. Lieutenant Vause's troop of African horse and a company of NNC went forward to join Durnford.

In the camp, before Pulleine's force – four companies of the 24th, two guns, two companies of NNC and a handful of mounted volunteers – could 'stand-to' (get ready in their positions), Zulus were clearly seen advancing about two miles (3.2 km) away. Pulleine's original orders were to defend the camp in a tight formation close to the hill, but he was also committed to supporting Durnford, now heavily engaged with the oncoming Zulu horde and falling back across the plain. Pulleine decided to deploy his infantry and guns forward, placing two companies of the 24th, commanded by Lieutenant Porteus and Captain Wardell, on either side of the two guns, between the Narrow and the Big Donga, with a company of NNC to their right. On the extreme right he placed Lieutenant Pope's

ABOVE: *The Zulu king Cetshwayo, c. 1870. Despite victory at Isandhlwana, he refused to celebrate, saying 'an assegai has been thrust in the belly of the nation'.*

company, also of the 24th. Pulleine's left was formed by Captain Reginald Younghusband's company. This was soon joined by Mostyn's and Cavaye's companies, which came running down from the spur to form part of the new firing line.

The Zulu advance is stalled

As the Zulus descended from the plateau, the guns opened fire with shrapnel. As the attacking Zulus closed to within 600 yards (550 m), the volleys fired by the imperial companies began to take effect, driving the Zulus back up the spur and halting the advance of their centre. The Zulu left horn, however, swept on in pursuit of Durnford's men, now riding hard back to the Big Donga. Reaching it, and joined there by Captain Robert Bradstreet's mounted rifles, Durnford dismounted his men and commenced firing. Supported by the fire of one of the two guns, Durnford's troops halted the Zulu left horn just south of the Conical Kop. By 1 p.m., Pulleine's line stretched 1.5 miles (2.4 km) from the north end of Isandhlwana Hill round in an arc down to Durnford's men in the Big Donga. The artillery fire and volleys of the British battalions were taking their toll: the Zulu advance had stalled on all fronts and their casualties were mounting. The whole Zulu line now lay roughly 400 yards (640 km) from Pulleine's, their dead and wounded piling up, unable to advance, unwilling to retreat.

Meanwhile, on the right, Durnford's men were running low on ammunition. He sent two officers back to resupply, but they were unable to find their own wagons. The men went instead to the quartermaster of the 1st/24th who refused to issue them with ammunition that was actually earmarked for his own battalion. According to a legend that persists to this day, the British infantry could not open their ammunition boxes, which were screwed down tight and banded with metal. It seems unlikely, though, that an experienced battalion such as the 1st/24th would have been guilty of such an elementary error.

By the time Durnford's officers returned – empty-handed – to the Big Donga, the entire Zulu line had risen up and launched a fresh attack. Once more it was halted on the Zulu right and centre but, noticing the slackening fire from the Big Donga, warriors of the left horn began to work round Durnford's right. Realizing he was in grave danger of being outflanked and running out of

Savage warfare

Colonial campaigns in the 19th century were characterized by attempts on the part of Europeans to bring on an early, decisive battle, rather than engage in a protracted guerilla war during which their soldiers might suffer from disease and the adverse effects of climate. Objectives would be selected – such as the Royal Kraal at Ulundi – which for emotional, spiritual or political reasons the enemy would have to defend. While at Isandhlwana, Pulleine misjudged the Zulus' tactics of encirclement and Chelmsford misjudged their strategy, splitting his force in search of an enemy that was, in fact, actively seeking him out.

ammunition, Durnford ordered his men to mount up and ride back towards the camp to form a new line in front of the tents.

'Usutu!'

Now only Pope's company of the 24th lay between the Zulu left horn and the camp. Pope had moved his company down to support Durnford, but in so doing had opened up a 700-yard (640-m) gap between his company and the next – Wardell's. Seeing that his entire line was in danger of being rolled up from the right, Pulleine ordered the 'retire' to be sounded and the whole of the 24th began to fall back.

> 'the Zulu centre swarmed forward shouting their war cry 'Usutu!'

The Zulus in the centre had been wilting under the 24th's volleys, so much so that a senior *induna*, Mkhosana, had run down from the plateau to urge them, in the name of Cetshwayo, to advance. As he did so, Mkhosana was shot through the forehead. Now, seeing their red-coated opponents falling back, the Zulu centre swarmed forward shouting their war cry 'Usutu!' The companies of the 24th retired towards the camp in rallying squares (hastily formed groups of men fighting back to back). The guns fired case shot (metallic cylinders packed with shot) into the advancing Zulu ranks until the very last minute before limbering up and galloping off. Although a few men were overrun in the initial rush, for the most part the companies reached the camp in good order. However, the Zulus were now intermingled with the British imperial troops and it was impossible to form a new firing line. The Zulus of the left horn were already among the tents, and Pulleine's regulars now stood where they could, fighting back-to-back.

Even before the Zulus reached the tents, men from the rear echelons – camp followers and some NNC – had started fleeing the camp, running down over the *nek* (mountain pass) behind Isandhlwana, towards Buffalo River. Soon, as the men of the 24th fought on desperately, it was every man for himself. Native Horse, NNC, Mounted Volunteers – anyone who had a horse – took the same route, many reaching the far side of the *nek* only to find their escape cut off by warriors of the Zulu right horn. Running the gauntlet between these and the Zulus of the left horn, 85 Europeans managed to cross the river to safety. Lieutenants Melvill and Coghill made a gallant attempt to save the Queen's colour (regimental flag) of the 1st/24th and remove it from the battlefield, but were killed at the Buffalo River.

Surrounded by assegais

For the remainder of the 24th, surrounded by Zulus and bound by regimental esprit, escape was not an option. Back-to-back they fought and died. A warrior of the umCijo later described the fighting: 'One party of soldiers came out from among the tents, and formed up a little above the ammunition wagons. They held their ground there until their ammunition failed them, when they were nearly all assegaied. Those who were not killed at this place formed again in a solid square in the neck of Isandhlwana. They were

'Escape was not an option. Back-to-back they fought and died.'

completely surrounded on all sides, and stood back to back, and surrounding some men who were in the centre. Their ammunition was now done, except they had some revolvers which they fired at us at close quarters. We were quite unable to break their square until we had killed a great many of them, by throwing our assegais at them at short distances. We eventually overcame them in this way.' Another Zulu of the Nokenke witnessed the last moments of Younghusband's company.'They fought well, a lot of them got up on the steep slope under the cliff behind the camp, and the Zulus could not get at them at all; they were shot or bayoneted as soon as they came up.

At last the soldiers gave a shout and charged down upon us. There was an *induna* in front of them with a long flashing sword, which he whirled round his head as he ran... Our people got above them and quite surrounded them; these and a group of white men on the *nek* were the last to fall.'

Not enough tears...

Of the 1,700 men Chelmsford had left to defend the camp, 52 officers, including Pulleine and Durnford, and 806 other ranks were killed, along with some 500 Africans. Of the six companies of the 24th, just two bandsmen and one private soldier survived. Alerted at 2.30 p.m. that the camp was in trouble, Chelmsford force-marched his column back, arriving in darkness, by which time the Zulus had departed. The horrors revealed by the dawn light are described in letters written home by Chelmsford's men:'It was a pity to see about 800 white men lying on the field cut up to pieces and stripped naked. Even the little boys that we had in the band, they were hung up on hooks and opened like sheep.'; 'What a state, 1,000 white men and 500 black men killed! Wagons broke! Bullocks killed! Tents all gone! It was the most horrid sight ever seen by a soldier'; 'Tell Harry not to enlist, for God's sake.'

'What a state, 1,000 white men and 500 black men killed! Wagons broke! Bullocks killed! Tents all gone! It was the most horrid sight ever.'

Zulu casualties are difficult to assess – certainly more than 1,000 warriors died, and many more suffered terrible wounds from which they would not recover.

It was noted that the main *impi* never attacked again with the determination it showed at Isandhlwana. Lord Chelmsford eventually engaged it at Ulundi on 4th July, gaining a victory that only partially restored his reputation. In the meantime, the Zulus would deliver more shocks to the British public, not least by killing the French Prince Imperial Louis Napoleon, son of the late emperor Napoleon III, who was attached to the British army. Cetshwayo, the Zulu king, was no fool, however – in the immediate aftermath of Isandhlwana he alone refused to celebrate. Appalled at the casualties that even a victory had cost, he perhaps foresaw the inevitable end of the old Zulu order. As he told his triumphant *indunas*,'An assegai has been thrust in the belly of the nation. There are not enough tears to mourn for the dead!'

'YOU CAN TAKE YOUR CLOTHES OFF NOW,
THE GERMANS ARE RETREATING'
GENERAL PAVEL RENNENKAMPF

TANNENBERG
1914

At the outset of World War I, the Russian general staff planned to contain the Germans in the north with one army while attacking the Austrians in the south with four. Under the terms of her alliance with France, Russia was committed to putting 800,000 men in the field within 15 days of mobilization. Russia failed to do so, but regardless, still decided to attack in the north to aid the French.

Plans for an offensive

The part of Poland then under Russian control formed a westward 'bulge' into Central Europe, surrounded on three sides by hostile territory: Austrian Galicia to the south and Germany to the west and north. The northern arm of Germany – bounded by the Baltic sea to the north, the River Vistula in the west and Russian territory to the east and south – was East Prussia. It was here that the Russians decided to launch their offensive.

The Russian conquest of East Prussia would eliminate any northern threat to their territory, including Warsaw. It would also strike a significant blow to enemy morale and straighten the frontier (assuming Russian armies to the south in Galicia were also successful) before a further advance on Berlin. Two armies were earmarked for the offensive – the 1st under General Pavel Rennenkampf and the 2nd under General Aleksandr Samsonov. Overall command would be exercised by General Yakov Jilinsky.

With Russian borders to the east and south, East Prussia was vulnerable from both directions, so the Russian plan was to attack on both these fronts. Rennenkampf would cross the River Niemen attacking westwards, driving the outnumbered Germans before him; meanwhile, to the south, Samsonov would execute a massive 'left hook', moving west and then sweeping north to cut the Germans off before they could retreat across the Vistula.

Illusory strength

On paper Russian strength seemed overwhelming, while in East Prussia there was just one German army to oppose them – the 8th Army, commanded by General Max von Prittwitz. The Russians would field nine corps and eight cavalry divisions against four German corps and only one cavalry division. But the Russian superiority was illusory. The German army was well-equipped, with artillery superior in both number (72 field guns per division against 48) and quality. In heavy artillery, the Germans outnumbered the invaders ten to one. In the German command were a number of officers of great ability, among them the corps commanders Otto von Below and Hermann von Francois, and Prittwitz's deputy chief of staff Colonel Max Hoffman.

Although much improved since its defeat at the hands of the Japanese in 1904–5, the Russian army still had its limitations. The Russian soldier was less

> 'Whole Russian regiments would blaze away at their own reconnaissance aircraft'

PREVIOUS PAGE: *German infantry advance during the Battle of Tannenberg. Outnumbered by the Russians in everything but – crucially – artillery, many of the German troops were fighting for hearth and home in East Prussia.*

sophisticated and technically competent than his German opponent. Russia's peasant soldiers, fifty per cent of whom were illiterate, differed little from their forefathers who had faced Napoleon at Borodino. Whole Russian regiments would blaze away at their own reconnaissance aircraft, convinced that such a wondrous machine must have been invented by a German. At higher levels, too, there were problems. Supply was chaotic; radio messages were sent in 'clear' or in simple codes that were easily broken by the Germans; there was a shortage of telephone cable; and the British liaison officer, General Alfred Knox, noted that the colonel in charge of the very small pool of staff cars could not read a map.

More seriously, the Russian plan required a great deal of co-operation between the two commanders, Rennenkampf and Samsonov, who detested each other. During the Japanese war they had come to blows on a station platform at Mukden, Korea. Worst of all, the advancing Russian armies would be split by the Masurian Lakes in the eastern part of East Prussia, a vast area of thick forests and lakes running north–south for some 500 miles (800 km).

Early Russian success at Gumbinnen

On the morning of 17th August, Rennekampf's army, the northern arm of the Russian pincer, encountered Francois' corps at Stalluponen, just inside the East Prussian frontier. Prittwitz ordered Francois to fall back to Gumbinnen, but Francois refused. He hit the Russians hard with a swift counter-attack and then fell back, taking 3,000 prisoners with him. At Gumbinnen three days later, Rennenkampf's army encountered Francois once more. Again Francois attacked, routing one Russian division and taking another 5,000 prisoners. At noon he was joined by two more corps, commanded by August von Mackensen and Otto von Below – but things began to go wrong for the Germans. The Russians halted Mackensen's attack and his corps faltered, one division fleeing in some disorder. Below's arrival came too late to restore the situation and the Russians, despite having lost 19,000 men, emerged the victors.

The abandonment of East Prussia in a retreat to the Vistula had always been the doomsday scenario for the German general staff. Disheartened by Gumbinnen and aware, now, of Samsonov's encircling manoeuvre to the south, Prittwitz telephoned the German commander-in-chief Helmuth von Moltke 'the Younger', nephew of the Helmuth von Moltke who had destroyed the French army at Sedan, to tell him that this was now his intention. Moltke had never had a high opinion of Prittwitz, an officer nicknamed 'Der Dicke' (Fatty), and whose promotion was generally ascribed to an ability to amuse the kaiser at the dinner table. If this judgement is a little harsh, it was nevertheless clear that Prittwitz had to go. To replace him, Moltke chose Prittwitz's brother-in-law General Paul von Hindenburg, a statesman and a retired officer of legendary imperturbability. Moltke appointed Erich Ludendorff, who had recently distinguished himself by capturing the fortress city of Liège, in Belgium, as Hindenburg's chief of staff.

The threat of the Cossack felt boot

On the train travelling east, the two men worked on a new plan, based partly on a pre-war scheme devised by the German strategist Alfred von Schlieffen and partly on their knowledge of the two Russian commanders. Since Rennenkampf was known to be the more cautious of the two generals, they thought it would be possible to hold him with a light screen of troops and to move the bulk of their forces, by road and rail, south of the Masurian Lakes to deal with Samosonov. It would be risky, of course – if Rennenkampf attacked, he could burst through the line and fall on their rear, but they calculated that he would not. Even as the two men were contemplating this strategy, Colonel Hoffman at 8th Army Headquarters had come to the same conclusion and decided to act on his own initiative, issuing detailed

> ' The cry "the Cossacks are coming!" induced panic among the German troops '

ABOVE: *Cossacks – the archetypal Slavic warriors. The very thought of them marauding among Junker estates created pressure on the German High Command to reinforce the Eastern Front – at the expense of the West.*

orders to Francois, Below and Mackensen, to dash with their corps to the south.

The Russian victory at Gumbinnen had one other effect that was, if anything, more far-reaching. East Prussia was the ancestral heartland of the Prussian aristocracy and their traditional outpost against the Slavic hordes. Throughout the campaign the cry 'the Cossacks are coming!' induced panic among the German troops and evoked ancient visceral terrors among the East Prussian population, now streaming westwards as refugees. Many among the German kaiser's entourage had estates in East Prussia, and the thought of these being trampled by the felt boot of the Slav led to a rising clamour in the highest circles 'for something to be done.' Yielding to this pressure, Moltke decided to reinforce the Eastern Front with two army corps and a cavalry division. This reduction of the Germany army from 34 divisions to 25 at a critical point on the Western Front seriously compromised the supposedly war-winning Schlieffen plan – Schlieffen's dying words had been 'Keep the right strong!' – and arguably retrieved the Allied situation there. By failing to win the war by the end of 1914, the Germans had, effectively, already lost it. Russia proved herself a good ally.

By the time Hindenburg and Ludendorff had reached 8th Army Headquarters, and endorsed all of Hoffman's dispositions, Francois' corps had already reached Tannenberg in the south and were preparing to taking up position on the right flank of General Friedrich von Scholtz's corps, which was fighting a rearguard action against Samsonov. Turning their backs on Rennenkampf and marching south from Gumbinnen, Below's and Mackensen's corps were to place themselves on Scholtz's left, prior to a combined attack against Samsonov. Did he but know it, all that was left of the German forces now facing Rennenkampf was a single cavalry division strung out over twenty miles (32 km). However, now enjoying the delights of the Dessauer Hof Hotel in Insterburg, a refreshing change from what Russian frontier towns had to offer, Rennenkampf was in no hurry. To a staff officer settling down to sleep fully dressed, he famously announced: 'You can take your clothes off now, the Germans are retreating.'

The Russians head for the trap

For a trap to work really well it helps if the victim willingly puts his head in the snare. At Russian headquarters, Marshal Jilinsky concluded that the Germans were indeed evacuating East Prussia and were retreating westwards. His only worry was that Samsonov would fail to trap the Germans before they reached the Vistula, so Jilinsky urged him to push his 20,000 men forward at greater speed. Samsonov drove his weary men on through the sandy terrain, hoping to capture even more Germans when he eventually swung north after an extended westward march. In fact, the Germans were not retreating westwards to the north of him, but southwestwards and *towards* him, and were about to descend upon his army with all the force they could muster.

Still convinced that he was pursuing just one single beaten body of men, XX Corps under Scholtz, Samsonov went on the attack. Although exhausted, disorganized and lacking supplies, the Russians fought with their customary gallantry and their numbers in the central sector told, driving Scholtz northwestwards. Scholtz's corps, though, was made up of local men, recruited in the district of Allenstein, who were fighting for hearth and home. Although hard pressed they did not break, continuing a fighting withdrawal ahead of Samsonov.

Ludendorff was still worried about the threat posed by Rennenkampf to his rear. 'Rennenkampf's formidable host hung like a threatening thunder-cloud in the north-east,' he wrote in his memoirs. 'He need only have closed with us and we should have been beaten.' With this in mind, on August 25th he ordered Francois to attack at once. Only a portion of Francois' corps and none of his heavy artillery had yet detrained and Francois, typically, refused. Hindenburg and Ludendorff visited him in person, with Ludendorff raging hysterically at his subordinate. Only when Colonel Hoffman produced an intercepted message, picked up by the German radio station at Königsberg, showing that Rennenkampf was moving at a leisurely pace and could not possibly threaten the German rear for at least two days, did Ludendorff relent, but he never forgave Francois. That same day Mackensen and Below arrived, and were soon in a position to attack Samsonov's right.

A village with history

In the rear of the German centre was the small village of Tannenberg where, 500 years earlier, the Teutonic Knights had suffered defeat at the hands of a Polish and Lithuanian army. A small monument marked the spot. Hindenburg, whose stolid demeanour had already done much to restore confidence in a jumpy 8th Army Headquarters, turned to his new staff and announced: 'We will give the name a new significance; the battle shall be called the Battle of Tannenberg.' That, at least, is one version – both Hoffman and Ludendorff would later claim to have chosen the name.

> ' We will give the name a new significance; the battle shall be called the Battle of Tannenberg '
> PAUL VON HINDENBURG

OPPOSITE: *The architects of victory – from left to right in the foreground, General Paul von Hindenburg, Colonel Max Hoffman, General Erich Ludendorff. All three would later claim to have named the battle.*

Samsonov realizes his predicament

Samsonov resumed his advance on 26th August. He was soon informed by one division of VI Corps, which formed his right flank, that they had seen German troops 6 miles (9.6 km) to their north. Assuming that these troops were fleeing from Rennenkampf, who must therefore be close at hand, the divisional commander turned to attack them, only to find his troops embroiled with Mackensen's corps. The other division on the right was force-marched back to assist their comrades, but ran into Below's corps. By the following morning the whole of VI Corps was falling back in disorder, leaving behind them thousands of dead and wounded. Samsonov's right flank was turned.

In Samsonov's centre, his two best corps commanders, Martos and Kliouev, continued to attack. Kliouev briefly took the town of Allenstein, but then moved to support the hard-pressed Martos. He thought that Allenstein would be taken over by VI Corps, but that corps was by was streaming to the rear in confusion. By evening it began to dawn on Samsonov that it was he who was in trouble. When he indicated to Army Group Headquarters a desire to slow his advance, he was accused by Jilinsky of cowardice and ordered to speed up his 'pursuit'. Instead of ordering an immediate withdrawal, which might have saved the bulk of his army, Samsonov decided to attack again in his centre on the following day. He was sure that

'By evening it began to dawn on Samsonov that it was he who was in trouble'

if he could hold the Germans just a little longer, Rennenkampf would arrive from the north to deliver a decisive blow. He was now placing his trust in Rennenkampf, along with his two centre corps and his left-flanking corps – I Corps. The latter was facing Francois' Corps, now fully detrained and ready to attack. Samsonov stressed to I Corps commander Artamanov the importance of holding Francois, telling him that the whole issue of the battle depended on I Corps holding firm.

The Russian steamroller

At the outset of the Great War, much faith was placed by the Allies in the 'Russian steamroller', which, it was hoped, would roll slowly and steadily to the very gates of Berlin. At the height of the crisis on the front at Ypres in 1914, Sir John French was telling his staff that it was now just a question of hanging on until the Russians won the war in the east. Although the steamroller fell apart on the roads of East Prussia in 1914, it did eventually reach Berlin, but it took 31 years and a change of regime to achieve this goal.

The Desperate Russians retreat

On the morning of 27th August Francois attacked, unleashing a seven-hour bombardment. Exhausted, starving and demoralized, I Corps gave way and fell back, leaving half their number dead in their trenches. Ordered by Ludendorff to march northeast to aid Scholtz's corps, which was still under pressure from Samsonov's centre, Francois once more disobeyed. Determined to outflank Samsonov's army and cut off his line of retreat, Francois struck eastwards, splitting his corps and stringing half of it out in a line of outposts. In the event, Scholz proved perfectly capable of holding his front unaided. Francois's disobedience ensured that Samsonov's left was now turned and his line of retreat cut off.

Samsonov's situation was desperate. Both his flanks had been turned, his cavalry were strung out and isolated, his men were starving, ammunition was running low and communications within his army were intermittent at best. His army was falling apart. Only his two centre corps, commanded by Generals Martos and Kliouev, were still putting up organized resistance. Samsonov telegraphed Jilinksy that he was going to the front to take personal command of the fighting. The British liaison officer, Knox, came upon him seated on the ground studying maps with his staff. Samsonov rose and talked to Knox, admitting that the situation was 'critical'. Since Knox's job was to report to the British government, Samsonov advised him to leave while there was still time. 'The enemy has luck one day,' he said, 'we will have luck another.' Sending his baggage and wireless equipment back to Russia, and thus cutting all his communications, Samsonov commandeered some Cossack horses for himself and his staff and rode towards the sound of the guns. When he reached General Martov's headquarters at the front, he embraced him and declared, 'You alone will save us.' That night Samsonov gave orders for a general retreat of the 2nd Army.

The trap snaps shut

If Samsonov still retained hopes that Rennenkampf was marching to his aid and would soon appear on his right, he was to be disappointed. Aware at last of the danger to his southern army, Jilinsky had ordered Rennenkampf to attack, but crucially to the west rather than the southwest. Samsonov and his army were doomed.

'A general has much to bear and needs strong nerves,' wrote Ludendorff in later life, but on the night of 28th August his nerve faltered. On hearing that a Russian force was marching up from Poland, Ludendorff decided against closing the ring around Samsonov's army. Hindenburg overruled him, but if Ludendorff had had his way, the bulk of Samsonov's army might have escaped through the forests, albeit with heavy casualties, to the Polish border. As it was, over the next two days, the Germans completed their encirclement and drew the net tighter. The bulk of Samsonov's army – in a cruel irony, the unfortunate part that had not crumpled and fled – was now herded into a vast, 200-square-mile (320-sq-km) wilderness of forest and marsh. Surrounded and under constant artillery bombardment, the Russians made numerous attempts to break out, some of them led by priests holding crosses aloft. But wherever they emerged from the forests, they were met by rifle and machine-gun fire from dug-in German infantry. One German regimental history described a typical incident. 'A long enemy column of all arms came slowly out of the woods without any protecting troops and offered a target that would never have been permitted at peace manoeuvres ... the general fire of both battalions and the machine-gun company was opened. This last was for the first time employed as a complete unit, and with all its six guns it opened continuous annihilating fire. A more fearful effect could hardly be imagined. The Russians tried to take refuge in the woods, abandoning vehicles and horses. The frightened and wounded animals rushed aimlessly over the country, wagons were upset, there was soon wild chaos. The units which were still armed sought to take positions on the edge of the woods, but they soon exhibited white cloths on poles and rifles.'

> ' The enemy has luck one day we will have luck another '
> GENERAL SAMSONOV

> ' Samsonov absented himself from his colleagues, walked off into the shadows and shot himself '

The best part of three Russian corps now dissolved into a confused mass, stumbling through the forests in search of a way out of the German net. On the night of 29th August General Martos was captured. Taken to a 'dirty little hotel' in a nearby village, he was subjected to a tirade by Ludendorff, who boasted that Russia was wide open to invasion, but Hindenburg spoke soothingly to the Russian, returned his sword and wished him happier times. That same night, in another part of the forest, Samsonov and his staff, now on foot, were also searching for a way out, Samsonov repeating constantly, 'The tsar trusted me. How can I face him after such a disaster?' At 1 a.m. Samsonov absented himself from his colleagues, walked off into the shadows and shot himself. His wife, who was in Germany at the time, dealing with matters relating to prisoners of war, was eventually able to trace his unmarked grave by a locket taken from his body.

The day of harvesting

Large gatherings of Russians reported by air reconnaissance caused alarm at 8th Army Headquarters until it became clear that these men had already surrendered – the glinting bayonets seen from above were the bayonets of their German captors. Bets were taken at headquarters as to the eventual number of prisoners, with expectations ranging between 20,000 and 40,000. The eventual number was 92,000 men and 500 guns, with the greater part, some 60,000 men, taken by Francois. The haul was such that 31st August would go down in German military history as 'the day of harvesting'.

In the days that followed, the 8th Army wheeled north to attack Rennenkampf. The two corps that Moltke had sent east enabled Hindenburg to hustle Rennenkampf back over the Russian border by the middle of September, leaving 30,000 prisoners behind him. Rennenkampf himself deserted his army and fled across the border in a motor car. Both he and Jilinksy were dismissed. The defeat at Tannenberg and the inadequacies it exposed in the Russian war machine led to calls for Russia to make peace. The tsar, reassured by victories against the Austrians and determined to stick by his allies, ignored these calls, condemning his regime to destruction.

A happy marriage

If Francois took the lion's share of the prisoners at Tannenberg, Ludendorff took the lion's share of the credit. Colonel Hoffman had already made many of the crucial decisions and issued orders before Hindenburg and Ludendorff arrived on the scene, and the encirclement and consequent huge haul of prisoners was the result of decisions taken by Francois. Nevertheless, Tannenberg propelled Hindenburg and Ludendorff to effective control of the whole German war effort. From then on their names became inextricably linked and by the end of the Great War they were exercising almost dictatorial power in Germany. Hindenburg described their relationship as 'a happy marriage'.

Although he was known as Marshal 'Was-sagst-du?' (What are you saying?) from his habit of addressing this question to Ludendorff, Hindenburg attained an ascendency in the eyes of the German public that even defeat could not diminish. In 1925 he became president of the German Republic, a post he was still holding when Hitler became chancellor in 1934. On the night Hitler's brownshirts staged a torchlight rally through the streets of Berlin, Hindenburg's mind, now failing, must have wandered back to the glory days of 1914. Watching the massed ranks pass below his balcony, he turned to an aide and remarked: 'I'd no idea we'd taken so many Russian prisoners!'

'THE STRAIN ON FRANCE HAS ALMOST
REACHED THE BREAKING-POINT'
Chief of German General Staff Erich von Falkenhayn

VERDUN
1916

With vast armies marching across Belgium and northern France, the war of manoeuvre that characterized the opening months of the Great War on the Western Front soon degenerated into trench warfare. Barbed wire and machine guns had given the defending forces a disproportionate advantage over the attacking, and by 1916 the opposing lines of trenches stretched from Switzerland to the North Sea. In effect, the war on the Western Front had become one great siege, though this was hardly recognized. Commanders on both sides, obsessed with military historian Clausewitz's 'Napoleonic' ideal of one great decisive battle, continued to launch bloody, fruitless offensives.

In the east, because of the much greater distances involved, open warfare continued, favouring the Central Powers. The much-vaunted Russian steamroller had been halted at Tannenberg, and the Germans had followed up their victory there with a further body-blow at Gorlice-Tarnów in the summer of 1915.

Falkenhayn's plan

Assessing the situation at the beginning of 1916, German Chief of General Staff, Falkenhayn, reasoned thus: the Russians had been effectively knocked out of the war for the foreseeable future, but ultimate victory would be hard to achieve. An advance on St. Petersburg would not end the war, while an advance on Moscow would only draw German forces deeper into Russia's vast interior. Hope in the east lay in Russia's political situation. As Falkenhayn wrote in a document for the kaiser at Christmas 1915: 'According to all reports, the domestic difficulties of the giant Empire are multiplying rapidly. Even if we cannot perhaps expect a revolution in the grand style, we are entitled to believe that Russia's internal troubles will compel her to give in within a relatively short period.' Germany's ally, Austria-Hungary, was pushing for a joint Austro-German offensive against Italy, which Falkenhayn felt would benefit Austria only and have little effect on the outcome of the war. Falkenhayn's eyes were turned to the Western Front. Here, about to be reinforced by the 24 divisions of Kitchener's 'New Army', the British were judged to be too strong. Any blow in the west must be dealt against France.

'As I have already insisted,' Falkenhayn wrote in the Christmas report, 'the strain on France has almost reached the breaking-point – though it is certainly borne with the most remarkable devotion. If we succeeded in opening the eyes of her people to the fact that in a military sense they have nothing more to hope for, that breaking-point would be reached and England's best sword knocked out of her hand. To achieve that object, uncertain method of a mass break-through, in any case beyond our means, is unnecessary. We can probably do enough for our purposes with limited resources.'

PREVIOUS PAGE: *Verdun 1916 – a French soldier and his horse, both wearing gas masks. Falkenhayn was relying on the 'remarkable devotion' of the French soldier to enable him to 'bleed the French army white'.*

Falkenhayn's plan was a simple one: pick a point that the French would have to defend, and threaten it. The French would pack it with infantry in fixed defences, and their army would then, in Falkenhayn's words, 'bleed to death'. The terrible doctrine of attrition had been accepted at the highest levels. However, attrition is a two-way process – unless one side decides to use firepower rather than manpower as its instrument. Falkenhayn's instrument was to be massed heavy artillery. Limited attacks by German infantry would keep the threat real, but be relatively inexpensive in terms of German casualties. In effect, Falkenhayn intended to create an 'artillery trap' – an area into which the French could be induced to feed division after division, to be slaughtered by German heavy guns.

The fortress on the Meuse

The point chosen was at the town of Verdun. Straddling the River Meuse, it had been a fortress since Roman times. Verdun's defences had been improved successively over the centuries – by Vauban, the great 17th-century military engineer, then by Napoleon III in the 19th century, and again in the 1880s, when a double ring of 21 small fortresses had been constructed on the heights surrounding the city. Sold to the German troops who would be assaulting it as 'the key to Paris', it was, in fact, nothing of the sort. Verdun was 138 miles (220 km) from the French capital – its capture would neither greatly benefit the Germans nor greatly inconvenience the French. Its importance lay in sentiment. For the French, Verdun was their ancient eastern bastion, facing its German rival Metz across the Franco-German border – its loss or abandonment was unthinkable. The Germans would present the French with a simple but brutal choice – give up Verdun or lose their army. There was little doubt which they would choose – French pride and the remarkable devotion of her troops would ensure that the French army would file obediently into Verdun's defences to be 'bled white' by massed artillery.

Verdun may have been a bastion for France in the past, but by 1916 the situation was quite different. The Belgians had placed great faith in their forts – in particular those protecting Liège. In the event, in August 1914 Liège had fallen in a matter of days to German 420 mm howitzers and 305 mm guns, produced by the Austro-Hungarian Skoda factory (forerunner of today's famous Czech vehicle manufacturer), which fired high-trajectory, armour-piercing shells. The cracking of this supposedly impregnable fortress sent shockwaves through military circles in Europe and made the name of the German commander, an up-and-coming staff officer named Erich Ludendorff. After Liège, the French commander-in-chief, General Joseph Joffre, lost faith in their forts as a means of defence and, believing that the guns could be better employed elsewhere, had most of them removed from Verdun's 21 forts. General Coutanceau, the military governor of Verdun, protested and was removed from his command. By 1916 Verdun was protected by only a single line of trenches. Lieutenant-Colonel Driant, an officer serving in the Verdun sector, who was also parliamentary deputy for Nancy, had the temerity to point this out, via political channels, while on leave. Word reached the Minister of War General Gallieni, whose inquiries to Joffre met with this classic reply: 'I cannot be party to soldiers placed under my command bringing before the Government, by channels other than the hierarchic channel, complaints or protests concerning the execution of my orders.' His leave over, Driant returned to his trenches in the Bois des Caures, a forested area north of Verdun, where he and his men would soon bear the brunt of the German onslaught.

Operation Gericht

For the Verdun offensive – nicknamed 'Gericht' (Court of Justice) – Falkenhayn had Prussian Crown Prince William's 5th Army at his disposal, plus ten divisions, bringing the total German strength to 140,000 men, supported by an unprecedented concentration of artillery. A total of 542 heavy guns, including 13 Krupp 420 mm and 17 Skoda 305 mm, were massed facing Verdun's eight miles (12.8 km) of perimeter, as well as the normal field and medium artillery. The Germans had stockpiled two-and-a-half million shells and were able to field one division and 150 guns to each mile (1.6 km) of front. So great was the concentration of guns that French aerial observers abandoned attempts to plot individual German battery positions – whole areas had become vast artillery parks.

Crown Prince William, the kaiser's eldest son, was portrayed by Allied propaganda as 'Little Willie', a vapid and foppish young man. In fact, like other German imperial princes in command of armies, he was kept on a tight rein by his chief of staff, General Schmidt von Knobelsdorf, and was in any case not without military ability. If he had won no battles in the opening years of the war, neither had he been defeated. The crown prince had his doubts about Operation Gericht, fearing that it would not just be the French who would be bled white. Both he and Knobelsdorf were unconvinced about the tactics of the forthcoming offensive – an advance on a narrow front on the east bank of the River Meuse only. He sent Knobelsdorf to General Headquarters to argue for a broader advance on both sides of the Meuse, but Knobelsdorf was won round by Falkenhayn's arguments for an advance on a limited front with crack troops supported by massed artillery. This, he told Knobelsdorf, would be the hammer that would pulverize the French on the anvil of their own positions, and, like his father, the crown prince allowed himself to be overruled by the professionals.

Operation Gericht was scheduled to begin on 12th February, but the weather intervened. Nine days of heavy rain imposed a delay – during which time the French, now alerted, began ferrying men and supplies into the threatened sector. Even so, by the third week in February, the French still only had two divisions with which to face the six German divisions now sheltering from the elements in underground bunkers.

The Germans unleash a devastating bombardment

The rain stopped on 19th February and, after allowing a day for the ground to dry out, the Germans opened their bombardment along a 15-mile (24-km) front at 4.00 a.m. on the 21st. High-explosive tear gas and choking agents rained on the French front, second lines and rear areas. A French eyewitness wrote: 'Without ceasing, shells of every calibre are bursting around us with tremendous hubbub, and the air is torn with incessant explosions. Thousands of projectiles are flying in every direction, some whistling, others

> '**Thousands of projectiles are flying in every direction, some whistling, others howling**'
>
> FRENCH EYEWITNESS

howling, others moaning low, and all this whistling, howling and moaning unites in one infernal roar... All these missiles of destruction flying over a fairly wide area burst one upon the other, so dense is the fire. Shell fragments fly on every side from the cloud of smoke and earth which soon becomes so persistent that it finally covers the earth like a thick fog.'

Within an hour, the French front line was isolated and all communication was by runner. In many places their trenches had been destroyed, wire cut and thick forest reduced to matchwood. The bombardment reached its peak between two and four in the afternoon, after which the German guns switched fire to the French rear areas and the first thin lines of grey-clad German infantry began to appear.

Had the Germans attacked from the start in full strength on both sides of the Meuse, there can be little doubt that Verdun would have fallen in the first few days, but that was not part of Falkenhayn's plan. It was the artillery that would 'bleed' the French – the infantry were merely to follow up and occupy the shattered trenches.

In the Bois de Caures, Driant and his regiment of Chasseurs fought on doggedly until the following day when, surrounded and about to be over-whelmed, they attempted to break out. Driant was killed – his last words were, 'Charge, my children! Long live France!' In one of the cruelest twists of fate and war, Driant and his Chasseurs died because of Joffre's error, while Joffre gained fresh kudos from Driant's sacrifice.

> '**Charge, my children! Long live France!**'
>
> LIEUTENANT-COLONEL DRIANT

The French defences fall

By the morning of 24th February the whole of the French trench line east of the Meuse had been overrun – only the forts of Vaux and Douaumont on the forward slopes of the Meuse Heights still held out. If they fell, German artillery observers on the Heights would be able to rain shells down on Verdun itself and on the Meuse bridges over which French supplies and reinforcements arrived.

On 25th February, Douaumont did fall, but almost by accident. The fort had just 23 gunners. Finding the drawbridge down and its few exhausted and shell-shocked occupants asleep, a small party from the Brandendburg Regiment took the fort without firing a shot. The official communiqué stated that it had been taken 'by assault' in the presence of the kaiser. With Douaumont in German hands, it seemed as if the fall of Verdun itself was imminent and the French bridges over the Meuse were prepared for demolition. With hindsight, such an outcome might well have been better for France. Assuming the nation's morale could have withstood such a blow, the loss of Verdun would have meant little more in military terms than a shortening and straightening of the salient (bulge in the front line) around the town – and an end to Erich von Falkenhayn's deadly game of attrition.

Pétain brings fresh spirit to the French

In the event, it was French courage that saved Falkenhayn's plan. Cometh the hour, cometh the man – and that man was Philippe Pétain. At the outbreak of war, Pétain had been a colonel of the 33rd Regiment, in which his young friend and protégé, Charles de Gaulle, was a lieutenant. By 1916 he had risen to become a corps commander. Summoned, it is said, from his mistress's bed to take command at Verdun, Pétain brought a fresh spirit to the defence. His motto – '*Ils ne passeront pas*' (They shall not pass) – became a national rallying cry. On his arrival in Verdun, Pétain immediately ordered the reoccupation and re-arming of the forts. Each garrison was given 14 days' supply of food and water and ordered never to capitulate. He then turned his attention to the supply lines. German artillery had closed all supply routes save for one light railway and the road to Bar-le-Duc 50 miles (80 km) away. The road was already breaking down under the constant traffic, so Pétain ordered a division of territorials to work full time on maintenance and to create parallel tracks. Henceforth the road itself – designated the *Voie Sacrée* (Sacred Way) – was to be for trucks only. Soon up to 6,000 trucks were using the road every 24 hours.

ABOVE: *German infantry attacking at Verdun on 15 March 1916. Gradually the Germans allowed themselves to be drawn into their own trap – and soon the French heavy artillery was taking its toll.*

Pétain organized his front into sectors, each of which was allotted its own heavy artillery. Soon it was the advancing Germans who found themselves coming under punishing bombardments. Coupled with a strategy of repeated and bloody counter-attacks, Pétain having already proved himself to be undismayed by heavy casualties, the bombardments brought the German advance to a halt.

German plans change

Historians are divided about how well Falkenhayn's plan was understood or supported in theory by the crown prince and his staff. To order troops to attack a position as though to capture it, but not actually to do so, is a difficult undertaking. This was effectively what Falkenhayn had asked the 5th Army to do. The Gericht offensive was designed to kill Frenchmen wholesale without attempting to achieve that holy grail of Western Front generals, a major breakthrough. Whether or not the crown prince or

‘ The capture of Verdun had now had now become a political necessity ’

Knobelsdorf understood this or agreed with it is doubtful. What is certain is that with the stalling of the German advance they now both began to argue forcefully for an extension of the offensive to the west bank of the Meuse. After all it was from here – from behind the heights crowned by the fort known as 'Mort Homme' (Dead Man) – that the French heavy artillery were now giving the Germans as good as they got. An attack on both sides of the Meuse, it was argued, would catch Verdun in a pincer – and pinch it out.

Also there was the political aspect to consider. The world had turned its attention to Verdun. If Falkenhayn's original conception of bleeding the French army white was working – and Falkenhayn's own figures told him that two-and-a-half Germans were dying for every five Frenchmen – to the world it looked as if the French were winning. Every day that Verdun continued to hold out boosted the Allies and diminished the Central Powers in the eyes of the world. The capture of Verdun – the threat of which had been a strategic ploy – had now very much become a political necessity.

Casualties continue to mount

On 6th March, after a two-day bombardment, the attack on the west bank of the Meuse began, although Falkenhayn would only commit four divisions. Two days later the offensive on the east bank was renewed. The initial objectives were to seize the *Mort Homme* on the west bank and the Poivre heights (also known as Hill 304) on the east bank. Both attacks failed with heavy

'the Germans found themselves throwing men as well as shells into the human mincing machine'

casualties. Worse still for the Germans, French heavy guns succeeded in destroying all the German 420 mm guns and blowing up the artillery park at Spincourt, containing 450,000 shells.

Just as Falkenhayn began to waver, however, and even to contemplate fresh efforts elsewhere on the front, the crown prince and his staff decided that the French were nearly spent. They urged that 'the destruction of French reserves ... should be completed by the employment of men, as well as of apparatus and munitions.' Falkenhayn allowed himself to be persuaded, and soon the Germans found themselves throwing men as well as shells into the human mincing machine they had themselves created.

As casualties mounted, even Knobelsdorf wavered, but on visiting Falkenhayn found him newly inspired – and the slaughter went on. On the French side Joffre intervened, promoting Pétain to commander of the Army Group and replacing him in the immediate command at Verdun by General Nivelle. Nivelle was an advocate of offensive *à l'outrance* (attack at all costs) – in the following year he was to launch a costly and futile offensive that would bring the citizen-soldiers of France to the point of outright mutiny. At that time, however, he seemed the ideal man to carry out Joffre's latest project: the recapture of Fort Douaumont. On 8th May a German ammunition store exploded inside the fort. On the 22nd the French attacked, capturing the outworks and even scaling the exterior before being bloodily repulsed. By another cruel irony, the forts of Verdun were proving both resistant to shellfire and, when held by seasoned troops, formidable bastions of defence. It gradually became clear that the problem with the Belgian forts had lain with the inexperience of their defenders. As the war progressed, troops (Belgians included), inured to the sight and sound of shellfire, proved far harder to dislodge from concrete defences than anyone had imagined in the immediate aftermath of Liège.

A French officer describing an attack by Bavarian troops wrote: 'The Germans attacked in massed formations, by big columns of five or six hundred men preceded by two waves of sharpshooters. We had only our rifles and our machine guns because the 75's [French Field guns] could not get to work. Fortunately the flank batteries succeeded in catching the Boches on the right. It is absolutely impossible to convey what losses the Germans must suffer in these attacks... Whole ranks of men are mowed down, and those that follow suffer the same fate. Under the storm of machine-gun, rifle and 75 fire, the German columns were ploughed into furrows of death. Imagine if you can what it would be like to rake water. Those gaps filled up again at once.' It is interesting to note that as late as 1916 the Germans were employing the same columns of attack used by their fathers against the French in the Franco-Prussian War of 1870–1, and by the Union troops at Fredericksburg in 1862.

A brief return to the age of chivalry

The most stubborn of the French forts on the east bank of the Meuse was Fort Vaux – the key to the Souville Heights. Held by Major Sylvain Reynal and 600 men, it was the object of an attack on 1st June by three German divisions. Surrounded and under constant bombardment, Reynal and his *poilus* ('hairy ones', the nickname for French infantrymen in the Great War) fought on amongst the piles of their own dead and wounded. It was only lack of water that forced them, in the end, to surrender. At Les Invalides in Paris, the Legion d'Honneur was presented to Reynal's wife. Reynal was informed of the award by his admiring captors, who included the crown prince himself. 'Little Willie' even presented Reynal with a sword to replace the one he had left in the fort.

This episode of chivalry over, the Germans turned to using chlorine gas as a means of attack. On 22nd June a massive German bombardment, employing 'Green Cross' gas shells, temporarily paralysed about a third of the French guns. With Fort Vaux in their hands, the Germans decided on a final push to seize the rest of the Souville Heights. If they could capture the Heights, the fall of Verdun could only be a matter of days.

Assault on Fort Souville

The attack was carried out by men of the elite Alpenkorps, among whom was a young officer by the name of Friedrich Paulus, who went on to command the German 6th Army at Stalingrad in 1942. At first all went well for the attackers. Deprived of artillery support, the French were pushed back, and the rooftops of Verdun seemed to beckon over the next horizon. At the fringes of Fort Souville, however, the attack ran out of momentum. Casualties, summer heat and especially thirst, the relentless, cruel enemy of soldiers through the ages, subsequently put an end to all further forward movement.

> ' the French had won a moral victory, but at a terrible price '

It had been a close-run thing. Pétain had been making preparations to evacuate the whole of the east bank of the Meuse, but by the following day the crisis was past. On hearing the news that the British had opened a huge bombardment on the Somme,

Fortress warfare

Verdun's forts proved more resilient than anyone had anticipated in the immediate aftermath of the fall of Liège. It was this realization that helped give birth to the Maginot Line – a belt of steel and concrete defences erected along France's border with Germany between 1930 and 1935. Much mocked now as an attempt to 'prepare for the previous war', the line's main fault – apart from its expense (7,000 million francs) – was that it did not extend far enough. The Belgians complained that if it continued along their frontier they would be excluded. Since Switzerland and Luxembourg also refused to be part of the line – on the grounds that it would compromise their neutrality – the line only covered the part of the French frontier that lies between these two countries. It was, in the words of one historian, 'impenetrable but not unavoidable' – the Germans went round it. It is interesting, though, to speculate how the Germans would have fared trying to batter a way through it in 1940.

Falkenhayne stopped the flow of ammunition to Verdun. No more German divisions were assigned to the Verdun sector, and after a final push on Fort Souville on 11th July, which was beaten off, the German offensive ground to a halt.

A terrible price

Between 21st February and 23rd June approximately 20 million shells had been fired into the Verdun salient, turning the countryside surrounding the town into something akin to a moonscape. Defending Verdun, the French lost approximately 377,000 men, more than the Germans – an unusual ratio in warfare, where the attacker usually expects to incur higher losses. The Germans, who had finally been drawn into their own trap, lost 337,000. Neither side had gained anything from the four months of slaughter – in a series of counter-offensives during the following autumn and winter, the French regained most of the ground they had lost. Their magnificent defence of Verdun had won the French a moral victory, but at a terrible price – the loss of hundreds of thousands of men and the demoralizaton of their army. In August Falkenhayn was dismissed, to be replaced by Field Marshal Paul von Hindenburg and Lieutenant-General Erich Ludendorff. At the end of the year Joffre was 'kicked upstairs' as 'Chief Military Advisor to the Government' and given the title of Marshal of France (a military distinction, not rank, granted for exceptional achievement) – the first since 1870. In the immediate aftermath of Verdun, however, the focus on the Western Front shifted northwest to where the British were about to launch their 'Big Push' on the Somme.

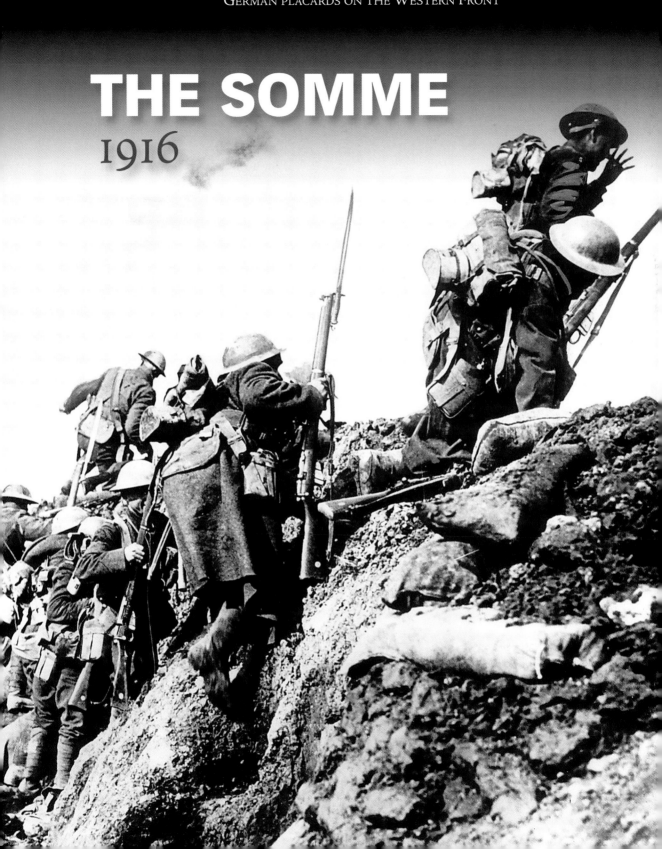

'COME ON, WE ARE READY FOR YOU'

GERMAN PLACARDS ON THE WESTERN FRONT

THE SOMME

1916

In December 1915, while General Erich von Falkenhayn
was assessing the situation on the Western Front in France, his
Allied opposite numbers were doing the same at Chantilly, near
Paris. Discussions dragged on, with Joseph Joffre, commander-
in-chief of the French army, calling for a concerted Allied
offensive in March and the Russians and the Italians preferring
to delay until mid-summer. The commander-in-chief of the
British expeditionary force, General Sir Douglas Haig, favoured
a British offensive in Flanders, while Joffre wanted the British to
take over a larger share of the trench lines, to assist in the wearing
down of the enemy. It was not until 14th February 1916 that a
compromise was agreed upon: a joint British and French
offensive in Picardy – *bras dessus bras dessous* (arm-in-arm).

The planned offensive

The British would attack with 25 divisions on a 14-mile (22.4-km) front between Arras
and Albert, north of the River Somme, while the French assault would be carried out
with 40 divisions on a 25-mile (40-km) front, south of the river. Within days of this
decision, however, Falkenhayn beat the Allies to the punch by opening his assault on
Verdun. As French reserves were drawn into the
fighting at Verdun, so their share of the planned
offensive shrank – their front reduced to 8 miles
(12.8 km) and the number of their divisions down
initially to 16 and, ultimately, to 5. The British would
now play the major role.

'Politically, the Germans could
afford to go onto the
defensive and consolidate
their trenches for a long stay'

The sector chosen for the attack was one of
the strongest on the enemy's line – on high ground, with multiple lines of deep
trenches and bomb-proof shelters connected by communication trenches, all protected
by two 40-yard (37-m) deep belts of barbed wire. Salients (bulges) along the line, from
which the Germans could fire both left and right onto the flanks of attacking infantry,
were turned into self-contained concrete fortresses, or redoubts, surrounded by mines.
With most of Belgium and a considerable part of northern France in German hands,
they were now looking for a negotiated peace based on territory held. Thanks to their
strong position, and now well established, politically, the Germans could afford to
go onto the defensive and consolidate their trenches for a long stay. For the British
and French, however, trench lines could only be regarded as a temporary measure –
a jumping-off point for a series of offensives that would ultimately drive the Germans
off Allied soil.

PREVIOUS PAGE: *British infantry leaving a trench and going 'over the top' – Somme front, 1916. Enemy front-line
trenches were often captured – but the dreamed-of breakthrough to 'green fields' proved elusive.*

THE SOMME – 1916

A patchwork army

The Allies believed that if the Germans were defeated here, it would be more of a blow to their morale than if they were beaten in any other sector of the front – and the British had supreme confidence in their newly reinforced armies. By June 1916, Sir Henry Rawlinson's 4th Army, which Haig allocated for the offensive, had grown to a force of half a million men comprising 200 battalions of infantry. Of the eleven divisions that would open the attack, three were composed of regular battalions, five were made up of battalions from the 'New Army' enlisted by Kitchener for the duration of the war, and three were a mix of regular, Territorial and New Army divisions. This was an army both undertrained and inexperienced. Even the ranks of the regular army battalions had to be brought up to strength with new recruits, the old pre-war regular army having been largely destroyed in the battles of 1914 and 1915. The Territorial and New Army battalions had little or no experience of battle. Morale, though, was high, particularly in the New Army formations. Many of these were 'Pals' battalions, special units made up of men from the same area who had enlisted together as part of local recruiting drives, with the promise that they would be able to serve together rather than being allocated to different army regiments in the conventional way.

A change of plan

The original plan had been for Rawlinson's army to break through on a front that was wide enough to allow the cavalry to exploit (push through into the enemy's rear areas), turn northwards and roll up the German front from south to north. By June, though, the strategy had been revised: the British 4th Army was now to attack 'in conjunction with the French 6th Army astride the Somme, with the object of relieving the pressure on the French at Verdun and inflicting loss on the enemy.'

> ' The Territorial and New Army battalions had little or no experience of battle. Morale though was high. '

The immediate objective of the 4th Army was the seizure of the high ground that the Germans held to their front – notably the Thiepval-Pozières Ridge – after which it was either to push on and achieve a breakthrough, or else continue to maintain pressure on the enemy from the ridge. Two of Rawlinson's divisions and his cavalry corps were taken to form a Reserve Army under General Gough, whose purpose would be to exploit any breakthrough. The British 1st, 2nd and 3rd Armies were to mount supporting and diversionary operations, with two divisions of the 3rd Army pinching out the Gommecourt salient, which bulged into the British line at the northern extreme of the proposed advance.

It was an ambitious plan, calling for an advance on a front of 14 miles (22.4 km) to a depth of between 1 to 2.5 miles (1.6–4 km), through heavily defended belts of German defences. The preparations for such an effort could hardly be concealed from the enemy, and at points along the German front line placards were erected proclaiming, 'Come on, we are ready for you!'

The artillery bombardment

Rawlinson requested a bombardment of seven days in which to cut the enemy wire, destroy enemy trenches, disrupt their rear areas (location of supplies and headquarters, etc.) and demoralize their troops. He was allocated 1,010 field guns, 182 heavy guns – 4.7 inchers and 60-pounders – and 345 heavy howitzers of 6-inch calibre and above. Although impressive on paper, he had been allocated less artillery than would be used for later offensives and, given the width and depth of the front, insufficient for the task. More than 1.5 million shells were fired in the week before the start of the offensive. Yet, due to inexperienced gunners, dispersal of effort and poor-quality ammunition (much of which remains unexploded to this day, lodged in the clay of the Somme), the bombardment failed to achieve what Rawlinson required.

Going 'over the top'

'Z' day, the day of the assault, was set for 29th June, but reports from patrols carried out by British infantry and the Royal Flying Corps indicated that much of the German wire remained uncut. 'Z' day was put back to the 1st July to allow for further bombardment. At 6.35 a.m. on the 1st, as the assault troops in the front trenches awaited the signal to advance, the Allied barrage reached maximum intensity. In the last quarter of an hour mines positioned along the front were detonated. At 7.30 a.m. the barrage lifted and the 60 battalions of the first wave went 'over the top'. From Gommecourt in the north to Montauban in the south, each battalion advanced in extended line on its own front of 400 yards (366 m). They moved slowly, burdened by the defensive materials – barbed wire, metal pickets (stakes), shovels and sandbags – they would need to convert the advanced in four waves, at a steady pace, to allow the men to arrive on the objective in good order and all at the same time. There was little attempt at fire and manoeuvre (units taking turns alternately to advance or provide fire cover), this being judged too complicated for inexperienced, non-regular troops.

As the British moved forward, the German infantry – battered, dazed and with many shell-shocked, but still alive – emerged from their shelters and raced forward to their battle stations. A German eyewitness – Lieutenant M. Gerster – described what followed in his sector, near Ovillers and La Boisselle. 'At 7.30 a.m. the hurricane of shells ceased as abruptly as it began. Our men at once clambered up the steep shafts leading from the dugouts to the daylight and ran singly or in groups to the nearest shell-craters... The machine guns were pulled out of the dugouts and hurriedly placed into position... As soon as in position, a series of extended lines of British infantry were seen moving forward from the British trenches. The first line appeared to continue without end to right and left. It was quickly followed by a second line, then a third, and fourth. They came on at a steady pace as if expecting to find nothing left alive in our front trenches.' This was what the British infantry had been led to expect – surely nothing could have survived the barrage. In fact

> 'They came on at a steady pace as if expecting to find nothing left alive in our front trenches'
> LIEUTENANT M. GERSTER

neither the German infantry, nor their artillery – much of it successfully concealed – had suffered to anything like the degree that the British tacticians had hoped.

> 'men could be seen throwing their arms in the air and collapsing never to move again'
>
> LIEUTENANT M. GERSTER

Gerster continues: 'When the leading British line was within 100 yards, the rattle of machine-gun fire and rifle fire broke out from along the whole line of craters... Red rockets sped up into the blue sky as a signal to the artillery, and immediately afterwards a mass of shells from the German batteries in the rear tore through the air and burst among the advancing lines... The advance quickly crumpled under this hail of shells and bullets. All along the line men could be seen throwing their arms in the air and collapsing never to move again. Badly wounded rolled about in their agony, and others less severely wounded crawled to the nearest shell-hole for shelter.'

Some success in the south

In the mythology of the Battle of the Somme, it is generally held that the British infantry were mown down in swathes along the length of their line, before they had been able to progress more than just a few yards from their trenches. In reality, along the 14-mile (22.4-km) front, the story was one of mixed fortunes – partial success in the south, but disaster in the north. To the south of the Somme, and to the north of it as far as Maricourt, the French attacked with both French and French colonial divisions. The Germans had not been expecting a French offensive, and this sector of the German line was more lightly held. The use of more flexible tactics by the French, combined with the element of surprise and heavier artillery support, enabled them to capture all their objectives as well as 4,000 prisoners. The British XIII Corps also achieved all their objectives, including the capture of the village of Montauban and keeping pace with the French on their right. Their advance was successful because the enemy wire had been cut and a 'creeping' barrage was used, where the artillery lengthened their range at staged intervals as the infantry followed close behind.

To the right of XIII Corps, XV Corps attacked the hinge of the German line – a maze of trenches and fortified houses with two bastions at Fricourt and Mametz. The British 21st Division managed to take ground to the north of Fricourt, penetrating 1.5 miles (2.4 km) into German lines. However, 7th division's attack on Fricourt itself was halted with severe casualties: the 7th Yorkshire Regiment (the Green Howards) lost 15 officers and 366 men in three minutes, and the 7th East Yorkshires coming up in support lost 5 officers and 150 men in the first few yards of their advance. Even so, the corps had managed to 'pinch out' the Fricourt bastion, which fell the next day.

Appalling casualties in the north

Fricourt, though, represented the northern limit of British success. Further north of the village it was a very different story. The route of III Corps' advance straddled both sides of the Albert–Bapaume road in the direction of the strongest German position at the villages of Ovillers and La Boisselle. Here, the creeping bombardment left behind the advancing infantry who, stumbling over broken ground and through uncut wire, could not keep up with it. The lengthening of the artillery's range was based on predicted timings and, as the battlefield communications of the time were not good enough, could not be adjusted to allow for the infantry's slow progress. The battalions of 34th Division attacked in four waves, but, lacking artillery support, suffered 80 per cent casualties within ten minutes. Two battalions of the Northumberland Fusiliers (Tyneside Irish) were cut to pieces by machine-gun fire before they had even crossed their start line. Despite appalling casualties, the division pushed on past La Boisselle as far as Contalmaison before being forced back. Meanwhile, the men of 8th Division were slaughtered in waves before Ovillers.

To the north of III Corps, X Corps attacked the Thiepval Ridge. If this attack succeeded, Ovillers, to the south, could be outflanked and the whole German line to the north 'rolled up'. The village of Thiepval, itself a complex of 60 fortified houses linked by tunnels, was attacked by the British 32nd Division. With a longer stretch of no man's land to cross than the troops attacking further south, they suffered heavy casualties. The 32nd broke into the German front lines, but, lacking artillery support could advance no further. The other assaulting division was the 36th Ulster Division, many of them wearing orange sashes in celebration of the forthcoming anniversary of the Battle of the Boyne. They crossed no man's land at speed and achieved an astonishing success, even gaining a foothold in the formidable Schwaben Redoubt before being halted by German reserves. Other assaults by the Allied forces, however, were not so successful. Observing two battalions of the Royal Irish Fusiliers and one of the Royal Irish Rifles apparently pinned down in open ground, an artillery observer asked

why they were not moving. 'Because they are all dead', he was told.

Further north the situation was even worse. The three assaulting divisions of VIII Corps – the 29th, 4th and 31st – were due to attack Beaumont Hamel and Serre, where no man's land was 500 yards (457 m) across. Muddled orders and adminstration caused the barrage in this sector to be lifted 15 minutes early, giving the German machine gunners even more time to deploy, and again the creeping barrage moved too fast, leaving the

ABOVE: *British troops move forward in single file through what was once a forest, but by the autumn of 1916 had become a muddy swamp. An offensive that had opened with high hopes petered out in mud and despair.*

infantry isolated. The casualties from German machine guns and artillery were appalling. The men of the 1st Royal Newfoundland Regiment were cut to pieces within yards of their own start line and the men of the Sheffield and Acrrington 'Pals' died in ranks before Serre. VIII Corps lost 14,000 men killed, wounded or missing,

'Of the 60 battalions of the first wave, perhaps 20 never even reached the German front line'

for almost no gain. At the extreme northern end of the British offensive, two divisions of General Allenby's army made an assault on the Gommecourt Salient. This attack was only ever intended to draw German reserves and artillery fire away from their 4th Army comrades to the south. Although 56th Division enjoyed some success, 46th Division's attack was repulsed with terrible casualties. The attack on Gommecourt was a bloody failure, and it is doubtful that it diverted a single German shell.

By 8.30 a.m. the British casualties were approximately 30,000 men, killed or wounded. Of the 60 battalions of the first wave, perhaps 20 never even reached the German front line. Those who had were now either digging in, mopping up – clearing bunkers and trench lines of snipers and stragglers – or desperately fortifying the newly captured trenches in preparation for German counterattacks. Rawlinson continued to feed battalions into the thick of battle until, by midday, 109 were engaged with the enemy.

The benefit of hindsight

It is easy to criticize Rawlinson for continuing to send troops into a battle that, with hindsight, we can see as a bloody failure, but a commander's job is to focus on victory, undeterred by mounting casualties, and surpress his personal feelings. 'Man cannot tell but Allah knows / how much the other side was hurt!' – Rudyard Kipling's words would have been familiar to British commanders. Throughout military history, many assaults that ultimately proved successful did not appear so until almost the last moment. The feeling that one last effort could break the enemy and that to call off all further attacks might be to concede defeat on the verge of victory has been a contributory factor in many a

Breaking the deadlock

The Somme saw the culmination of a process that began with the invention of the breech-loading rifle – a weapon that could be loaded and fired lying down. At a stroke, defending troops gained a significant advantage over attacking forces, since lying in a prone position they presented a much smaller target. The process continued during the 19th century with the development of machine guns, barbed wire, concrete and indirect-fire (firing at targets the gunners cannot physically see) – ending in 1914 with the deadlock of the Western Front. It was the British, with the invention of the tank, and the Germans, with their deep infiltration 'storm' tactics, who found a way to break the stalemate. When, between the wars, the Germans combined the two in their 'Blitzkrieg' strategy they became, for a time, completely unstoppable.

seemingly pointless slaughter. Besides, those battalions who had succeeded in penetrating enemy lines were now under increasing pressure from artillery fire from German guns pre-registered (sighted) on their own front-line trenches (in the event that their trenches should be captured), as well as from counterattacks by German reserves, sniper fire and bombing by isolated German groups who had been missed or bypassed in the initial advance. The fresh battalions thrown in by Rawlinson were desperately needed to consolidate the few gains that had been made, to replace casualties or to help extricate the troops of the first wave, who now found themselves being pushed back out of objectives they had gained at such a high cost.

Reinforcing failure

Where Rawlinson may perhaps be criticized is in his failure to exploit his army's success in the south. The French had seized all their objectives. Along 6 miles (9.6 km) of Rawlinson's southern front, British troops were practically looking at open, undefended country. The French were calling for a further push from the British, but corps commander General Sir William Congreve would not depart from the plan. His orders were to capture Montauban and consolidate the position. There was to be no further advance until the second phase of the offensive had been fully prepared. Despite French protests, Rawlinson would not budge, and an opportunity was lost that might have swept the Allies forward to Ginchy, Guillemont and even Combles.

'Reinforce success, don't reinforce failure' is a well-known military maxim, but it was forgotten in the only British success north of Fricourt. With the men of 36th Division hanging on grimly in the Schwaben Redoubt, their corps commander chose to send his reserve division to the aid of the 32nd Division, who were stalled on the Thiepval spur. As a result, the Ulstermen of the 36th were slowly driven out of the redoubt and off the ground they had won earlier in the day.

The blackest day

By nightfall the British had lost 57,470 men – killed, wounded or missing – for a penetration of the enemy line just 1 mile (1.6 km) deep and 3.5 miles (5.6 km) wide. 1st July 1916 was, without doubt, the blackest day in the history of the British army. Of 129 battalions, 32 had lost more than 500 men. Worst hit was 10th Battalion, the West Yorkshire Regiment, which lost 710 men. Censorship sheltered the British public from the extent of the disaster – until the casualty figures were posted. The grouping of men into 'Pals' battalions meant that some communities suffered disproportionately – whole streets, villages, towns and cities went into mourning.

The offensive grinds on

If Haig had a plan for failure – disengagement, and a fresh offensive in Flanders – he had none for what was the more likely result on the Somme, a mixture of failure and success. The 'bulldog' nature of his character, which would show to advantage in the crisis in March 1918, prevailed, and he decided to continue with the offensive, capitalizing on successes in the south. At Rawlinson's suggestion, the two left-hand corps of the 4th Army – X and VIII – were placed under Gough's command and incorporated into Gough's Reserve Army. Rawlinson was all for a further push by Gough in the northern sector on 2nd July, but Gough demurred and nothing further happened that day. On the 3rd, Joffre visited Haig and insisted that the ridge from Thiepval to Pozières, in the British centre, should be taken before any advance was made on the right. Joffre raged at Haig, ordering him to make the assault, after which Haig calmly reminded him: 'I am solely responsible to the British government for the actions of the British army.'

The Germans had been badly shaken and their reserves were few, but these delays allowed them time to recover by thickening up the thin line of men and guns that stood between the Allies and open country in the southern sector. Even so, over the next few days the Germans were steadily driven back by a series of attacks, mostly by XV Corps. On 14th July a brilliantly executed attack by XIII Corps – a swift, 'hurricane' bombardment followed by a dawn infantry attack – took the Germans by surprise and

carried the British into High Wood, just south of the Albert–Bapaume road. A squadron of the 7th Dragoon Guards accompanied the advance, the first appearance of British cavalry on the battlefield since 1914, but the success caught the British by surprise, too, and no reserves were available to exploit it. The offensive continued throughout July, but all hopes of a breakthrough were by now abandoned and the aim was mere attrition. With the Germans forced into making repeated counterattacks, they, too, suffered heavy losses, and casualties on both sides rose to 90,000.

Drawing in South African, Canadian, Australian and New Zealand troops, the fighting continued into September. On the 15th of that month Haig deployed a new British invention, the 'tank' – so named because for deception purposes it was designated a 'self-propelled water carrier'. Some local successes were achieved and hundreds of German prisoners taken, but Haig has been much criticized for employing a secret weapon before it was fully developed and present in sufficient numbers to affect the outcome of the battle. Fortunately for the Allies, the Germans' military conservatism led them to disregard the tank's potential. When tanks were employed en masse at Cambrai the following year, the effect was as great as if the Germans had never seen them before.

Bloody graveyard

Not until November, by which time the mud of the Somme had already acquired its terrible reputation, did the offensive finally peter out in exhaustion and despair. By that time, the British and French had lost approximately 600,000 men, and the Germans about the same. The British had advanced between 5 and 7 miles (8–11.2 km) along 10 miles (16 km) of the 14-mile front, but beyond relieving the pressure on the French at Verdun, no strategic advantage had been gained. As a consequence of the Battle of the Somme, British troops lost much of their patriotic ardour, as well as their confidence in their commanders, and conscription was introduced in Britain shortly afterwards to make up the loss of manpower. There were however no winners on the Somme. A historian of the German 27th Division wrote: 'In the Somme fighting of 1916 there was a heroism that was never again found in the division'. The German High Command declared that 'the Somme was the bloody graveyard of the German army'.

'the Somme was the bloody graveyard of the German army'
GERMAN HIGH COMMAND

OPPOSITE: *In a shallow trench in a ruined landscape, British troops await the order to advance. As summer turned to autumn, the battle drew in Dominion troops – Canadians, Australians, South Africans and New Zealanders.*

'RUSSIA WILL THEN BE TO US WHAT INDIA
IS TO THE BRITISH!'
ADOLF HITLER

STALINGRAD
1942

In Spring 1942, having failed to capture Moscow the previous year, Hitler turned his gaze southwards. While Stalin expected and prepared for a renewed German offensive against Moscow, Hitler was planning to take possession of Russia's economic assets – the wheat lands and mines of southern Russia and, most importantly of all, the oilfields of the Caucasus. Seizing these would secure Germany's fuel supply and deny it to the Russians. Once his panzers had captured Baku on the Caspian Sea, as Hitler told Goebbels, 'Russia will then be to us what India is to the British!'

Operation Blue

This was the basis of Hitler's spring offensive, codenamed Blue. Following the capture of Sevastopol in the Crimea, four German armies – Army Group B including the Fourth Panzer Army and the Sixth Army, and Army Group A, including the First Panzer Army and the Seventeenth Army – were to advance eastwards across the River Donetz and encircle and destroy Marshal Timoshenko's armies. East of the Donetz is a vast plain of open grassland stretching roughly 100 miles (160 km) westwards to the River Don and 800 miles (1,280 km) southwards to the Caucasus. General Hermann Hoth's Fourth Panzer Army was to help establish a blocking position at Voronezh on the Don. The Fourth Panzer and the Sixth Army, commanded by General Friedrich von Paulus (who had also been at Verdun), would then advance south-eastwards down the 'corridor' between the Don and the Donetz to seize Stalingrad on the Volga. These two blocking positions – Voronezh on the Don and Stalingrad on the Volga – would shield the left flank of Army Group A, which would push on south to conquer the Caucasus.

Operation Blue opened on 28 June 1942 and at first all seemed to go well. Within a week, Field Marshal Manstein had captured 170,000 men in the Crimea, though Sevastopol held out until July. At the Stavka, Stalin's advisors had persuaded him that orders to commanders not to yield an inch of ground merely played into the enemy's hands. Even so, Hoth's panzers became embroiled in vicious street fighting in Voronezh, where the Russians put up unexpectedly stiff resistance.

In the planning for Operation Blue a swift advance to Stalingrad by Paulus's Sixth Army and Hoth's Fourth Panzer Army was envisaged. However, in his impatience to push on into the Caucasus, exacerbated by the news that his panzer divisions had been halted at certain critical moments by fuel shortages, Hitler now ordered Hoth's panzers south to assist Army Group A's drive to the Caucasus. This fatally slowed the advance of Paulus who plodded on alone towards Stalingrad. It would not be until the end of August that Paulus's advance guard reached the outskirts of the city.

OPPOSITE: *Russian soldiers firing from a damaged building. Having cleared the Russians from one street, by the next day the Germans would find they had 'run back like rats in the rafters'.*

Paulus miscalculates

At a conference on 8th September at Hitler's new Werwolf headquarters at Vinnitsa in the Ukraine, Paulus told Hitler that he would need 14 days to regroup and a further 10 to take the city.

Paulus's estimate was over-optimistic for two reasons. Firstly, in the wake of the spirited defence their troops had mounted at Voronezh, the Russians had come round to the idea that defending cities was a more effective strategy than fighting the Germans in open country. The despatch to Stalingrad of the 10th NKVD Rifle Division (as the KGB was then called) was an early indication that they were preparing to mount such a defence there. These were Interior Ministry troops whose main role was to 'encourage' defenders and civilians and enforce party discipline behind the lines. An even stronger indication came with the removal from command of Timoshenko and his replacement by the man who had successfully defended Moscow the previous winter – Marshal Georgi Zhukov.

The second reason why Paulus's estimate was mistaken was the state of Stalingrad itself. On Hitler's orders General Wolfram von Richtofen's Fourth Luftflotte (Air Fleet) had already reduced Stalingrad to rubble. By the time Paulus was briefing Hitler at Vinnitsa, the fighting in Stalingrad had already begun. On 23rd August Paulus's advance guard, the Sixteenth Panzer Division, advancing to the Volga, had been halted by Richtofen in person. Within hours the delighted panzer crews were cheering and waving as wave after wave of Junkers 88s, Heinkel IIIs and Junkers 87 'Stukas' flew over en route to Stalingrad.

'Richtofen's bombers had presented the city's defenders with a gift'

Richtofen's air assault completely overwhelmed the city's anti-aircraft guns, manned by girls barely out of school. This was a terror raid – half the bombs dropped were incendiaries. By the time the Sixteenth Panzer Division reached the heights above the Volga, 40,000 civilians were dead and the city was in flames. The city's wooden buildings were mostly burnt to the ground, while the part that was built of brick and stone was reduced to rubble, but this was much more suitable for defensive fighting. Richtofen's bombers had presented the city's defenders with a gift.

Morale, however, was high among the German troops, the *Landsers* (the nickname for the German infantry), many of whom thought the war was as good as over. 'The whole city is on fire,' one soldier wrote home, 'on the Führer's orders our Luftwaffe has sent it up in flames. That's what the Russians need to stop them resisting.' The Russians did not stop resisting, though. Sixteenth Panzer had to fight its way into the city's suburbs 'shot for shot' as the young women manning the flak guns levelled them to aim at ground targets and fought on until all 37 Russian guns were knocked out. On 25th August the Soviet Regional Party Committee declared a state of siege.

A trophy city

Both sides gradually seemed to reach the conclusion that the key to the whole war in southern Russia was Stalingrad. The city of Stalingrad straggled for 25 miles (40 km) down the west bank of the Volga. A centre of communications and armaments manufacturing, it produced a quarter of the Red Army's tanks. In its northern sector were four great factories: the Dzerzhinsky tractor plant – transformed into a tank factory; the Barrikady arms plant; the Red October steelworks; and the Lazur chemical plant. All four were now being converted into fortresses. Further south, beyond the 107-metre (350-ft) Mamayev Kurgan, an ancient burial mound but now a park, was the city centre – an ugly sprawl of shops, government buildings and two railway stations. The ferries that connected the city with the eastern bank of the river (there was no bridge) ran from here. As long as the ferries were operating, Russian forces defending the city on the west bank could be resupplied and reinforced from the east bank. Unless the Germans could cross the Volga themselves, Russian artillery on the east bank could support their comrades on the west.

> 'The slogan for the defence was "There is no land beyond the Volga!"'

Stalingrad had a special significance for Stalin himself – as Tsaritsyn (its original name), the city had seen of some of his finest hours in the Civil War of 1917–19, and the city had been renamed after him in 1928. Now he designated it Russia's southern bastion. To command the defence of the city itself, Andrei Yeremenko, commander of the South-eastern Front, chose General V.I. Chuikov who was to assume command of the 62nd Army. All Stalingrad's citizens were enlisted to work on the city's defences. All men and boys, regardless of age or physical condition, were conscripted into the infantry, while women were enrolled as nurses, unit medical orderlies and signal troops. It was impressed on the garrison that there would be no retreat. Commissar General Nikita Khrushchev ensured that every jetty on the east bank was patrolled by NKVD troops – anyone crossing the river from west to east without good reason would face summary execution. The slogan for the defence was 'There is no land beyond the Volga!'

For Hitler, too, the city was symbolic. Indeed, in the past, the Führer had shown a weakness for 'trophy cities', although neither Moscow nor Leningrad in the north had yet fallen to his forces.

The bombardment begins

By now, the panzers of Army Group A had crossed the bend of the Don and seized the destroyed oilfield of Maikop, and Bavarian mountain troops had planted the swastika on the summit of Mount Elbrus, north of the main range of the Greater Caucasus. However, the Russians had clung on tenaciously to the Caucasus passes and the German advance had ground to a halt. When General Alfred Jodl reported to the Führer that the army had no hope of breaking through to the oilfields before winter, Hitler accused him of behaving 'like Hentsch'. His choice of insult is significant. Hentsch was the staff officer who had ordered the German retreat from the Marne in 1914. A Great War infantryman himself, Hitler remembered that at the Marne a German advance had been foiled by a counterstroke launched from an uncaptured city – Paris. With its 300-mile (480-km) lines of communication, could his army in the Caucasus now be vulnerable to a similar counterstroke from the uncaptured city of Stalingrad?

By 25th August the whole of Paulus's forces were arrayed before the city, along with Hoth's Fourth Panzer Army, which had been brought back from the south. On 12th September Hitler issued Paulus with orders for the capture of the city, at the same time reassuring him about the security of his northern flank – the line of the River Don. The 'satellite armies' of the Hungarians, Rumanians and Italians would soon be arriving to guard that flank.

That same day, General Chuikov crossed the Volga by ferry to enter Stalingrad – now under heavy bombardment by Paulus's guns. Chuikov and his staff could feel the rise in air temperature from the flames, and shrapnel and shell fragments splashed into the waters of the Volga, breaking the surface 'like trout'. Chuikov's situation was dire – with three of Paulus's infantry divisions and four of Hoth's panzer divisions about to

ABOVE: *In the middle of the devastated city, Russian troops storm an apartment building. For both Hitler and Stalin, the fighting in Stalingrad had become an almost personal trial of strength and will.*

assault from the west and south, the total German strength deployed against the city had risen to 200,000 men. As he set up his first headquarters in the Mamayev Kurgan, Chuikov had a mere

55,000 exhausted men and women and 40 tanks, many of them now immobile and dug in. Nevertheless, he declared: 'We shall defend the city, or die there!'

The following day, in the Kremlin, Zhukov met with Stalin and outlined to him a plan far bolder than the mere defence of the city. Zhukov foresaw that the fighting in Stalingrad could suck in so many German troops as to render both their northern and southern flanks vulnerable. His intention was to defend the city with as few men as possible, feeding just enough troops across the river to prevent it from falling, while simultaneously building up powerful forces north and south of the city preparatory to a double envelopment – a 'Cannae on the Volga', which would destroy Paulus's Sixth Army. Stalin took some persuading – like Hitler he was obsessed with the city itself, but Zhukov was able to convince him both that such an encirclement was feasible, and that the necessary forces could be mustered.

Rattenkrieg

On that same day, 13th September, Paulus began his first drive into the city. Preceded by a barrage from artillery and Stukas, German infantry and panzers fought their way in towards Stalingrad's city centre. The Gorki Theatre and the Univermag Department Store were left in ruins. The Mamayev Kurgan changed hands several times and only by ferrying across the river 10,000 men of the elite 13th Guards was Chuikov able to hold onto it.

This was a new form of fighting to the German troops, and one they had difficulty adapting to. *Blitzkrieg* – 'lightning war' – was replaced by *Rattenkrieg* – 'rats' war'. A German officer, General Doerr, later wrote: 'For every house, workshop, water-tower, railway embankment, wall, cellar and every pile of ruins, a bitter battle was waged, without equal even in the First World War with its vast expenditure of munitions. The distance between the enemy's army and ours was as small as it could possibly be. Despite the concentrated activity of aircraft and artillery, it was impossible to break out of the area of close fighting. The Russians surpassed the Germans in their use of the terrain and in camouflage and were more experienced in barricade warfare for individual buildings.'

Having secured much of the southern part of the city in the first three days' fighting, Paulus struck again on 17th September, this time in the north of the city, towards the factory district. German tactics were crude, battering a series of narrow corridors through the city down towards the river, rather than attacking along the riverbank from north and south and cutting its defenders off from the river. As a result, the Germans reached the banks of the Volga at various points, once again celebrating 'the end of the war', but found themselves surrounded by hostile territory. Nowhere did the Germans reach the bank in sufficient strength to interrupt the continuous supply of men and munitions that were nightly ferried across from the east bank. Nor did their artillery or Richtofen's Luftflotte succeed in suppressing the Red Army's guns on the east bank.

Unaccustomed to street fighting and forced for the first time to operate without the support of large concentrations of tanks, the *Landsers* adopted the 'storm' tactics their fathers had used, forming *Kampfgruppen* of a dozen or so men armed with light machine guns, flamethrowers and grenades. For their part, the Russians set up 'breakwaters' – areas of houses and ruins that were heavily mined, and through which only they knew the way – to channel German attacks into killing zones. 'We would spend a whole day clearing a street from end to end,' wrote a German officer, 'but at dawn the Russians would start firing from their old positions at the far end... They had knocked holes between the garrets and attics, and during the night would run back like rats in the rafters.'

Struggle without end

On 4th October Paulus launched the heaviest attack yet, this time on the factory district. The offensive was preceded by attacks by massed Stukas and again relied on the application of massive force. Paulus sent in five infantry and two panzer divisions, reinforced by police battalions and engineers, specialists in street-fighting, on a 3-mile (5-km) front. Slowly the Germans ground their way towards the Barrikady arms plant, the Red October steelworks and the tractor plant from which newly finished tanks would roll off the production line straight into battle.

An officer of the Twentyfourth Panzer Division wrote of the fighting: 'There is a ceaseless struggle from noon till night. From storey to storey, faces black with sweat, we bombard each other with grenades in the middle of explosions, clouds of dust and smoke, heaps of mortar, floods of blood, fragments of human beings. Ask any soldier what half an hour of struggle means in such a fight. And imagine Stalingrad: eighty days of hand to hand struggles. The street is no longer measured by metres but by corpses.' By 14th October, half of the Red October steelworks and most of the Barrikady plant

ABOVE: *In front of the Red October steelworks – Russian troops adapted far better than their opponents to the street-fighting at Stalingrad. Those fighting in the city – on both sides – were unaware of Zhukov's impending counter-stroke.*

'The street is no longer
measured by metres
but by corpses'
GERMAN PANZER OFFICER

was in German hands. The Russian presence on the west bank of the Volga was reduced to one enclave eight miles (12.8 km) long and one mile (1.6 km) deep, and an even smaller one in the far north.

They did not know it, but the Germans had now reached the easternmost point of their advance into Russia. German propaganda proclaimed, with echoes of Verdun, that the Soviets were being 'bled white' – in fact both sides were exhausted. 'The two armies were left gripping each other in a deadly clutch,' wrote Chuikov, '...the front became virtually stabilized.' The strain had started to tell on both commanders: Paulus had developed a nervous twitch in his left eye and Chuikov's hands were covered in eczema.

Operation Uranus strikes back

At this stage Chuikov was still not aware that his army was the bait in Zhukov's trap. While the Volga ferry boats had been making their 35,000 runs across to the west bank of the Volga, ferrying some 122,000 men into the city, and while the city and its defenders had been fighting, Zhukov had been amassing an army for his counterstroke. By mid-November he had gathered more than a million men, 13,500 heavy guns, 900 tanks and 11,000 aircraft. Stalingrad had become, for both dictators, the focus of a personal trial of strength. Hitler had insisted on feeding more and more German troops into the city, as large parts of the rest of the 300-mile (480-km) front were held by the less committed 'satellite' armies of Romanians, Hungarians and Italians. On the morning of 19th November, after a night of bitter cold, Zhukov's counterstroke, 'Operation Uranus', hit the Romanian Third Army, 100 miles (160 km) north of Stalingrad. After a 3,500-gun bombardment, massed T34 tanks and waves of white, winter-camouflaged infantry rolled over the hapless Romanians. Ordered up to support them, the Twentysecond Panzer Division found that they could not even start some of their engines. The division had been idle for two months due to lack of fuel, and the straw packed round the engines to protect them had attracted mice, which had gnawed through the wiring. The Romanian army broke, opening up a 50-mile (80-km) gap in the Axis line.

The following day Russian armies in the south opened their offensive, rounding up 10,000 prisoners and pushing 30 miles (48 km) into German territory in two days. Zhukov's plan was for 1st, 5th and 21st Armies, attacking from northwest of Stalingrad, and 57th and 51st Armies, attacking from the south, to link up west of the city, trapping Paulus's Sixth Army and part of Hoth's Fourth Panzer Army in a giant pincer. On 23rd November, advancing from opposite directions, Red Army units met near Kalach, some 40 miles (64 km) west of Stalingrad, trapping 250,000 Germans and Romanians in the city.

As with Nicias at Syracuse, having been the besieger, Paulus now became the besieged. From his headquarters at the Gumrak railway station, Paulus signalled to the Führer: 'Army heading for disaster. It is essential to withdraw all our forces from Stalingrad.' At Vinnitsa, however, Goering assured a shaken Führer that the Luftwaffe could supply the Sixth Army from the air until relief arrived and the city finally fell. It was an absurd claim. To provide Paulus's army with the 120 tonnes of fuel and 250 tonnes of ammunition it required every day, let alone supply it with food, would have required every JU 52 transport plane the Luftwaffe possessed – and hundreds were already deployed in North Africa. The attempted airlift was a disaster from the start – aircraft losses were heavy and even on the best days only 140 tonnes of supplies got through. As the temperature dropped to minus 22 °F (minus 30 °C) the wounded, lined up in their hundreds at Gumrak Airfield, froze to death awaiting aircraft that never came. Those who didn't freeze, starved. The men of the Sixth Army were now existing on *Wassersuppe* (water soup) – chunks of the remaining draught horses boiled in water. Exacerbated by exhaustion and typhus, and without winter uniforms, the physical condition of the men deteriorated rapidly.

A chance to break out

To relieve the garrison, Hitler combined the Romanian armies, the Sixth Army and Hoth's Fourth Panzer into a new army group, Army Group Don, under the command of Field Marshal Erich von Manstein. Manstein planned to use those of Hoth's panzers that were not trapped in Stalingrad to drive a corridor northwestwards towards the city to enable Paulus and what remained of his army to break out. Operation Wintersturm was launched on 12th December. Hoth's panzers penetrated 40 miles (64 km) into the newly liberated Russian territory before Russian reinforcements stopped them between the Rivers Myshkova and Alksay just 30 miles (48 km) short of the city. This was Paulus's chance to break out towards Hoth with what remained of his forces, but he refused to do so without Hitler's order. His decision doomed the Sixth Army – on 23rd December, unable to wait any longer, Manstein ordered Hoth to withdraw.

Final surrender

On 8th January the Russians gave Paulus the opportunity to surrender. When he rejected the offer, they opened an intense bombardment and a renewed offensive. Still the Sixth Army, low on ammunition, hands numbed by frostbite, fought on, inflicting 26,000 casualties on the Russians as they pressed in from all sides. By now, Goebbels' propaganda machine was describing the defenders as sacrificing themselves to help stabilize the front – making comparisons with the Spartans at Thermopylae. To emphasize the point, on 30th

'the wounded froze to death awaiting aircraft that never came'

January Hitler promoted Paulus to the rank of field marshal. The message was clear: no German field marshal had ever surrendered. Paulus was to fight to the death or commit suicide. Instead, on the following day – with his defensive perimeter now littered with dead and his army reduced to 108,000 frostbitten, starving and demoralized men – the newly promoted Field Marshal von Paulus stepped out of his headquarters in the Univermag Department Store and surrendered to the commander of the 64th Army.

Manning the front

In Russia, Hitler faced the same problem that had beset Napoleon – an ever-expanding front. Given primitive communications and the slow speed of armies in the 19th century, it was possible for Napoleon's 'Army Groups', and those of the Russians, to operate over Russia's vast distances with open flanks. By 1941, modern communications, railways, motor transport and aircraft meant a continuous front had to be maintained. Hitler's only way of matching Russia's manpower reserves was to employ auxiliary armies – Italian, Spanish, Hungarians and Romanians, who were poorly equipped and less motivated than their German allies. Throughout the war on the Eastern Front we see German units winning stunning operational victories, only to be forced to retreat because flanking satellite units had been defeated.

On the whole of the Stalingrad front the Germans and their allies had lost approximately 750,000 men; the Russians roughly the same. Paulus's Sixth Army, comprising 250,000 men in 22 divisions, had ceased to exist. Of the 108,000 men who surrendered with their commander, only 5,000 survived the march to captivity and the NKVD camps. The following month, Chuikov and his 62nd Army, now redesignated the 8th Guards Army, left Stalingrad en route for the Donetz. The next streets they would fight through would be those of Berlin.

'THIS MUSN'T FINISH
WITH A WHITE FLAG'
GENERAL COGNY

DIEN BIEN PHU
1954

On their return to Indo-China in 1946, the French

found the Vietnamese nationalists were now armed and ready to fight for independence under their leader Ho Chi Minh. The nationalists had already waged a guerrilla war against the occupying Japanese who had garrisoned the country since the French defeat in 1940. Ho Chi Minh's People's Army was led by General Vo Nguyen Giap – now recognized as a master of guerrilla warfare, but dismissed by one French general as 'a non-commissioned officer learning to handle regiments'.

This contempt for an under-trained, under-equipped foe was typical of French opinion at the time, but by 1953 the People's Army (part of the Viet Minh) was receiving material support from both the USSR and communist China, and was learning fast. Short of manpower, the French relied on superior mobility through the deployment of airborne troops and firepower. They had enjoyed some spectacular successes. Airborne operations had destroyed a number of Giap's supply bases and, at Na San in late 1952, inflicted heavy casualties on the Viet Minh (League for the Independence of Vietnam).

A 'hedgehog' in the highlands

Despite this French success, Giap's army was still a force to be reckoned with and, in the highlands of Upper Tonkin, posed a threat to Laos, also part of the French Indo-Chinese Federation. The French commander in Indo-China, General Navarre, conceived a plan whereby Giap's army might be lured into the kind of direct, confrontational fight that the French had always won. By placing in the highlands a defensive 'hedgehog' (a strong, all-round defensive position), supported and re-supplied from the air, he could defend Laos from a Viet Minh invasion and inflict a bloody and, hopefully fatal, defeat on the People's Army. A second aim – not proclaimed publicly, but of equal importance – was to protect the lucrative opium trade of Upper Tonkin (in northern Vietnam) and deny it to the enemy. This trade was largely in the hands of the local *montagnard* (highland) tribes, traditional enemies of the Vietnamese and, therefore, allies of the French. With a perhaps exaggerated belief in the achievements of the French maquis in France in the Second World War, French commanders saw the *montagnard* maquis as vital to an eventual victory over the Viet Minh. For the site of this *base aero-terrestre* (fortified air-land base), Navarre settled on a remote Second World War supply base called Dien Bien Phu, in a small valley 200 miles (320 km) from the French headquarters at Hanoi.

The opposing forces

For the operation, nicknamed 'Castor', Navarre could call on a variety of French and colonial troops. His 'seize and hold' troops would, of course, be his elite parachute battalions – French, colonial (including Vietnamese) and Foreign Legion. To consolidate

PREVIOUS PAGE: *Reinforcements for the garrison at Dien Bien Phu – French paratroops land near a blockhouse on 23 March 1954. Even when it was clear that the garrison was doomed, volunteers parachuted in to rejoin their units.*

and hold the position required more heavy infantry battalions. Again the Foreign Legion was a significant factor. Legion battalions were at this stage 50 per cent German – men too young, for the most part, to have fought in World War II but led by NCOs who were, in many cases, ex-Wehrmacht and SS. Other battalions were made up of French conscripts and colonial troops. The latter – Moroccans, Algerians, Vietnamese and West Africans – varied in quality and motivation, but, when well led, proved the equal of their European comrades.

Giap's army has best been described as an army of peasant farmers. By late 1953 he had at his disposal five Viet Minh divisions comprising approximately 22,000 men in 28 battalions. This gave him a three-to-one superiority – a ratio that was not overwhelming, but one that conventional military wisdom holds necessary for a force attacking prepared positions. These were backed up by some 60,000 male and female auxiliaries, mobilized to build roads and carry ammunition. Giap also had a distinct advantage in artillery – with the end of the Korean War, communist China had begun to supply the Viet Minh with heavy guns. Against the French at Dien Bien Phu, Giap could bring an additional 36 x 105 mm guns, 24 x 75 mm howitzers, 50 x 120 mm mortars and 6 x 75 mm recoilless guns. In heavy guns – those of more than 75 mm calibre – he outnumbered the French by more than two to one. All these guns were dismantled and laboriously carried through the jungle to the hills around Dien Bien Phu where they were reassembled and emplaced. Crucially, Giap also had at his disposal more than 180 anti-aircraft guns of varying calibres. These he also disposed in the hills surrounding the French *base aero-terrestre*.

'this was a well-led army with high morale, fighting on and for home ground'

Unlike the French, Giap had no tanks and no air support. Only rarely had his infantry attacked French positions of much greater than company strength, and when they had they had done so they were defeated with heavy casualties. However, this was a well-led army with high morale, fighting on and for home ground.

The French build up their base

Operation Castor began on 20th November 1953 with a parachute drop of three French battalions comprising 1800 men onto the airfield at Dien Bien Phu. The French quickly chased off two Viet Minh companies that were training in the area and began setting up a defensive perimeter. By 24th November, the airstrip was ready to receive aircraft, and reinforcements were rapidly bringing the base up to full strength. For the next three months, the build-up continued, with the arrival of four battalions of the Foreign Legion; a battalion each of Vietnamese, Thai and Moroccan infantry; a sapper battalion; and a transport company with 127 vehicles. By March 1954, the force – commanded by a dashing and distinguished cavalry officer, Colonel Christian de Castries – had swelled to 10,133 men, with 60 guns. At De Castries's request, his counter-attack

'Confident in the strength of their position, the French awaited the coming battle'

capability was reinforced with ten
American M24 'Chaffee' tanks, which were
flown in as components and assembled on
site. The garrison was to be supported by
six napalm-carrying fighter bombers, four
C-47 transport aircraft and one casualty-
evacuation helicopter, all based at the
airfield. In addition there were fighter
bombers and supply planes based in the
Tonkin Delta and on the French aircraft
carrier *Arromanches*.

The village and airfield were ringed
with defensive 'hedgehogs', all given
women's names. Clockwise from 12 o'clock,
the inner circle consisted of Huguette,
Dominique, Eliane , Claudine and
Françoise. Each of these was sited for all-
round defence, with trenches, deep
underground bunkers and barbed wire, and
connected to the others by communication
trenches. North of the inner circle were
two more positions: Ann-Marie to the
northwest and Béatrice to the northeast.
At the top of the valley, forming a triangle
with these two, was Gabrielle. Three miles
to the south of the inner ring, at the
bottom end of the valley, was Isabelle,
which guarded a second airstrip. The
whole defensive perimeter, from Gabrielle in the north to Isabelle in the south, was
roughly nine miles (14.4 km) long and two miles (3.2 km) across. Confident in the
strength of their position, the French awaited the coming battle.

An intense Viet Minh bombardment

Giap was also building up his forces, and by the second week of March he was ready to
take up Navarre's gauntlet. He opened his offensive with a long-range bombardment
that continued throughout the 12th and 13th March, destroying two C-47s and a
fighter-bomber on the airstrip. At 5.15 p.m. on 13th March, the bombardment was
suddenly intensified, employing the full weight of Giap's artillery. For the first time the
French became aware of just how many guns Giap had at his disposal. Within minutes
the French headquarters, bunkers, artillery positions and defensive positions were
deluged with shells. On Béatrice, at the easternmost extent of the northern triangle,
manned by 450 soldiers of the Foreign Legion, the defending force could see hoards of

Viet Minh infantry coming down through the trees and filing into the assault trenches at the foot of the hills. The Viet Minh liked to attack in late afternoon, to give the French as little time as possible in which to use their air power before darkness fell. While the legionnaires of Béatrice bore the brunt of the bombardment, their own artillery, stunned by the intensity of the shellfire and with communications disrupted and spotter planes grounded, proved incapable of locating and destroying the Vietnamese guns. The French had been relying on firepower to win this battle, but already they were losing the artillery duel.

Assault on Béatrice and Gabrielle

At about 6.30 p.m. on the 13th the Viet Minh attacked selected points on the perimeter, using overwhelming strength on a narrow front. French commanders in the main base could do nothing to help as the legionnaires fought on in a series of brutal, hopeless 'corporal's battles' (small-unit fights). Communications were briefly restored when they

ABOVE: *Infantry of the Vietnamese People's Army attack a French stronghold on Dominique, one of the defensive 'hedgehogs' that protected Dien Bien Phu village and the airfield.*

heard a German voice report over the radio, 'C'est tout le monde mort – Alles Tot!' ('all are dead') then silence reigned once more over the airwaves. By 9.30 p.m., the French headquarters at Dien Bien Phu was only in contact with one outpost on Béatrice, and by midnight that too had fallen silent. Eventually, 200 survivors managed to 'exfiltrate' themselves through enemy lines to rejoin the main garrison – the remainder were dead, wounded or captured. Within 48 hours of the opening of the Viet Minh offensive, one of Dien Bien Phu's main bastions had fallen.

'he retired to his bunker, pulled the pin from a grenade with his teeth and with his one remaining arm clutched it to his chest'

The following day another French parachute battalion – the 5th Vietnamese – landed on Dien Bien Phu, just in time to participate in the next battle. At 6 p.m. the Viet Minh attacked the northernmost outpost, Gabrielle, with eight battalions. The attack followed the same pattern as that of the previous day. As with Béatrice the Viet Minh had reconnoitred the position thoroughly and, during another intense bombardment, had dug the final approach trenches from which their infantry could 'jump off' into the assault. After their engineers had blown gaps in the French wire with 'Bangalore torpedoes', at the blow of a whistle, the assault troops climbed out of their trenches and charged towards the French positions. It was a method of attack that had changed little since World War I and, as in that war, the barbed wire was littered with corpses as the Algerians replied with rifles, machine guns, mortars and recoilless guns. By 2.30 a.m. the Viet Minh assaults seemed to have foundered – but the French had underestimated Giap's willingness to take heavy casualties. At 3.30 a.m. the bombardment opened up again with new intensity. Viet Minh infantry now attacked the position from the north, as before, and the southeast. The exhausted French gunners supporting Gabrielle resorted to firing 'airburst' shells over their own positions, now swarming with Viet Minh, but by 7 a.m. the People's Army flag was flying over Gabrielle's headquarters. A hastily improvised counter-attack by two Foreign Legion companies and the newly arrived Vietnamese paratroopers, supported by six 'Chaffee' tanks, succeeded in extricating Gabrielle's last 150 men, but it was small recompense for the loss of their northern outpost.

Besieged and demoralized

In the aftermath of these defeats French morale plummeted. The artillery were particularly hard-hit hit by their failure to neutralize their Vietnamese counterparts. Their commander, Colonel Piroth, an experienced officer who had lost an arm in earlier fighting against the Viet Minh, toured the positions, encouraging his officers and men and apologizing to the infantry. On the evening of the 15th he retired to his bunker, pulled the pin from a grenade with his teeth and with his one remaining arm clutched it to his chest. His death was put down to 'enemy action', but the truth was soon being whispered around the garrison, lowering morale further. Also particularly hard-hit were the colonials and Allies. On the night of 16–17th March, a Thai battalion on Ann-Marie abandoned its positions and melted away into the night. They were later followed by numbers of North Africans and Vietnamese, who hid and scavenged along the River Nam Youm.

The following day, 18th March, after another hurricane bombardment, Giap's infantry swarmed over Ann-Marie, capturing the third and last of the northern triangle of outposts.

Spectacularly successful as Giap's initial offensive had been, it had been costly. The People's Army had lost 2,500 men and many more had been wounded. Giap now reverted to traditional siege warfare, 'sapping' (digging cover trenches) and moving slowly forward to allow assaulting troops to attack from as close to French positions as possible. During this lull, the French garrison was reinforced by a French colonial parachute battalion and a field hospital with staff.

By 28th March, thanks to Giap's heavy artillery, the main airfield was unusable – from now on all French supplies and reinforcements would have to be dropped in by parachute. A high proportion of dropped supplies went astray, sometimes as much as 40 per cent. These either landed in Viet Minh lines, where the artillery shells and fuses were particularly welcomed by Giap's gunners, or in no man's land from where they had to be recovered by night patrols. Tactical air support suffered too – fighter-bombers from the Tonkin Delta and the *Arromanches* now had to run a gauntlet of anti-aircraft fire from the surrounding hills.

Success at last for the French

On 29th March, early monsoon rain set in, degrading the French trenches and turning Dien Bien Phu into a sea of mud. The following night the results of the Viet Minh's tunnelling were revealed when a mine exploded under Eliane, one of the two easternmost bastions of the inner circle of 'hedgehogs'. This was the signal for an assault by five Viet Minh brigades comprising 15 battalions on Eliane and Dominique, the other eastern bastion. They followed the usual pattern – a ferocious bombardment followed by 'human wave' attacks. The attack on Dominique began just as a battalion of Vietnamese paratroopers were relieving a battalion of Algerian *tirailleurs* (light infantry). The fighting was confused and bloody, with a supporting battery of West African gunners firing at point-blank range, their shells, with timers at the lowest setting, exploding just yards in front of the guns' muzzles. The combined firepower of this and supporting batteries, and the rifles and machine guns of the Vietnamese and Algerian defenders, cut swathes through the Viet Minh assault columns, which wavered and finally fell back. It was a similar story on Eliane and, the following night, on Huguette, as Giap tried to press home attacks from three directions. From the night of 30–31st March to 5th April the fighting was almost continuous, but this time things went according to the original French plan. The defensive perimeter had shrunk by almost half, but firepower won the day, inflicting heavy losses on Giap's army – probably in the region of 10,000 killed or wounded.

'Verdun ... without the Sacred Way'

There was little optimism, though, within Dien Bien Phu. De Castries called it 'Verdun ... without the Sacred Way' and it was now openly referred to – with memories, perhaps, of

Sedan – as 'la cuvette', the toilet bowl. Most now recognized that the garrison was doomed. On the night of the 5–6th April what was to be garrison's the last major reinforcement arrived: two companies of the Foreign Legion and two companies of colonial paratroops, many of them making their first jump. Small groups of volunteers would continue to jump into Dien Bien Phu almost to the last hours of the siege. That many of these were men who had been detached from their battalions for various reasons and now chose to rejoin them to be with their comrades at the end says much for the *esprit de corps* of the units defending Dien Bien Phu.

The legionnaires and colonial Vietnamese paratroopers dropped on the night of the 5–6th were only just in time – Giap was already planning his final offensive. On 26th April the Geneva Conference on the Far East opened. Indo-China was to be debated on 8th May and Giap was afraid that the Western powers would insist on a ceasefire based on the status quo, allowing the French to save face and extract their garrison, in so doing cheating the People's Army of a famous victory. On 1st May Giap began his final push in the accustomed fashion, with a massive bombardment late in the day. This was longer and more intense than any before – described as being like an 'earthquake' – and ranged over all the defensive outposts and the centre of the position. After the bombardment came the 'human waves', again from the east, against the core of Dien Bien Phu's defensive perimeter – Dominique and Eliane,

> ' Dien Bien Phu was now openly referred to as *'la cuvette'*, the toilet bowl '

and Claudine at the heart of the position. The units defending these strong points – French and Vietnamese paratroops on Eliane, Algerians and Thais on Dominique – were mere skeleton formations, known as 'the remains of the remains'. The men were exhausted, shell-shocked, hungry and low on ammunition. Nevertheless they fought hard, the Thais redeeming the reputation lost by their comrades' desertion of Ann-Marie. By dawn, however, the Viet Minh had overrun the greater part of both positions. In the west, Viet Minh attacks were stalled by the legionnaires defending Huguette but at a high cost – they lost the equivalent of a battalion, which the garrison could ill-afford.

Albatross – survival of the fittest

2nd May brought heavy rain, which, apart from the almost constant shellfire and harassing attacks, gave the defenders a brief respite. The commanders used the time to consider a break-out plan, codenamed Albatross, in which the fittest men – some 2,000–3,000 paratroops and legionnaires – would fight their way out of the encirclement to the south. Their retreat would be covered by a sacrificial rearguard commanded by De Castries himself. The wounded would also remain behind.

De Castries's command had largely been usurped during the later fighting by two of the more forceful parachute colonels – Langlais and Bigeard – but his courage and composure in this situation recalls that of the Athenian Nicias at Syracuse. Having fought their way through the Viet Minh encirclement, the break-out force would march towards Laos to rendezvous with a relief force of some 3,000 irregulars (Meo and Lao

'firepower won the day, inflicting heavy losses on Giap's army' tribesmen and other *montagnards*) and one battalion of French regulars under Colonel Godard. By a supreme irony, the Dien Bien Phu garrison, which had been inserted in part to support the *montagnards*, was now pinning its few remaining hopes on rescue by those same forces. The French high command in Hanoi was not keen on Albatross, fearing the propaganda implications of their troops abandoning their wounded and being hunted through the jungles like deer by the Viet Minh, but the plan was nevertheless, scheduled for 15th May.

'Stalin organs' deliver the final blow

Giap, though, had his own schedule. Another massive bombardment on the night of 4–5th May heralded a series of assaults on the western sector – Huguette and the western part of Claudine. These attacks were beaten off by a force of legionnaires and Moroccans, but for a loss of a further 200 men. A day of violent storms on the 5th brought little relief to the garrison, now confined to a half-mile (0.8 km) square around the southern end of the airstrip and subjected in the evening to yet another bombardment. In Hanoi the French high command frantically sought American military intervention in the form of carrier-based bombers, or even, as a last resort, nuclear weapons. However, the Americans, who had supplied the French with arms and supplies, refused to become directly involved. The fate of Dien Bien Phu was sealed.

At 4 p.m. on 6th May the Viet Minh bombarded the whole of the perimeter with a new intensity. Giap was playing his trump card. He turned the six newly arrived Russian-designed Katyusha rocket launchers, nicknamed 'Stalin organs' by the Germans, on the fortifications of Dien Bien Phu's central sector. Within two hours, almost the last of the garrison's reserve ammunition and medical supplies had been destroyed. A mine detonated under what remained of Eliane was the signal for infantry assaults that continued through the night and into the morning of the 7th.

White flags in place

Giap's plan had originally built in a pause of two or three days to regroup for the final assault, but by midday on the 7th it was clear that Dien Bien Phu was about to fall. By mid-afternoon, having discussed and rejected one last suicidal attempt at a break-out, the French commanders decided that further resistance was pointless. The artillery fired off all their remaining rounds, the tanks had their engines drained of oil and then raced till they seized and Colonel Langlais burned his red beret. By 5.30 p.m. De Castries was on the radio to his commander, General Cogny, in Hanoi. Cogny told his subordinate: 'There mustn't be any raising of the white flag; the firing must be allowed to die away – but don't surrender. That would debase everything magnificent that you've done up to now... this mustn't finish with a white flag. What you've achieved is too good for that. Do you understand old boy?' De Castries indicated that he did, to which Cogny replied, 'Well... *au revoir*, old boy.'

In fact, white flags were already flying over what remained of the French positions as the legionnaires and paratroopers, French conscripts, Algerians, Moroccans and West Africans, who had defended Dien Bien Phu with incredible bravery for 56 days, now sat out in the open awaiting their captors. Many fell asleep.

'Within two hours, almost the last of the garrison's reserve ammunition and medical supplies had been destroyed'

Vietnam divided

Of the garrison at Dien Bien Phu, approximately 3,000 men died during the fighting, while a further 10,000 died or disappeared during the march to captivity and Viet Minh 're-education'. Only around 3,000 eventually re-emerged from captivity. Viet Minh casualties were estimated at 8,000 killed and 15,000 wounded. On 2nd June, in Geneva, the French and Viet Minh began talks, which ended on 21st July with the division of Vietnam into two states – a communist north and an 'anti-communist' south. The French withdrew their troops from Indo-China, but retained 'advisors' in the south, as well as Laos and Cambodia. The United States, which had not signed the agreement, provided South Vietnam with military equipment and economic aid. American intervention in the form of waves of bombers flying from US aircraft carriers might have saved the garrison of Dien Bien Phu, but for President Eisenhower's opinion that white troops could not defeat the Vietnamese in their own country. His opinion would be ignored by his successors who, again relying on mobility and firepower, would commit American ground forces to a further, bloodier Vietnamese war.

Underestimating the enemy

It is dangerous, and often fatal, to underestimate an enemy, and yet it has occurred again and again throughout military history. It may be the belief in the superiority of their own civilization, or in a technological or organizational advantage, or even simply in a history of success against a particular foe that leads commanders to misread a situation. A good 'track record' against an enemy has led many to a misplaced belief in a force's invincibility and its ability to take on the enemy in almost any situation at almost any odds. In the 19th century, imperialism and theories concerning racial superiority, combined with a record of battles easily won against ill-armed foes, led many Europeans to assume that victory over non-Europeans was inevitable. Underestimating Asiatic enemies proved fatal to the Russians in their war with the Japanese in 1904–5, and to the British in Singapore in 1942. So, ultimately, was it to be for the French at Dien Bien Phu.

INDEX

Page numbers in **bold** text refer to main entry.
Page numbers in *italic* indicate illustration.

PICTURE CREDITS

Quercus Publishing Plc
21 Bloomsbury Square
London
WC1A 2NS

First published in 2010

Copyright © Julian Spilsbury 2010

The moral right of Julian Spilsbury to be identified as the author of this work has been asserted in accordance with the Copyright, Design and Patents Act, 1988.

Editorial and project management: JMS Books LLP
Design: Justin Hunt
Picture research: Emma O'Neill

A catalogue record of this book is available from the British Library

ISBN: 978-1-84866-039-7

Printed and bound in China

10 9 8 7 6 5 4 3 2 1